D0757694

The Political Economy of Gunnar Myrdal

The Political Economy of Gunnar Myrdal

An Institutional Basis for the
Transformation Problem

James Angresano

John Brandt Professor in Economics, Albertson College of Idaho, US

Edward Elgar
Cheltenham, UK • Lyme, US

© James Angresano 1997

All rights reserved. No part of this publication may be reproduced, stored in a retrieval system or transmitted in any form or by any means, electronic, mechanical or photocopying, recording, or otherwise without the prior permission of the publisher.

Published by
Edward Elgar Publishing Limited
8 Lansdown Place
Cheltenham
Glos GL50 2HU
UK

Edward Elgar Publishing, Inc.
1 Pinnacle Hill Road
Lyme
NH 03768
US

A catalogue record for this book
is available from the British Library

Library of Congress Cataloguing in Publication Data
Angresano, James, 1946–
   The political economy of Gunnar Myrdal: an institutional basis
for the transformation problem / James Angresano.
   Includes bibliographical references.
   1. Myrdal, Gunnar, 1898– . 2. Economists—Sweden—Biography.
3. Economic policy. 4. Social policy. 5. Institutional economics.
I. Title.
HB116.5.M9154 1997
330.1—dc21   97–12121
                                                         CIP

ISBN 1 85898 530 7

Typeset by Manton Typesetters, 5–7 Eastfield Road, Louth, Lincolnshire LN11 7AJ, UK.
Printed and bound in Great Britain by Biddles Ltd, Guildford and Kings Lynn

Contents

Tables

Preface

For more than 60 years Gunnar Myrdal (1898–1987) contributed to social science and societal reform as a researcher, teacher, and government official on the national and international level.[1] His bibliography includes over 1000 citations. Recognition came in the form of more than 30 honorary degrees, the Nobel Memorial Prize in Economics, and such accolades as being considered 'the leading economist and social scientist of his epoch' (Kindleberger 1987, p. 393). Another fitting tribute proclaims that

> [a]t one time or another ... [Myrdal] has worked seriously at history, politics, and sociology ... It is hard to think of any other economist of our generation who would have had the courage, competence, and energy to carry through studies of such sweeping scope, in which the purely economic component is kept always in proper perspective. (Reynolds 1974, p. 488)

This book focuses on Myrdal's intellectual development and contributions to transformation policy making throughout the world. His professional life was primarily devoted to extensive studies of broad societal issues that included analysis of development in Sweden, United States race relations, post-World War Two European reconstruction, and poverty in underdeveloped nations. As the consummate political economist he transcended his analysis to formulate and implement transformation policies. Today, however, his perspective, conclusions, and policy measures generally are ignored – most notably in graduate economics programs and transformation policy making in Central and Eastern Europe (CEE).

This book's main theme is that economists, despite being trained in the orthodox neoclassical tradition, can develop an alternative perspective which is more relevant and appropriate for transformation analysis and policy making than the narrow 'economic' view being taught in graduate school and applied by Western economic advisors throughout the world, especially in CEE. Since Myrdal is a prime example of an economist who abandoned the neoclassical perspective in favor of an institutional perspective, this book stresses his intellectual development and contributions to transformation issues. These are discussed within their historical context, with Myrdal's own interpretation emphasized.[2] An explanation is provided concerning how and why he rejected the neoclassical perspective in favor of an institutional perspective towards broad social problems.[3] To illustrate its contemporary relevance and usefulness Myrdal's institutional perspective of economics and economies is offered as an alternative basis for CEE transformation policy.

There is considerable contemporary relevance in Myrdal's intellectual development and contributions to transformation policy making throughout the world – perhaps more than at any time since his birth in 1898. Change within economics education and in the orthodox perspective towards economics, as well as transformation policies for economies throughout CEE and underdeveloped countries (UDCs), are prime issues for the 21st century – more so than any 'ism' regarding how to regulate an economy. Therefore, this book should be of particular interest to economists who, having been imbued with the orthodox perspective of economics and economies with an emphasis upon narrowly focused economic models, now find this perspective both irrelevant and inappropriate for analyzing and recommending policies for broad societal issues. They will discover that a study of Myrdal offers an alternative perspective as well as an example of how someone with a graduate school education similar to that of nearly all contemporary economists was able to develop his own holistic, interdisciplinary approach to economic analysis.

According to John Kenneth Galbraith, economists tend to be 'economical' regarding their investment in an economics education,[4] with nearly all clinging for their entire professional career to the neoclassical perspective they learned in graduate school.[5] John Maynard Keynes noted that among practitioners of economics 'there are not many who are influenced by new theories after they are twenty-five or thirty years of age' (Keynes 1964, pp. 383–4). It was postulated by Joseph Schumpeter that the important contributions of great authors occurred when they were young, during the years he referred to as the 'sacred fertile third decade' (Harris 1951, p. 2). Myrdal, while 'skeptical of Schumpeter's theses that the original scientific contributions are only made in very young years', nevertheless believed that 'the embryonic germs that later would develop into full-scale theorems must be present in youth' (Myrdal 1972).

Clinging to an orthodox perspective learned in graduate school for an entire career can create problems, particularly when the economist attempts to apply that perspective in a canonical fashion while advising other nations or teaching graduate students. The inclination of such economists is to 'arrive at general propositions and then postulate them as valid for every time, place and culture. There is a tendency in contemporary economic theory to follow this path to the extreme' (Todaro 1989, p. 12) despite the fact that many theories are designed for the special conditions common only to wealthier nations such as those belonging to the Organization for Economic Cooperation and Development (OECD).

The development of a holistic approach to societal problems is the distinguishing aspect of Myrdal's career. He is one of the few economists whose perspective towards and approach to economics, economies, and what economists should do changed dramatically during his career. Although his graduate education was in the neoclassical tradition, albeit with some modifications offered by his Swedish mentors, he eventually rejected the perspective held by practitioners of the neoclassical school concerning method of analysis, what economics should be and what economists should do, and the neoclassical conceptualized reality.[6] He began as a theoretical macroeconomist in the neoclassical tradition, a member of the 'Stockholm School' who focused on macroeconomic theory. Seeking an answer to the question of values in social science research, he searched (albeit unsuccessfully) for a method to assure objectivity on the part of the social science analyst.

During the late 1920s and early 1930s Myrdal's approach to economics tended toward that of a political and social economist. He became devoted to the transformation of the Swedish economy from a predominantly market-oriented economy with a modest agenda for the state to an economy subject to democratic, social control in which the state played a significant role redistributing income while providing extensive social insurance and welfare benefits to all citizens. Working within the Social Democratic Party Myrdal was instrumental not only in promoting the macroeconomic stabilization policies that he helped develop while a theoretical economist (in the neoclassical, Wicksellian sense), but also in laying the foundation for the social insurance and welfare programs that were gradually introduced in Sweden after the rise to power of the Social Democrats in 1932.

In the late 1930s Myrdal was invited by the Carnegie Foundation to become the principal contributor to a landmark study of race relations in the United States. During his study he became an institutional economist with ultimate and instrumental goals for reform, a conception of the existing socioeconomic reality, and a theory of societal transformation that are consistent with those of American institutionalists Thorstein Veblen, Clarence Ayres, and John R. Commons. Myrdal's subsequent work with the United Nations (1947–56) and underdeveloped countries (1957–75) embodies the institutionalist perspective, especially in his belief that there are no economic, social, or political problems – only problems which are complex. His later contributions to the history of economic thought, such as his reexamination of the role of values in social research and a critical analysis of orthodox economic thought, also are presented from this perspective. The theory and policies Myrdal developed concerning transformation issues are presented both within their historical context, and collectively in terms of his goals, conceptualized reality, theories and policy prescriptions for societies in the process (or in need) of transformation. His experiences spanned analyzing

Sweden's poverty conditions in the 1930s, race relations in the United States, post-World War Two European reconstruction, and problems and obstacles to development in poor nations.

Chapter 1 distinguishes transformation from evolution of economies, and identifies transformation issues pertinent to CEE and China. A comparative analysis of the performance of CEE and China's economies under alternative transformation policies follows. Based upon this comparison a case is made for a new perspective towards societal transformation, and it is argued that comprehension of Myrdal's intellectual development and contributions to transformation policy can provide the basis for such a perspective. As one scholar argues, while Myrdal does not provide the 'analytical tools capable of rationally solving problems in the sense that price theory and national income theory purport to do ... [he does offer] the perspective of the institutional approach [which] can help provide a setting in which civilized, understanding, and conciliatory people will be more likely to work out viable policies' (Gordon 1980, p. x).

The next three chapters focus on Myrdal's intellectual development, which can be divided into three distinct, but slightly overlapping, periods during which his employment history corresponded to each particular period in this development: Gunnar Myrdal I (GM I) the pure theorist, 1915–33; Gunnar Myrdal II (GM II) the political and social economist in transition, 1929–38; and Gunnar Myrdal III (GM III) the institutional economist, 1938–87.[7] Each of these three chapters contains a biographical sketch, including a description of the academic and government positions Myrdal held, his intellectual concerns, the general approach to economics he adopted (that is, his method of analysis), his major contributions to theory and policy, and the unique features of his intellectual development and career. Chapter 2 analyzes GM I's graduate education, theoretical macroeconomic research, and initial attempt to establish the basis for objective economic analysis.

In Chapter 3 GM II's work as a policy maker with the Swedish government during and after the Great Depression is emphasized. Factors contributing to his intellectual development moving in the political and social economist direction are identified, while his transition to GM III, an institutional economist, is the focus of Chapter 4. This chapter also outlines the main intellectual concerns during the post-1938 period of his life – particularly his landmark studies of regional, national, and global poverty and racial issues.

Chapter 5 summarizes and analyzes Myrdal's contributions to transformation issues and their particular relevance for CEE. Offering a separate chapter on such contributions avoids taking individual points out of context, and enables the informed eye to evaluate them after having explored Myrdal's matrix of thought within which his transformation contributions properly fit. Since Myrdal dealt with many social issues and his ideas evolved on many different planes over a number of decades, his transformation contributions are abstracted in Chapter 5 from their original context in Chapters 2–4 in a manner justifiable by previous analysis of his intellectual development. Each of the countries or regions with which he worked had a common problem – poverty. Seeking to alleviate that problem, Myrdal developed his own perspective, while offering a vision for each society's future: a conception of the institutional conditions and behavior of the economic order that had to be transformed; his method of analysis and theories to explain the behavior of such societies; and policy prescriptions to transform the troubled societies. Each of these elements will be presented, emphasis being placed upon features common to each of his studies.

Chapter 5 explains how Myrdal's approach to transformation issues can be applied to CEE. The post-1989 CEE transformation goals and policies which have been adopted by CEE authorities and their advisors are critiqued from a Myrdalian perspective. A critical evaluation of contemporary economics education follows, with an alternative program suggested which Myrdal would have endorsed. Overall, this final chapter offers a Myrdalian perspective towards social science research which should appeal to analysts seeking to broaden their own research method.

Primary material is drawn from Myrdal's books, professional journal articles, public lectures, the author's two interviews with Myrdal (the texts of which are contained in the Appendix), and from professional and personal material from Myrdal's complete collection stored in the Labor Organization Archives in Stockholm (where the author has done research on two separate occasions). Secondary material consists of articles written concerning Myrdal, including three by the author, as well as the author's published work about Sweden, research in Sweden, work experience in Central and East Europe, and material from courses taught pertaining to comparative economics, economic development, history of economic thought, and Myrdal's analysis of race relations in the United States.

Acknowledgements

I wish to extend my appreciation to the following institutions for their support: Albertson College of Idaho, the Center for Post-Soviet and East European Studies at the University of Texas at Austin, Central European University in Prague, and the Labor Organization Archives in Stockholm.

Special thanks for reading parts of the book to Kathy Seibold, JuNelle Harris, and Chris Barnes. Chris was responsible for the arduous task of preparing the camera-ready copy of the book for publication.

The works of Gunnar Myrdal and the perspective they provided were the initial impetus for writing this book. Furthermore I was fortunate to have been given permission by Gunnar Myrdal to interview him on two occasions. Owing to Alva's and his generosity I received funding to travel to Sweden from Svenska Handelsbanken in Stockholm. This bank has been given the responsibility of administering research grants to interested scholars from a fund established by the Myrdals.

It would have been difficult to complete the book without the continued moral support and encouragement provided by my children, Nicole and Michelle. Their interest and enthusiasm for the project was a constant source of inspiration.

Of great significance to the author has been the exemplary written works, classes and endless professional advice provided by Hans Jensen. He has been an ideal role model not only for myself, but for countless graduate students through his teaching, research, and personal life.

Finally, thank you Elizabeth for being you.

1. Transformation policy: searching for a useful perspective

THE ECONOMY AND THE PROCESS OF EVOLUTION OR TRANSFORMATION

A useful economic perspective contains a realistic conception of the socio-economic reality that can serve as the basis for both analysis and sound policy making. In order for a new perspective to establish itself as a serious, viable alternative to the neoclassical perspective, thereby becoming part of *the* paradigm for social science practitioners in the academic community, it must offer a more realistic conceptualized reality than the neoclassical perspective provides. This new perspective would give its adherents an alternative, more accurate understanding of an economy's principal institutions and working rules (than that which is currently provided by neoclassical economics), thereby offering a sounder basis for developing public policies to achieve their normative propositions.

Despite being imbued with the neoclassical paradigm during his graduate education and macroeconomic policy development work during the early 1930s, Gunnar Myrdal realized this paradigm was inadequate for analyzing broad economic issues. He began to develop his own conception of the socioeconomic reality, stating his normative propositions, critique of neoclassical economics, and method of analysis. Myrdal's conception of the socio-economic order convinced him that 'economic' problems could not be studied in isolation, but only in their demographic, social and political setting. With this conception as the basis for his analysis Myrdal was instrumental in promoting macroeconomic stabilization policy for Sweden during the early 1930s depression, and in laying the foundation for the social insurance and welfare programs that Sweden gradually implemented thereafter. He combined the same conception with an interdisciplinary method of analysis in his landmark examination of race relations in the United States, implementation of economic recovery measures in Europe after World War Two, and investigation of the causes of poverty in underdeveloped nations.

Myrdal's perspective towards an economy was evolutionary-institutional.[8] He viewed the economy not as a static entity, but as an ongoing process comprised of the aggregate of institutions which perform economic functions and determine economic conditions. These institutions behave according to working rules, many of which are established by authorities who allocate scarce resources while answering questions pertaining to production and distribution of goods and services.[9] Working rules establish rights and duties of the economy's participants, and serve to create order among conflicting interests while strengthening the social process for coordinating economic (as well as social, political, and cultural) matters by outlining the boundaries of behavior for economic activity. Societies establish institutions and working rules in an attempt to achieve order – predictability without rigidity and flexibility without chaos.

Working rules are both formal and informal, and exist at different levels (for example, household, firm, nationwide) either with or without sovereign power exercised by the state. The formal regulations recognized and sanctioned by society establish every member's rights, duties, and liberties and what members can expect the state to perform in the collective interest. Formal rules establish a legal structure within which property rights are defined and transactions can be undertaken. Participants in economic activities face a choice of opportunities and exercise their economic power within the working rules established by authorities. Arbiters may become necessary to settle disputes between transacting parties. The informal rules (opinions, or attitudes[10] in public opinion which identify society's important problems and what should be done to alleviate them) provide some basis for the establishment of working rules.

The institutions which comprise an economy are interrelated in order to define the choice sets of economic actors behaving independently, and indicate the rules regarding economic decisions as well as the cost of each decision. Taken together these institutions provide formal rules and attitudes for all economic activities in which a society's members engage. Either profound, new technology or a sustained, unusual performance of an economy (changes in pertinent social and economic indicators) stimulate development of new attitudes (informal rules), which can lead to subsequent modification or replacement of the economy's (formal) working rules, and thereby its principal institutions.[11]

Whether an economy is in the process of an evolution or transformation is a matter of degree. All economies are characterized by ongoing processes of dynamic change as working rules and institutions are modified or replaced. When institutional change is gradual, the economy in question is considered to be evolving, such as the United States or Swedish economies since 1932. However, when in response to a political or economic revolution comprehensive institutional change ensues throughout an economy, this process can be considered a transformation. While transformation may or may not include dramatic changes in the political structure, it generally features the introduction of a radically different philosophical basis[12] for the economy with a commitment to establish fundamentally new principal institutions and working rules consistent with this new philosophy. The two most dramatic contemporary examples of transformation are Central and Eastern Europe (CEE) countries since 1989, and China since 1978 – albeit without significant changes in its political structure.

TRANSFORMATION ISSUES IN CEE AND IN CHINA

Significance of the Comparison

Since 1989 attention throughout the academic and public policy making community concerning transformation has been riveted on CEE. The results of the initial transformation policy measures have been noted, and subsequent policies proposed based upon those results. Many have credited the type of transformation policies introduced in Poland and the Czech Republic with the realization of the positive performance indicators over the past few years in those nations – especially their respective rates of economic growth. However, improved economic performance in other CEE nations which have adopted similar policies, particularly Bulgaria and Russia, has not been nearly as marked. Nevertheless, the same advocates of the initial transformation policy packages enthusiastically endorse the continued implementation of similar policies in all CEE nations, despite the expansion of poverty and political unrest throughout most of the region.

The transformation experience of China has been given much less attention. The significance of comparing the transformation strategies and experiences of CEE nations and China for those interested in transformation policy has largely been ignored. As the fastest growing economies in their respective continents the relative performance of the Polish economy and that of China is important for other transforming nations. If evidence indicates that the gradual transformation strategy adopted in China can contribute to improvements in performance indicators comparable to improvements realized in similar performance indicators in Poland – but at a lower cost (as indicated by lower rates of unemployment and poverty) – then comparing the two nations' perspective of an economy and its evolution or transformation, the transformation policies based upon that perspective, and the subsequent performances of those economies will yield lessons which can be of benefit to policy makers in other transforming nations.[13]

It must be kept in mind that the performance of any economy is influenced by three factors: its institutions and working rules, economic policies, and exogenous factors – including the economic environment within its trading

partners. It is difficult to isolate which of these factors influence the performance of any economy, and to what extent. All three are rarely stable for any
length of time. This has been especially true throughout CEE. Therefore no
firm conclusion can be drawn concerning which of the three factors is the
primary cause of an economy's performance. Nevertheless, it is the *perception* of a policy's impact that is important, for example the implications
illustrated by the Laffer Curve and its use by American policy makers in
support of tax cuts and other supply-side economic policies in 1981. Many
macroeconomic policies are adopted based upon a perception of the policy's
impact rather than hard evidence of the proposed policy's effectiveness following analysis of actual experience.[14] Therefore a comparison of the relative
performance of the CEE and Chinese economies under different transformation perspectives and policies plays an important role in the search for a
useful transformation perspective and policies.

The Transformation Perspective of CEE Policy Makers

The task faced by policy makers in 1989 was unprecedented. Many daunting
problems and obstacles had to be surmounted before a successful transformation of the former 'command' economies could occur.[15] These included (1)
reducing state influence over particular sectors in the name of greater economic efficiency and distributional equity; (2) softening the recessionary
effects due to the breakup of COMECON; (3) compensating for workers and
managers who were inexperienced and unskilled for functioning effectively
in a competitive economy; (4) establishing a stable economy which faced an
inevitable increase in unemployment and inflation – especially following the
privatization or bankruptcy of obsolete, revenue-losing enterprises; (5) coun-
tering resistance to abandoning all aspects of the Marxian philosophical
basis, especially state ownership of property, for fear that a 'capitalist' class
would emerge to exploit the working class and assume control over authorities through domination of the 'superstructure' – just as Marx had argued; (6)
face the difficulty in establishing a social and psychological environment in
which faith in government was sufficient to give it the possibility of leading
the country out of its economic difficulties; and (7) making the nation's
currency freely convertible on the international market and grafting it onto
the 'brain-dead socialist economy'.[16]

Political realities posed another obstacle. Reformers feared the ruling bureaucrats would fight a shift of their authority to those lower in the social
structure, and would seek to reintroduce central controls if the economy
failed to perform well immediately following introduction of reforms – thereby
aborting the reforms 'that threaten[ed] the current property-rights structure'
from which they had directly benefited.[17] Those involved with the second

economy also had reason to resist reform. Their competitive position vis-a-vis legal suppliers and their profit margin on goods sold would be adversely affected if free entry of other suppliers was permitted. Consequently, many of the millions engaged in the second economy would, in a manner consistent with the theory of rent-seeking behavior, seek to retain 'their little illegal or gray niches and rackets' which had been carefully 'cultivated' over the years rather than become subject to unknown competitive forces (Grossman 1990, p. 51).

Additional obstacles included the monopoly structures and obsolete technology pervasive among state-owned enterprises. These conditions, when combined with indifferent management and worker attitudes, resulted in the production of low-quality goods at high cost per unit produced. Such conditions discouraged these firms from adapting to the foreign technology, and discouraged foreign investment in them. It was expected that foreign investment would also be inhibited by bureaucratic delays and the absence of local finance for those foreign firms seeking working capital. Anticipated bureaucratic delays were attributable to the retention of ministries and large staffs which were expected to continue interfering in the production and distribution process.

Recognizing these obstacles and realizing that the philosophical basis and performance of their pre-1989 economies was both bankrupt and inadequate, CEE authorities sought a new ideology. No pragmatic alternatives (such as state-guided industrial policies adopted by Japan in the 1950s) were given serious consideration. Instead, the choice was seen as 'either socialism or a market economy'. Establishment of a *free market economy* (FME) was the stated goal of many CEE authorities and their Western advisors, albeit without any formal description provided. Desire to establish such an economy contributed to policy proposals which sought to introduce institutions common to the textbook FME model, reducing all economic problems to a matter of optimum allocation of resources in the process. It was assumed that efficiency would be established once perfectly competitive markets and free individuals seeking to maximize utility were created or emerged. Thus, transformation of the economies was perceived as following a mechanical, simplified pattern. Policy makers adopted an inductive method of reform, believing that certain stimuli, consisting of such available tools as stringent monetary and fiscal policy and liberalized prices, would quickly induce desired changes throughout CEE economies. It was assumed that using the proposed stabilization measures as stimuli, the desired changes in economic behavior were virtually guaranteed, even as a chemist's combination of particular elements is certain to produce a specific reaction.

The architects of Poland's 1990–92 transformation policies led the CEE transformation charge. They held a neo-classical conception of human behavior, socioeconomic order and economic history. They assumed Polish economic agents would behave rationally, and that a FME would emerge following the dissolution of state-owned and controlled institutions. According to this conception 'economic systems are perceived reversible and path-independent. Since economic agents behave rationally, economic regularities are conceived universal and non-historic. Therefore, a strong belief in the ability to construct a market prevails. The nature of transition (i.e., [transformation]) [is assumed to be] a matter of instantaneous adjustment of rational agents without a past and essentially entails the implementation of new rules and the elimination of political resistance. From this, it follows that the transition should be as quick as possible, i.e. by the application of a shock therapy' (Hoen 1995, p. 66).

Poland's advisors anticipated a quick recovery based upon an assumption that 'destruction' of state owned enterprises would soon be followed by 'creation' of new private enterprises to offset the loss of output, income and employment. Furthermore, it was believed that the private sector would quickly prosper, thereby generating tax revenue that could offset anticipated decreases in revenues from the public sector. Combined with this assumption was a strong doctrinaire belief that only liquidation or a rapid, radical overhaul of state-owned enterprises was viable.[18] Such a perspective assumed that the transformation of Poland's economy was primarily 'a matter of [achieving macroeconomic stabilization and] demolishing those institutions which belong to a central planning and changing the rules of the game … a matter of quickly removing non-budgetary and non-technical constraints for agency behaviour' (Hoen 1995, p. 74).[19] The main advisors to Poland and Russia (prior to their replacement in 1994) continued to predict that 'the service sector will ultimately expand to provide jobs for [unemployed] workers who, inevitably, will be released from the industrial sector' (Lipton and Sachs 1992). Unfortunately, reformers failed to recognize the enormous magnitude of structural adjustment required, particularly in the industrial sector, and therefore did not predict ensuing high, persistent rates of unemployment and growing incidence of poverty. Despite evidence that China has experienced the world's highest rate of sustained economic growth (while holding the rate of unemployment far below rates prevailing throughout CEE) since introducing different transformation policies in 1979, Western advisors argued that Chinese gradualism had 'little relevance' for CEE.[20]

Transformation Policies in CEE

The key issues faced at the beginning of CEE's transformation were which new institutions and corresponding working rules would be chosen, how this choice would be made, and what would be the rate by which the selected institutions and rules would replace existing ones. It was unfortunate that the process of selecting a transformation goal and policies for its achievement became a 'reductionist debate [throughout CEE in 1989 and 1990], implying a simplistic choice between shock and gradualism, [which] hid the necessary sequencing and speed of the components of an overall policy package' (Islam 1993, p. 60). Intellectual dogmatism led to the dichotomy view and simple, 'catch slogans like "shock therapy" versus "gradualism" as they derive from simple intellectual schemes or models incapable of handling country-specific complexities' (Laski 1993, p. 2).

Since the 'shock approach' and its inherent economic political ideology consistent with laissez-faire provided a simple resolution to these issues within prevailing political philosophy, it influenced the most pervasive set of policies introduced.[21] It was initially proposed by Polish authorities, Western academics serving as their advisors, and international agency 'experts'. They argued that 'the introduction of a set of simple initial macroeconomic conditions' such as rapidly privatizing state property, eliminating subsidies to enterprises and households, restricting growth of the money supply, reducing the budget deficit, reforming the tax system and rules for accounting, liberalizing prices, making the currency internally convertible while stabilizing the exchange rate, holding down wage increases, and opening up the domestic market by eliminating tariffs and subsidies 'would provide the framework in which the operation of individual initiative rewarded by economic success in competitive market conditions would be sufficient to initiate the transformation process' (Kregel and Matzner 1992, p. 33). Liberalization of domestic and international markets and macroeconomic stabilization through restrictive monetary and fiscal policies were viewed as the most urgent problems. The two nominal 'anchors' for these programs were stabilization of the exchange rate, the goal being the reduction of inflationary expectations by linking the CEE nation's currency with foreign currencies, and restraint of nominal wages – the intention being to discipline state-owned enterprises and reduce inflationary pressure.

When Poland began to formulate its initial transformation policies IMF support was needed not only to obtain additional financial credit, but to facilitate Polish policy makers' ability to gain credibility from the international community for implementation of their transformation policies. In response to Poland's request for assistance the IMF introduced their standard program with its interrelated components: (1) stringent fiscal policy and monetary policy, (2) achievement of a favorable external balance of payments as well as the opening of Poland's borders to foreign trade while achieving a stable (and subsequently convertible) zloty, (3) establishment of an incomes policy to combat inflation, and (4) structural and institutional changes. Targets and corresponding policy measures were established. In Poland, shock therapy 'recommended the use of massive monetary squeezes to shock these economies to life' (Hanke and Walters 1993, p. 52).

Similar transformation policies have been formulated and implemented throughout the rest of CEE, with some variation among nations regarding the extent of privatization and reduction of subsidies to state-owned enterprises. It was decided throughout the region (with the exception of Hungary) that management of the transformation would be 'top-down ... rigorously structured and regulated by a central plan' (Dallago 1992, p. 273). Meanwhile, policy implementation would be rapid to break the 'treadmill of reforms' characteristic of the pre-1989 period and to take advantage of public acquiescence to 'radical, pro-capitalist reform' while denying interest groups opposed to the reform time to 'coalesce into effective blocs'.[22] The plan was bold and created an aura that transformation was a technical, 'economic problem'.

From the point of view of one Polish economist, transformation policy measures similar to Poland's shock therapy program were both politically successful and appealing, albeit narrow in focus. 'The boldness of the plan, fearfulness of its creators (who were able to convince society about the lack of credible alternative to the plan), and external support ... helped to create the belief that the plan was purely a matter of the technical skills of its authors' (Surdej 1992, pp. 32-33). The plan's efficiency effects were strongly emphasized, while its distributional effects were ignored so as to establish a rational economic order.

The Transformation Perspective of China's Policy Makers

During the late 1970s there was a change in China's transformation perspective. New authorities decided that for the Communist Party to survive and retain control over a nation whose economy had been performing poorly compared to the rest of Southeast Asia the best alternative was to promote economic reforms that were market oriented while retaining social control over the economy. They recognized the economy's poor performance was due primarily to the dominance of public ownership, commitment to an egalitarian distribution of income, low productivity and the absence of managerial initiative. Seeking a different 'true' transformation path for China to follow, authorities chose to replace Party emphasis upon ideology and idealism with economic and political pragmatism. Their belief was that whatever works was the basis for truth – exemplified by Deng Xiaoping's statement that the color of a cat is not important as long as it catches mice. The official party intention was not to transform the economy to resemble that of Japan, Hong Kong or Taiwan, but to permit the establishment of some institutions and working rules similar to those of China's much wealthier neighbors that would enhance the economy's performance while preserving Party officials' security within the political structure. The Chinese perceived Taiwan as a vulgar example of the American brand of 'capitalism' which they sought to avoid, particularly the ability of some to exploit others by operating selfishly and unconstrained within an unregulated market economy (Metzger 1996, pp. 3–23).[23] Consequently, they chose to establish a '"new socialist market economy" seeking growth with equity, combining free enterprise with planning, and based on a complex mix of ownership forms' (Metzger 1996, p. 2).

China thereby developed its own transformation perspective which stood in contrast to the ideological CEE linear approach, especially its dichotomous 'market versus state' viewpoint. The 'ideological underpinnings' (philosophical basis) for the transformation would be to continue Chou En-lai's 'Four Modernizations' which pertained to agriculture, industry, science and technology, and defense (Metzger 1996, p. 2). In addition, they would follow the 'Four Cardinal Principles' of Deng Xiaoping who advocated that the country 'must adhere to the socialist path, the dictatorship of the proletariat, the leadership of the Party, and the thought of Marx, Lenin, and Mao' (Metzger 1996, p. 2). Both China's ruling authorities and intellectual elite sought to avoid the negative aspects of Western modernization by 'accommodating the market without fully institutionalizing it' (Metzger 1996, p. 3) and by only modifying (rather than abandoning) their unique culture in the most efficient pursuit of their economic goals.

Rejecting the 'cookbook approach' to transformation in favor of treating transformation much as one plays a game of chess, Chinese policy makers nurtured the development of traditional market-oriented institutions and working rules which suited the Chinese economic, political and social environment. They chose to rely upon common sense and experience rather than upon any abstract theoretical economic model. In the process they developed a transformation perspective which has been relatively less ideological and more measured, experimental, evolutionary and pragmatic than that of CEE policy makers.

Transformation Policies in China

China's 'reflective practitioner' approach (Marquid 1995, p. 7) to transformation strategy relies on 'learning by doing', which has given them a strong willingness to modify transformation policy measures when necessary to maintain political and macroeconomic stability. Chinese policy makers avoided large-scale reform experiments by experimenting on a small scale at the local level, and only after the experiment was deemed successful would a transformation policy be introduced over a broad geographic area. In this manner China developed some distinct, viable new institutions (such as the township-village enterprises) not common to the economy of any OECD country.

Unlike CEE authorities, Chinese policy makers have not abandoned a strong state role in transforming the economy, perhaps because they recognize that while the 'advanced countries espouse free competition ... [these nations] exhibit pervasive oligopolistic business practices and extensive active government involvement in shaping and directing the economy' (Amsden et al. 1995, p. 4). Instead, they have focused on a 'dual-track' approach whereby the state sector's scope remains relatively constant while resources devoted to non-state activity have increased (Li 1995). The result has been a steady increase in the private sector's importance. It is difficult to determine the size of China's private sector because of the unique institutions characterized by multiple ownership forms which have coexisted since the reform period began. If the private sector is defined to mean privately managed enterprises outside of state influence, that is, all of those institutions that are not state-owned, then about 60% of China's industrial output comes from the private sector (Young 1995).

Rather than risk a serious recession, and recognizing that the initial conditions of their economy in 1978 meant that rapid introduction of policies similar to shock therapy would likely be followed by a large recession, Chinese policy makers chose to continue subsidizing state enterprises while encouraging private sector expansion. This policy has had two significant benefits. First, in guaranteeing preservation of the interests and living standards of those managing and working in the state sector, policy makers have been able to introduce economic reforms (such as permitting state-owned enterprises to sell their above quota output among themselves at market prices) aimed at gradually transforming state enterprise while helping to integrate them with the private sector. Second, although there has been a 'massive diversion of supplies to the market from the plan in the late 1980s, there was no dramatic collapse in the output of state enterprises' (Liew 1995, pp. 885–7). Additional transformation stimulus came from entrepreneurs within China and 'capitalists' (Chinese expatriates from Hong Kong, Singapore and Taiwan) who have funded the entrepreneurs' ventures. China's transformation policies have permitted cadres to make the transition to private sector entrepreneurs, even if corruption was an interim stage in the process. As Liew argues (in a way similar to what Friedrich Hayek argued re competition as a discovery process) '[t]he market provides a window [of opportunity] to these employees – it reveals what is potentially possible. It provides employees of state enterprises examples, as well as opportunities, for potentially higher living standards'. As a result, thousands of officials have left state-sector jobs for private sector jobs (Liew 1995, p. 888).

Performance of the CEE and Chinese Economies[24]

Evaluating the relative performance of the CEE and Chinese economies following implementation of transformation policies based upon their respective transformation perspectives will contribute to the search for a useful transformation perspective. Four steps need to be followed when evaluating and comparing the performance of selected economies (see Angresano 1994 a, c, d, pp. 23–38). First, the selection of criteria which, taken together, comprise the analyst's definition of performance; second, the identification of performance indicators for each criterion; third, measurement of these performance indicators; finally, compilation of a performance index. This index consists of the quantitative performance measures of each criterion weighted according to its relative importance. This step can be taken if performance indicators lend themselves to quantification.

This procedure raises objectivity issues, for the particular criteria chosen, the method of measurement, and the relative importance attached to each performance criterion will be influenced by the analyst's viewpoint.[25] Myrdal would argue that as a result the analyst can be neither neutral nor objective since 'the choice of a viewpoint establishes a set of standards or norms by which any candidates for answers to the questions with our viewpoint will be deemed to be good answers or bad' (Dykema 1980, p. 149). Analysts may purport to be engaging in positive analysis, but their 'hidden values', such as a preference for a laissez-faire domestic economic and social policy, privately owned enterprises, and the belief that the institutions of a FME tend towards a stable equilibrium, can lead to conclusions which he believes are 'biased' (Myrdal 1957e, pp. 138–47).

To achieve greater objectivity Myrdal calls for analysts to explicitly identify their desired performance criteria (such as a preference for high rates of economic growth) or what he calls 'value premises', in order to purge the analysis, to the extent possible, of distorting biases by specifying the analysts' relative norms. Doing so 'unmasks two methodological errors that follow from … [an] ethnocentric position: the analysis of development based on a selection of exclusively economic variables, and the attribution of universal merit to the process of Western development' (Ethier 1992, p. 69), both of which overemphasize technique to the neglect of open discussion of critical social issues, including economic imperialism.[26] The following two evaluations identify explicitly the desired performance criteria which stem from a particular view. The first is derived from a Myrdalian view, and compares the post-transformation performance of five CEE economies to that of China. The second focuses on the Polish and Chinese economies' performances from the view of the International Monetary Fund (IMF).

EVALUATION OF CEE AND CHINESE ECONOMIES FROM A MYRDALIAN VIEW

CEE countries selected for analysis are Bulgaria, the Czech Republic, Hungary, Poland, and Russia. The evaluation process begins by specifying the performance indicators selected, followed by an evaluation of the selected economies' actual performance. Myrdal, having selected similar criteria of performance for countries as diverse as Sweden, the United States, and Asian underdeveloped countries, undoubtedly would have applied the same criteria to CEE. These criteria (Myrdal 1968, pp. 54–69; 1975a, pp. 212–13; 1975b, p. 50) and their corresponding indicators of performance are presented in Table 1.1.[27] Myrdal believes these criteria to be interrelated, so that improvement in one or a few contributes to improvement in others. Nearly all are deemed of equal importance, with two exceptions. Social and economic equality is considered a 'supreme ideal', reflecting his strong egalitarian value that is shared by many CEE citizens. The existence of political democracy (rather than an authoritarian regime), while preferred, is not considered essential for positive trends in the other performance indicators.

When using these criteria to evaluate and compare the selected CEE economies a few problems arise. Only the first four correspond to performance indicators for which data are available. Furthermore, some of the obtainable data, particularly that pertaining to wealth and income distribution, poverty rates, involvement in the 'social' and 'uncivil' economies (see below) and tax avoidance is only partially complete, and may not be totally reliable. Nevertheless, conclusions have been, and will continue to be drawn from similar information for the purpose of evaluating transformation policies and determining their efficacy for being continued or implemented in another country seeking to transform its economy.

Table 1.2 has been constructed with these caveats in mind. Where possible, data provided by organizations not directly involved with CEE policy making, such as the OECD and *The Economist* Intelligence Unit, and UNICEF have been selected in the interest of greater objectivity. Rather than compiling an index for each CEE economy, they will be evaluated together. Emphasis will be placed upon identification of common features and tendencies.

Further elaboration of some performance indicators is warranted. A common argument is that the extent of participation in the 'social' economy and 'uncivil' economy means that GDP, poverty, real income, and unemployment data overstate the degree of misery. While this may be the case, one must be careful not to overestimate the ability of a typical household to supplement its income through such participation (beyond what it did before 1989) since many households' members have been engaged in these unofficial economies for the past four decades (and longer in Russia).[28] Some households actively

Table 1.1   *Criteria of performance and corresponding performance indicators*

Criteria	Performance indicator
Social and economic equalization Regarding status, opportunities, wealth, income, and levels of living	Distribution of wealth and income
Rise of productivity Increased output per capita	% change in GDP/capita
Rise of levels of living Prerequisites for rising efficiency and improved productivity of labor	Incidence of poverty Real wages Unemployment Inflation
Improved institutions and attitudes Want people who are efficient, diligent, orderly, punctual, honest, rational, self-reliant, energetic and enterprising, and have a long run outlook	Number of new firms developed Crime rates Involvement in social and uncivil economies Tax avoidance
Social discipline, rational planning Establish coordinated economic policies by procedures based upon sound critical reasoning. Compliance does not require compulsion	Procedure and basis for democratic development (transformation) policies
National independence Effective formation and execution of national policies	Political stability and ability to legislate
National consolidation United, cohesive, and effective national system of government, legal system, and administration with unchallenged authority within boundaries of the state	Ability to enforce laws
Political democracy National regime viewed as legitimate and accepted by a majority of the public.	Extent of democracy in willingly political system and public attitude towards governing authorities

Table 1.2   Performance of selected CEE nations

	Bulgaria	Czech Republic	Hungary	Poland	Russia
GDP[a]	%	%	%	%	%
1985–88	3.7	2.5	1.0	3.8	2.5
1989	–0.3	2.4	0.4	0.2	1.6
1990	–9.1	0.8	–3.3	–11.6	–4.0
1991	–12.0	–14.9	–12	–9.0	–5.0
1992	–8.0	–7.0	–3.0	2.6	–15.0
1993	–4.0	–1.0	–0.8	3.8	–9.0
1994	1.4	–1.0	2.9	5.3	–13.0
1995	2.6	5.2	1.5	7.0	–4.0
1996*	2.0	4.0	2.0	6.0	1.0
Poverty[b]	%	%	%	%	%
1989	–	5.7	10.1	20.5	27.1
1991	–	19.4	21.3	38.8	28.7
1992	62.7	18.2	–	42.5	77.1
Real Income[c]	%	%	%	%	%
1989	100.0	100.0	100.0	100.0	100.0
1991	58.5	88.5	96.5	71.8	105.3
1992	60.8	94.0	91.8	70.3	61.7
Unemployment[d]	%	%	%	%	%
1990	1.6	–	1.6	6.1	0.0
1991	11.7	–	7.5	11.5	0.0
1992	15.0	3.0	12.0	15.0	1.0
1993	17.0	3.5	12.0	17.0	1.0
1994	17.0	8.0	13.0	16.0	6.0
1995	17.0	7.0	12.0	15.0	8.0
1996*	18.0	7.0	12.0	15.0	9.0
Inflation	%	%	%	%	%
1990	26.0	–	28.0	585.0	5.0
1991	334.0	–	35.0	70.0	103.0
1992	90.0	11.0	23.0	43 .0	2000.0
1993	64.0	18.0	23.0	37.0	1000.0
1994	96.0	14.0	19.0	28.0	307.0
1995	62.0	8.0	28.0	22.0	198.0
1996*	50.0	9.0	24.0	21.0	80.0

Notes:

*   Estimated – some figures are the average of the OECD and *The Economist* Intelligence Unit forecasts.

[a]   Annual percentage change in per capita real GDP. In Bulgaria, Hungary and Russia the population has declined slightly since 1989. Pre-1989 data is for Czechoslovakia.

[b]   Percentage of households earning less than 45% of 1989 average wage (35% for Czechoslovakia).

[c]   Index of per capital real income; 1989 is the base year.

[d]   If those working on partial shifts and those on paid or unpaid leave are included, another 3% to 5% of the labor force are either unemployed or underemployed.

Sources: OECD, *The Economist* Intelligence Unit, 1994a,b, 1995a,b, 1996a,b,c,d,e; UNICEF, 1993; World Bank, 1993; Lipton and Sachs, 1992; Mokrzycki, 1993; Surdej, 1992; Klusak and Mertlik, 1992; and Brady, 1993.

involved in these economies before 1989 have actually suffered from the transformation. Their previous ability to supplement their official income was due to their having access to hard currency and the means to obtain consumer goods not available in their country, both of which were inaccessible to the typical CEE household at the time, but neither of which is inaccessible today.

Poverty[29]

Indicators such as declining real income,[30] rising percentages of consumption devoted to food, changing composition of food purchased (which indicates an aggravated dietary imbalance), reduced average calories consumed per capita, high and persistent unemployment, and growing inability to pay rent demonstrate that poverty has 'increased massively' throughout CEE, particularly in rural areas (UNICEF 1993, pp. 7, 20, 81). In 1995 while real incomes rose in Russia (for the first time since 1989, after falling 13% in 1994), Poland, and the Czech Republic, real incomes declined in both Bulgaria and Hungary. Hungarian living standards were 'hit hard' in 1995, with a fall of 6% in average real incomes (*The Economist* Intelligence Unit 1996c). Homelessness is a growing problem. Only the Czech Republic has experienced improved welfare conditions for a large majority of its population. Although deterioration in welfare conditions has 'stabilized' in Poland the past two years, the levels are below those which prevailed in 1989 for many Poles. Unemployment in Poland, despite the economy's rapid rate of growth, remains over 15%, and except for the Czech Republic is 9% or greater in the other CEE countries. Furthermore, official unemployment figures do not include the percentage of the labor force (about 4%) who are underemployed or on administrative leave. Poverty among children is growing throughout the region, while health and educational standards as well as spending on other social services are falling (with pervasive per capita cuts in health and education), with extensive structural unemployment exacerbating the problem. Poverty can be expected to rise dramatically in Bulgaria where the 'economy is crumbling . . . [and] salvaging disaster will mean hard times' (*The Economist* Intelligence Unit 1996b).

Distribution of wealth and income

There appears to be growing 'sharp divisions in standards of living (Ringen and Wallace 1993, p. 7) in all CEE nations. While some stronger and shrewder individuals are profiting from expanded market opportunities, many are not. Throughout CEE, state governments are passing along responsibility for providing social services to local governments and private firms, as well as asking the public to pay a greater share of the costs. Since many firms cannot afford to provide such services and a growing number of households are unable to pay, the effects of growing disparity in wealth and income are exacerbated.

Crime

There are strong indications that throughout CEE the breakdown in civil authority combined with growing poverty, job insecurity, and expanded opportunities for quick profits has contributed to an expansion of criminal activity (although some argue corruption may have always been high, but is now more openly acknowledged). In all countries the sharp, steady growth of crime rates has been of 'precipitous proportions'. Using 1989 as the base year to compute an index (100.0) for the number of crimes reported, the index in 1992 was 394.6 in Bulgaria, 285.8 in the Czech Republic, 198.4 in Hungary, 178.1 in Poland, and 169.4 in Russia (UNICEF 1993, p. 87). Smuggling, sales of narcotics, and organized crime networks are pervasive. Opinion polls indicate this is particularly true of Russia. Murders in retaliation for legitimate merchants' refusal to pay protection money are not uncommon, and the murder rate is now double that of the United States.[31] Bribery of public officials and theft of money by tax and bank officers also are widespread activities. Throughout CEE the extent of organized crime and bureaucratic corruption is such that bribery has become a necessary part of doing business, particularly in Bulgaria, the Czech Republic, and Russia.

Democracy and public support for authorities

Democratically elected regimes characterize CEE, but negative public attitudes are growing in the face of the pervasive economic crises throughout the region. Feelings of hopelessness and persistent stagflation make conditions ripe, in the opinion of some, for a dictatorial government to assume power. Blaming 'free market' reforms for the declining standards of living, CEE voters have responded by electing former communist party members to lead their government in all but a few countries.[32]

SUMMARY

One conclusion that can be drawn from this evaluation is that based upon the Myrdalian criteria for performance and corresponding performance indicators, the CEE economies' performance since 1989 can be considered relatively poor.[33] This follows from the negative assessments which Myrdal would give to social and economic equalization, rise of productivity, rise of levels of living, and social discipline and rational planning. On the other hand, positive and negative aspects can be identified for each of the other four criteria.

Using comparable performance indicators, trends in China, except for inflation (which has averaged almost 12% since 1990) and political democracy, are either similar or more positive than corresponding results in CEE (see Table 1.3 below).[34] In nearly every year since 1978 China's actual performance has exceeded planned performance. The country's performance has been 'unpredicted and astounding', a 'success ... since the 1980s in creating a fast-growing economy animated by much free enterprise' (Metzger 1996, p. 1). 'Another glorious year' (*The Economist* Intelligence Unit, 1996a) hailed one description of the Chinese economy's 1995 performance during which GDP grew 10.2%, exports rose 23% from 1994, and foreign direct investment was up almost 12% from the previous year. On the other hand, in almost every CEE nation the decline in economic activity following implementation of transformation measures has consistently exceeded the most pessimistic forecasts of policy makers and their foreign advisors. Consequently, the social and economic costs born by the Chinese during their transformation have been much lower. This evaluation calls into question the efficacy of CEE policies based upon the assumption that transformation requires rapid privatization, elimination of subsidies to state-owned enterprises, and stabilization measures prior to institutional reforms, or that the state should assume a passive role in supply-side responses during the transformation process.

EVALUATION OF POLAND'S ECONOMIC PERFORMANCE FROM AN IMF VIEW

The few quantitative IMF criteria adopted for evaluating performance in countries where IMF policies have been implemented are (1) an upper limit for the cumulative change in net credit of the banking system to the government; (2) an upper limit for the cumulative budget deficit of the government; (3) an upper limit for the cumulative change in the net domestic assets of the banking system; (4) a lower limit for the cumulative change in convertible currencies of the banking system (Gomulka 1995, p. 328). The performance criteria adopted primarily for Poland focused on the inflation rate and the country's external position. Reduction of inflation was treated as a policy objective but no quantitative criteria were established.

Poland's policy makers, with considerable IMF influence, established the following performance criteria with which to monitor the effectiveness of their transformation policies. These criteria included 'macroeconomic consistency conditions' (Gomulka 1995, p. 324) such as income, disposable income, demand for money, net government revenue, the stock of bank credit to the non-financial sector of the economy, and expected inflation rate. The key criteria were the budget deficit (fiscal measure), interest rate (monetary measure), exchange rate and stock of net international reserves (external measures), and wage rate (incomes measure). The 'nominal anchors' of the stabilization program were the exchange rate and wage rate, as policy makers sought to establish a fixed nominal exchange rate as the main policy instrument for reducing inflation.

Growth

According to official Polish estimates annual growth of GDP has been increasing since early 1992. There is reason to believe the 1996 rate may be close to the 7% rate achieved in 1995, making it the fastest growing country in Europe. Growth in the industrial sector is strong, with real industrial production up over 10% in 1995 (Delegation of the European Commission in Poland 1995).

Inflation

Following a period of hyperinflation during the early stages of the shock therapy, annual inflation has fallen, albeit at much slower rates, to just under 30% in 1995. Long range forecasts vary widely due to different evaluations of the extent to which inflationary pressures such as a high inflow of foreign currency and growing increases in salaries will manifest themselves in rising consumer prices. Polish analysts believe persistent inflation is cost induced, placing particular blame on the combination of high interest rates, a 'significant encumbrance of salaries with taxes paid by employers (which exceeded 48% in 1994), and a highly energy-intensive economic structure' (Central Office of Planning 1995b, p. 15).

Restructuring the economy

Most analysts would agree that 'structural adjustment has been the dominant economic process in Poland' (Berg 1994, p. 38). The percentage of GDP accounted for by the private sector grew from about 30% in 1990 to over 60% by the end of 1995, with private sector employment increasing to more than 65% as compared to a 46% rate in 1989 (Central Office of Planning Poland 1995a, p. 7). Relatively less efficient economic units unable to compete in the new environment have been gradually eliminated. Indirect instruments of monetary control and reform of the banking system have also been established – including 'the establishment of a central bank accounting system; the development of a money market and a government securities market; and the emergence of a stock market' (Chopra 1994, p. 23).

For both political and economic reasons privatization of state-owned assets has been slow. Some Polish experts disagree with the emphasis placed on comprehensive privatization which will eliminate all state-owned enterprises.

One argues that in 1992 the profitability rate of these enterprises was about the same as that of private firms, with only the private firms in construction and transportation doing better than state-owned enterprises in this regard (Mujzel 1993, p. 19). There is support for this position: a comparative performance of the private and public sector indicates that in 1994 productivity of the public sector (in constant 1992 prices) rose 16% (partly due to shifting of labor from state-owned enterprises as well as to hardening of enterprise budget constraints), nearly as much as that of the private sector which increased more than 19%. This performance together with the Polish government's principal economic advisor, Jerzy Hausner's assessment that direct privatization of the state-owned giants 'is impossible' (Hausner 1995, p. 3) suggests that the Chinese experience, where state-owned enterprises have been retained and phased out gradually to mitigate the unemployment and poverty problem while the private sector is encouraged to grow, may be quite relevant for all CEE nations.

Zloty stability and convertibility
In 1990 a fixed exchange rate of 9500 zloty to the dollar was selected, but soon after shock therapy was implemented it was devalued by 31.6%. After subsequent devaluations totaling about 18% in 1992 and 1993 the zloty has stabilized while the basket has remained unchanged.[35] Analysts forecast that the zloty will continue to appreciate in real terms and become fully convertible within the next few years.

Fiscal trends
Poland's state budget deficit has improved since the depth of the recession in 1992, rising from a deficit of 6% of GDP to a deficit under 3% before the 1995 election year. For most of 1995, spending cuts were taboo due to the October–November 1995 presidential election and 1996 parliamentary election. In terms of expenditure, 'the structure of state budget revenues has shifted steadily in the direction of that usual in a market economy: more indirect and personal taxes (which now account for over 2/3 of revenues versus about half in 1990)' (OECD 1994, pp. 33–5). The fiscal deficit has contributed to reduced funding for programs in education, health care, welfare, and unemployment as well as in the state's ability to promote culture. Policy makers will be hard pressed to further reduce the deficit due to fiscal pressure from the number of pensioners which is growing faster than the number of contributors in the labor force.

Incomes
Average incomes declined almost 30% from 1989 to 1994, with the most dramatic decline in 1990 following the first round of shock therapy.[36] By

1994, however, real monthly net salaries began to increase. Poland's 'real' wage growth (nominal wage rise deflated by change in the exchange rate) over 1993–4 was 22.3% (*The Economist* Intelligence Unit 1995a, April 17, p. 1).

Consumption
Among the positive results has been the elimination of the necessity to shop for many goods on the black market at exorbitant prices as well as the need to purchase excess quantities of goods in anticipation of a shortage; a greater range and quality of goods and services; much less time spent queuing to purchase goods and services; and the absence of low quality consumer goods subsidized by the government. Using data on purchases of consumer durables there is evidence that 'the increase in consumer durables' holding between 1990 and 1993 … [was] "substantial"' (OECD 1994, p. 32).

Productivity
While capital productivity growth has been weak, productivity of labor has rebounded after the initial impact of shock therapy. Part of the improvement in labor's performance is attributable to the decrease in state-owned enterprise employment, as labor productivity rose over 11% following a decline in employment of about 10%. Labor productivity in the private sector has increased by around 20% since early 1992 while employment in that sector was increasing by 13% during the same period (OECD 1994).

Investment
Like the pattern of other performance indicators, investment rebounded sharply in 1994 following dramatic declines in 1990 and 1991. Uncertainty in industries such as electronics, telecommunications and power generation concerning ownership and control, as well as reductions in subsidies, dampened the growth of domestic investment, but foreign investment has increased considerably. Attracted by Poland's skilled labor and relatively low real wages, investors in industries where real wages are a high percentage of production costs (such as textiles) have set up outward trade processing systems in which goods are made in Poland to Western specifications, usually from semi-finished materials, and then re-exported for sale to wealthier nations.

External financial conditions
The reduction in Poland's foreign debt obligations has been significant – as the total debt and debt-service reduction as a percentage of debt restructured was over 63% (IMF 1995, pp. 14–15). Perhaps as compensation for accepting foreign-endorsed shock therapy policies,[37] as a percentage of commercial debt the reduction for Poland, over 49%, exceeded that of all other major

debtor countries including Brazil and Mexico (Mesjasz 1995, p. 13). Negotiations with the 'London Club' and 'Paris Club' of creditors has resulted in
Poland's obligation to repay diminished to less than $7 billion for principal
and interest of its debt (about 10 per cent of foreign exchange earned from
exports) during the 1990–94 period rather than the more than $32 billion the
nation was scheduled to repay (Central Office of Planning 1995b, p. 4). In
1991 alone Poland's total debt service was nearly $9 billion, but by 1994 it
had been reduced to just over $3 billion – although obligations will increase
considerably beginning around the year 2000.[38]

Some non-IMF performance criteria and corresponding data
The aforementioned criteria and data correspond to Polish policy makers'
goals and priorities. There are other criteria that some Polish and outside
analysts believe should be taken into account in assessing the performance of
the economy after shock therapy was introduced. These include unemployment,[39] income distribution, and changes in overall welfare – including the
incidence of poverty.

The rate of unemployment grew steadily worse, rising from 1.5% in the
first quarter of 1990 to 15.4% during the third quarter of 1993 (Ministry of
Economic Affairs 1995a, p. 44). After a decrease the following quarter the
rate grew to 16.7% in early 1994, and declined slowly to 14.8% late in 1995
(Central Office of Planning 1995a, p. 10). It then rose back to 15.4% by mid
1996. In part due to a lack of labor force mobility and difficult housing
market conditions there is a high concentration of unemployment in rural
areas and in some clustered peripheral economies in the northeast region of
Poland, many of which with unemployment rates exceeding 25%.[40]

Some offsetting aspects of Polish unemployment are noteworthy. On the
positive side, around half the unemployed do some work for remuneration
according to one free market research institute. Overall, an estimated one
third of the adult population receives income from firms with fewer than five
employees and perhaps also through informal economic activity of some type
(*The Economist* Intelligence Unit 1995b). In addition, in a 1994 survey, the
OECD predicted a 'steady fall in joblessness' (OECD 1994, pp. 55–6). On
the other hand, the rate of unemployment would be even higher had not
Poland lowered its retirement age in 1990–92 in an effort to generate employment – resulting in pension costs which constitute a percentage of GDP that
ranks among the highest in CEE (Fox 1995, p. 36). In response to the current
labor market situation, the leading Polish economic advisor to the government argues that unemployment 'has already become ... [the economy's]
most difficult problem to solve' (Hausner 1995, p. 6).

Income distribution
In 1989 Poland's distribution of income featured a low Gini coefficient, 0.24
(World Bank 1991, p. 262). The evidence concerning the change in income
distribution since shock therapy is not clear. Most agree that those on fixed
incomes, the unemployed, and rural households which rely on agriculture
have suffered the most (the latter following large reductions in agricultural
subsidies), and that the Gini coefficient has increased (Berg 1994, p. 412).
There are indications that while a 'narrow segment of the population have
made fortunes, ... the majority are much worse off; they must bear the burden
of the high social cost of shock treatment' (Adam 1994, p. 615).[41]

Social costs: poverty, changes in the standard of living
Unfortunately, there is growing evidence 'the Polish experience suggests that
the social and economic costs of reform [policies] now appear to be much
greater than originally anticipated' (Dhanji 1990, p. 13), and that there has
been 'a high social cost of economic transformation' (Central Office of
Planning 1995b, p. 19). In addition to high unemployment and growing disparities in income distribution, unexpectedly high costs include a growing
percentage of individuals subsisting on low or sub poverty level incomes,
with 'about 30% of households hav[ing] fallen into the low income bracket'
(Central Office of Planning 1995b, p. 19).[42] Performance indicators do not
suggest that the essential needs of most Poles are unsatisfied, but while
average per capita caloric intake has risen and significant improvement in
purchasing power has been realized by many Poles, there appear to be strong
indicators that compared to 1989 10% or more of the population is living in
poverty. Statistics seem to reinforce this picture of a society impoverished by
the market, with 'a third of the population living below the poverty line' (*The
Economist* Intelligence Unit 1994b, p. 5).

SUMMARY OF THE POLISH ECONOMY'S
PERFORMANCE SINCE 1990

Using the aforementioned performance criteria and corresponding data, an
analysis of Poland's performance following shock therapy by proponents
and opponents of the initial transformation policies leads to two broad
performance assessments. The policy makers and their supporters conclude
that the performance has been favorable, and therefore that shock therapy
was a success. They reach this conclusion by heavily weighting performance indicators such as the rate of GDP growth, expansion and growing
significance of the private sector, a redirection of most trade by private
Polish entrepreneurs with private sector counterparts outside of CEE, and

financial stabilization concerning the rate of inflation, zloty, fiscal deficit and international debt.[43]

Other analysts who emphasize the importance of different performance criteria argue that a number of unfavorable economic and social conditions have ensued following implementation of the initial transformation policies – particularly high and prolonged unemployment, a rising Gini coefficient, and much greater than anticipated social costs as manifested by higher rates of poverty. In the opinion of these analysts the high social costs more than offset the favorable trends in the IMF-type criteria endorsed by architects of shock therapy. It appears that a majority of the population believes the social costs which coincided with the introduction of shock policies have been excessive and unnecessary – manifested by the election of former communist party member Aleksander Kwasniewski as President to replace Lech Walensa. Many observers believe the outcome of this election, which witnessed the highest voter turnout since voting was permitted after 1989, reflects a backlash against the rapid, negative impact of shock policies and the desire for a leader who would endorse policies designed to ease the shock of transformation.[44]

THE PERFORMANCE OF CHINA'S ECONOMY

Based upon performance indicators consistent with those of either Myrdal or the IMF (see Table 1.3), the Chinese economy has realized a favorable economic performance since 1978 while transforming itself towards greater reliance upon market institutions and working rules. Growth has been 'phenomenal' as real GNP has risen at an average annual rate of greater than 9% since 1978, by far the highest in the world during that time period (Liew 1995, p. 883). China's economy is now the world's third largest, and its gross national product is almost half that of the United States. The value of China's exports places it tenth in the world. Since 1980 the dollar value of its exports has increased from less than $20 billion to about $100 billion, primarily due to growth of labor productivity (which increased almost as fast as that of Korea and Taiwan during the same period), inexpensive labor, and currency depreciation (which fell from about 5.5 RMB per dollar in 1980 to less than 1.5 in the early 1990s) (IMF 1995, p. 82). China's credit rating has recently been upgraded by Moody's Investors to single-A-3 (Prybla 1995, p. 125). Due in part to these favorable trends, China has received more foreign direct investment than all CEE nations combined. In comparison to Poland, China has experienced a decline in its average real exchange rate while Poland's has appreciated. China's long-term private capital inflow rose 5% from 1990–94 versus only 1% for Poland (although Poland's rose 7% in 1995), and its 1994

Table 1.3   Chinese performance indicators

GDP growth	1980–91	9.4%
Poverty*		
Infant mortality (rate per 1000)	1981	71
	1991	38
Life expectancy at birth	1981	67
	1991	69
Incidence	1978	28.0%
	1990	8.6%
Average daily calorie intake		
per capita	1965	1931
	1988	2632
Real income (increase in average per capita)		
urban	1985–90	48.3%
rural	1978–90	135%
Inflation (average annual rate)	1980–89	5.8%
	1990–95	11.7%

Note: *Between 1981 and 1991 China raised the incomes and welfare standards of the poorest 40% of the population, as noted in the improvement in 'basic needs' such as greater calorie intake, reduced infant mortality, and higher average life expectancy (Nolan 1995, p. 12).

Source: Nolan 1995, pp. 11–14; World Bank; *The Economist* Intelligence Unit.

current account to GDP ratio was 0.1 compared to Poland's –3.0 (Dadush and Brahmbratt 1995, p. 5). The absence of human rights is often cited as a strong negative feature of China's. Many characterize the Chinese regime as 'turbid' and 'oppressive'. While virtually no analysts disagree with this assessment, some point out that if a broad definition of such rights included not only the right to vote but the right to an improved standard of living and an environment with a low violent crime rate, then China's 'human rights' record is better than that of Russia and some other CEE nations (Nolan 1995).

It appears that China possessed no relative advantage in its initial conditions (obstacles and problems faced) in 1978 compared to CEE in 1989, and actually was at a relative disadvantage when faced with the challenge of transforming its economy (Nolan 1995). To the extent that China's economic performance can be considered favorable, it has been in spite of, rather than because of the initial conditions faced on the eve of its transformation period. China was able to take advantage of what few advantages it may have had because it possessed a stable government whose authorities were able and willing to introduce pragmatic, non ideological transformation policies.[45] Included among the benefits of political stability in China is the ability to preserve fiscal stability and to experiment with reforms on a small scale before introducing them over a broad area. These experimental policies generated a Myrdalian spread effect as the initial favorable performance initiated self reinforcing trends throughout the economy.

Compared with Polish policy makers and their Western advisors, Chinese policy makers (as well as those in Japan and Vietnam) have been far more pragmatic – relying on 'common sense and experience rather than a high level of economic theory' (Nolan 1995, p. 60). Reforms were measured and introduced in an experimental, evolutionary manner. Rather than 'regard the economy as a simple mechanism akin to perfect competition', Chinese policy makers developed their own transformation program which featured an eclectic blend of economic philosophies (Nolan 1995, p. 60).

In addition to this pragmatism other factors have been credited for the country's economic performance. These include the rapid expansion of the private sector driven by entrepreneurial activity; continued government support of state-owned enterprises; relatively easy access to credit for new enterprises; and a large volume of foreign direct investment[46] – with many of the investors being Chinese expatriates residing in Hong Kong, Singapore, and Taiwan who invest in the mainland through family networks. The relative size of China's private sector is perhaps not as important as its demonstration effect. More rapid growth in the private sector than the state sector has had an ideological impact on managers and workers. Meanwhile economic decision making at lower level enterprises has increasingly been turned over to managers who, in reaching cooperative agreements with private enterprises, have begun learning how to respond to market forces. In the process, the private sector has become intertwined with enterprises featuring all other forms of ownership. This phenomena has influenced the subsequent evolution of state-owned enterprises and collectives in a market-oriented direction.

The state sector has been aided by pragmatic, supportive state policies for development of the private sector.[47] While this authoritarian political structure forbids groups from offering any challenge to its authority, it 'otherwise allows its citizens much [economic] freedom' (Metzger 1996, p. 29). Acknowledging that their authority could be maintained in the absence of economic disaster, and astutely recognizing that the initial conditions of their economy in 1978 meant that a rapid introduction of policies similar to shock therapy would likely be followed by a large recession, Chinese policy makers chose to continue subsidizing state enterprises while encouraging private sector expansion. This policy has had two significant benefits. First, in guaranteeing to preserve the interests and living standards of those managing and working in the state sector, policy makers have been able to introduce economic reforms aimed at gradually transforming the state enterprises while helping to integrate them with the private sector. Second, although there has been a 'massive diversion of supplies to the market from the plan in the late 1980s, there was no dramatic collapse in the output of state enterprise' (Liew 1995, p. 887). The growing private sector has afforded many workers with an opportunity to moonlight, gathering income which may now comprise a substantial portion of the average family's income.

SUMMARY – POLAND VS. CHINA

Shock therapy in Poland, aided by certain external factors, appears to have stimulated favorable trends in many of the criteria deemed important by the nation's policy makers – albeit at the expense of higher than anticipated social costs. China's policies have done likewise without contributing to, or coinciding with a severe recession – albeit at the expense of political freedom. These respective transformation experiences provide lessons which are useful for transformation policy makers.[48]

1. *Ideology remains an important aspect of policy formulation and evaluation of performance, and is instrumental in promoting the view that 'transition orthodoxy' manifested in shock therapy policies is the most suitable approach to transformation.* The Chinese experience indicates otherwise. An important lesson for policy makers is to avoid ideologically based policy measures which rely exclusively on deductive 'economic' models based upon a neoclassical perspective. Shock therapy was not adopted because of any analytical proof or empirical evidence that it would achieve the objectives of Poland's policy makers. It was adopted because of the belief held by many Western economists that a rapid, linear transformation path to a 'free market economy' without the transforming nation experiencing extensive social and economic costs was both possible and desirable. If a gradual transformation without extensive social costs is preferred, then a 'rejection of dogmatism, and implementation of a comprehensive, efficiency-oriented systemic reform of publicly-owned enterprises' (Mujzel 1993, p. 22) offers an alternative to treating privatization as an end in itself.

2. *Shock therapy appears to have had both a positive and negative impact on the performance of Poland's economy.* This point follows from Poland's experience since 1990, as well as from that of Latin American nations where

similar policies were implemented. If policy makers wish to pursue a more gradual transformation, then an alternative approach is to compensate losers in the state sector so that relatively few people become materially worse off during the transformation period as a result of stringent macroeconomic or structural policies. Otherwise institutional resistance to reform will ensue as social costs mount, among other problems.

3. *Strong state support can contribute favorably to economic performance of transforming economies.* China illustrates that a strong central state can be efficacious for transformation, especially in its ability to eliminate some otherwise powerful forces resisting institutional change. To the extent that there is relatively little resistance from those in the state-enterprise sector, credit can be given to Chinese policy makers' use of a combination of incentives for integration of state-owned enterprise managers and workers and the growing private sector with guarantees that existing entitlements, including employment, will be maintained.

4. *Promotion of the private sector and competition from below can contribute more favorably to performance than privatization or destruction of state-owned enterprises.* It appears that while privatization may not be crucial to a successful transformation, competition is. Therefore, instead of concentrating on privatizing existing state assets, policies which encourage entrepreneurial activity to expand within the private sector, at the same time maintaining but integrating and gradually reducing support for the state-owned sector, can be consistent with favorable performance trends without extensive social costs.[49]

EFFICACY OF CONTINUING THE INITIAL TRANSFORMATION POLICIES IN CEE

The previous section demonstrated that China's transformation policies have coincided with a performance level at least equal to that of Poland (from the IMF view), and which exceeds that of all CEE countries (from a Myrdalian view). Unlike many CEE nations since 1989, China has been 'developing' in the Myrdalian sense. Its economy's performance has been achieved without its transformation policies contributing to, or coinciding with severe recession and corresponding high social costs. This calls into question the efficacy of continued reliance upon CEE transformation policies based upon the neoclassical perspective which assumes that transformation requires rapid privatization, elimination of subsidies to state-owned enterprises, stabilization measures prior to institutional reforms, and a passive state role in supply-side responses during the transformation process.[50]

Four additional points lend support to replacing the existing transformation perspective and policies characteristic of the CEE region. First, the belief that neoclassical 'transition orthodoxy' manifested in shock therapy policies is the most suitable approach to transformation for any country is rooted in an ideological perspective that is inappropriate for the region. Transformation goals for CEE in the early 1990s were biased toward Western interests, ridden with inherent ideological assumptions in neoclassical theory such as a desire to secure markets for Western exports and access to CEE's raw materials, and strengthen political influence throughout the region.[51] The treatment of stabilization measures as themselves ends in the short run and the claim that these means can be separated from the ultimate goal (namely, the specific type of economy to be established) run counter to the Myrdalian belief that development should be defined by societies' needs, not abstract targets, and that means and ends cannot be separated.[52]

Second, the strong technical bent of Western advisors, combined with behavioral assumptions and policy prescriptions rooted in traditional neoclassical theory, are at best questionable and at worst completely inappropriate for CEE. The neoclassical perspective leads to policies which seek to introduce institutions derived from the textbook FME model, reduce all economic problems to a matter of optimum allocation of resources, and assume that efficiency will be established once perfectly competitive markets and free individuals seeking to maximize utility are created or emerge. This approach is both 'simplistic' in its formulation of policies and representative of a 'revival of a monolithic and deterministic vision of the economic system and the way it works' (Dallago 1992, p. 268). Economists familiar with comparative economic studies who do not allow ideological preferences to cloud their analysis recognize that identical reform policies introduced in multiple economies are likely to generate dissimilar outcomes. No single set of 'economic' policies can serve as a 'universal panacea' for CEE (Barry 1993, p. 2). However, the CEE transformation policies 'make no allowances for cultural and historical differences between the countries and ethnic group' (Pejovich 1993, p. 76). This has been manifested by the 'arrogant messianism of shock therapy' introduced throughout most of CEE as a 'sweeping prescription' (Koves 1992, pp. 17, 29).

Third, in Russia, where the belief that shock therapy justified the neoclassical 'transition orthodoxy' was advocated by many Western advisors, shock therapy policies were implemented with disastrous results.[53] The performance of Russia's economy suggests that there are significant problems with the assumptions and methodology underlying the neoclassical transformation perspective. The attempt to establish a FME in Russia based upon the assumption that economic growth and system transformation would ensue quickly following the dissolution of the state and establishment of efficient markets, was misguided. Some of the transformation policies were large-scale, 'dangerous [economic and political] reform experiments' introduced in a cookbook manner. The irony of the Russian case is that it constituted a 'great leap forward' which had the same results as China's ill-fated 1950s leap.[54]

The final supporting point for replacement of the neoclassical transformation perspective is that such a view encouraged policy makers to naively expect that economic rationality in every country would be the only guiding force of the transformation. This assumption followed from their 'underestimat[ing what de Tocqueville and Myrdal[55] called] the "soft" factors of habits, mentalities, cultural routines' (Sztompka 1992, p. 2). From the CEE countries' historical legacy, many values, norms, and standards for behavior persist which constitute the primary impediments to development. These include the absence of individualistic competitiveness that is achievement oriented, lack of a civic culture in which people willingly adhere to a rule of law, and absence of a business culture where people are clean, orderly, neat, and eager to satisfy consumers. Where legislation was passed and implemented with the intention of creating the desired 'free market' institutions, policy makers failed to account for the institutional legacy of the previous economy – with high social costs born by many citizens as a result.

Overall, evidence supports the need for a new transformation perspective. To maintain this perspective means continued application of rules for economizing from microeconomic theory to a very large issue – advocated by 'experts' who themselves took a great leap from their own special fields to offer 'grand simplistic generalizations' for CEE nations (Nolan 1995, p. 312). While such generalizations have often been proven incorrect in institutional economic development literature, the experts never doubted that their policies would succeed. Such misguided confidence manifests an absence in understanding among many orthodox economists concerning the manner in which culture, politics, and social structure interact within an economy.

TOWARDS AN INSTITUTIONAL BASIS FOR A USEFUL TRANSFORMATION PERSPECTIVE: MYRDAL'S POLITICAL ECONOMY

A useful transformation perspective for any nation must go well beyond specifying methods for achieving macroeconomic stabilization and establishing a FME. It must incorporate certain lessons from the development experiences of other nations, recognize the essential features of a realistic theory of societal change, and initiate social interaction through dialogue among interest group representatives. It would include a holistic conception of societal development, and could be based upon the 'Popperian principle of experimentation' (Nolan 1995, p. 311), which would contain an evolutionary approach toward transformation policy. Such a perspective also would be rooted in 'intellectual and institutional history combined with considerable immersion in the [country's] ... history, thought, and current situation' (Metzger 1996, p. 7) of the country to be transformed.

Analyzing Myrdal and identifying his contributions can provide a foundation for developing such a transformation perspective. He relied heavily on history, and was influenced by (and sought to account for) the economic, political, and social conditions of the era in which he was writing.[56] His conception of behavior included the view that forces in addition to self-interest (including emotion and interpersonal relationships such as trust) influence the economic decisions of societal members. Unlike recent advisors to Central and East Europe, Myrdal does not believe that a large number of profit-oriented entrepreneurs offering supply-side innovations can be expected to emerge quickly in every nation – particularly in a nation whose economy is performing poorly and suddenly seeks to stimulate investment while transforming its principal economic, political, and social institutions. Citing differences in conditions between Western industrialized nations and the rest of the world such as availability of raw materials, climate, population growth, government honesty and stability, as well as social motives and mechanisms, he argued against expectation that some latent entrepreneurial class exists which will respond spontaneously and rationally to investment opportunities in all nations.

In the Myrdalian view a causal interrelatedness exists among technological, attitudinal, and institutional factors during the process of societal change. Unlike most economists, he argues that the original stimulus for initiating cumulative change within a complex social mechanism will stem from changes in attitudes and institutions rather than from technological or economic variables (such as prices or interest rates). Those seeking to direct the transformation of an economy, he argues, must recognize that attitudinal and institutional change must precede changes in economic variables. He was adamant that there are no 'economic problems', but that social systems have mixed and complex problems with economic, political, social, and cultural components – all aspects of which are highly interrelated and need to be studied in their cultural context. It is necessary for the analyst to identify causal relationships among these variables before proposing policies consistent with a society's attitudes and institutions.[57] Myrdal recognized significant attitudinal and institutional differences among societies, and argued that no single set of policies would provide a panacea for any nation. He was especially critical of policies based upon narrow, closed economic models which emphasize easily quantifiable variables at the neglect of non-economic factors such as attitudes, health, and education. He considered such policies inappropriate and misguided because they ignore the primary impediments to societal transformation and development.

He would have adamantly opposed the transformation perspective and policies characteristic of CEE, for Myrdal's criticism of neoclassical economics was extensive.[58] He recognized the inadequacy of its static equilibrium approach to analyzing broad societal problems, especially its assertion that the typical process by which social change occurs in one basic, endogenous economic factor generates subsequent adjustments in other economic factors (such as a change in relative prices or privatization of previously state-owned enterprises).[59] He chided neoclassical policy makers for reducing all problems to a matter of optimum allocation of resources and for assuming that efficiency and favorable economic growth would ensue following the establishment of competitive markets. A further criticism was leveled at neoclassical economics for being ahistorical, with proponents advancing their theories as universal propositions valid for every time, place, and culture.

Social scientists seeking a new, more useful transformation perspective should be encouraged about the potential for developing such a perspective by the contributions of Myrdal. The following chapters will demonstrate that his interdisciplinary, dynamic, long-run perspective which accounts for historical, political, and social aspects of the society being studied, can be the basis for a useful alternative to the reductionist neoclassical economic perspective – and would include a more realistic understanding of economies as well as a method of analysis capable of providing a sound basis for transformation policy formulation.

2. Gunnar Myrdal I: 1915–33, the years of 'High Theory'

INTRODUCTION

Gunnar Myrdal believed that his professional life consisted of three distinct periods, each characterized by a different stage in his intellectual development. These periods overlapped slightly. This chapter will present the formative years of Gunnar Myrdal I (GM I): 1915–33, 'economic theorist'. The following two chapters focus respectively on the transition period of GM II – 1932–38, 'political economist'; and GM III – 1938–87, 'institutional economist' (Myrdal 1969b, p. 10), an unorthodox and anti-orthodox social scientist with global concerns. The analysis of each Gunnar Myrdal contains a biographical sketch and summary of his major contributions, identifies the unique features of his methodology, explains his pedigree, and outlines his most important policy prescriptions.

BIOGRAPHICAL SKETCH AND MAJOR CONTRIBUTIONS

Pre Dissertation

Reflecting upon his career, an 84-year old GM III described himself as a 'fundamentalist', pointing out that there are 'fundamental things which go through my life' (Appendix, Myrdal Interview 1982). Two of these fundamental things were the optimistic philosophy of the Enlightenment taught to him as a *gymnasium* student by his history and geography teacher, John Landquist, and an interest in social policy issues.[60] Despite having focused on natural science and mathematics throughout *gymnasium*, the Enlightenment belief in the ability of people to improve society through reason, combined with an interest in determining how 'law, politics, and society function' (Jackson 1990, p. 45) led GM I to enter the Law School of Stockholm University in 1918 (Appendix, Myrdal Interview 1980). After receiving his law degree in 1923 he held various legal positions (including clerk, magistrate, and public prosecutor) during the next few years.[61]

In retrospect, GM III credits his law studies with having two lasting beneficial effects upon his career (which he believes eventually pointed him in the
'institutionalist direction'): one, 'to mark words', that is to 'be clear about the
meaning of words', and two, 'to get hold of what is the central problem' after
sifting through all the evidence (Appendix, Myrdal Interview 1980). Sensing
that her husband found the legal profession 'boring and [that he] was deeply
depressed and intellectually frustrated' (Jackson 1990, p. 53) while sharing
his desire to comprehend the rules which governed changes within society,
Alva Myrdal convinced GM I to study economics 'since it was much more
like mathematics and natural sciences' (Appendix, Myrdal Interview 1980)
and offered greater potential to improve society than a legal practice.[62] Consequently, Myrdal began reading economics in 1923, and soon thereafter
entered the University of Stockholm as a full-time student.

In 1925 he traveled to England, doing research in Cambridge and London
on the classical economists. During the following two years he carried out
dissertation research at universities and libraries in Germany and France,
while expanding contacts among European academic circles. In 1927 he
received his *juris* doctor degree in economics, and was appointed Assistant
Professor of Political Economy at Stockholm University. Analysts credit GM
I with making many significant contributions to theory and policy making
during this theoretical segment of his career. These contributions were in
microeconomic and macroeconomic theory, objectivity in economic analysis,
and international trade theory.

Dissertation

GM I's intellectual concerns were in 'pure theory'. GM III describes his
dissertation, *Prisbildnings problemet och föränderligheten* (Change and the
Problem of Price Formation) as a 'highly theoretical' analysis of the importance of risk and uncertainty – albeit an analysis that GM III claimed he
could 'hardly understand today' (Myrdal Interview 1980). The study is a
microeconomic analysis of planning decisions made by individual business
enterprises, and represented his 'first major theoretical work on the [system-
atic] integration of anticipation into the theory of price formation' (Myrdal
1958a, p. 242).

This manuscript contains 'two important innovations: the importance of
ideas about the future and the uncertainty of the future, although previous
events helped in the forming of an opinion' (Ohlin 1981, p. 196). Some
consider it to be 'the cornerstone of the [innovative findings of the] Stockholm School[63] ... where the main contribution was the construction of the
"method of expectation"', while others describe it as 'the opening ground of
a new epoch in Swedish economics' (Dostaler 1990, p. 199). GM I succeeded

in 'dynamizing [Gustav] Cassel's formulation of a Walrasian system of prices' (Streeten 1992, p. 120). Crediting his dissertation director Cassel, considered by some to be the world's leading economist during that era, for influencing his own 'general approach' (Myrdal 1958a, p. 242), GM I analyzed 'how prices are formed, profits occur, and capital value changes come about as consequences of *anticipation* of future changes in market conditions and technical development' (Lundberg 1974, p. 472). Using his dynamic model he concluded that anticipation influences pricing plans made by entrepreneurs, and therefore their anticipation is one determinant of price formation – a conclusion that could not be reached from the static neoclassical model. Myrdal stressed the distinction between *ex ante* decisions and *ex post* measurable, actual values. He explains these concepts as follows: 'quantities defined in terms of measurements made at the end of the period in question are referred to as *ex post*, quantities defined in terms of planned at the beginning of the period in question are referred to as *ex ante*' (Myrdal 1939a, pp. 46–7). This distinction 'provided a deeper understanding of the behavior of economic agents and of the institutions in which they operate' (Dopfer 1988, p. 228).

The ability of Myrdal to have 'brilliantly amplified' (Streeten 1992, p. 133) Cassel's earlier contribution resulted in his being one of only two Swedish economists (Knut Wicksell was the other) during the era of Swedish economic eminence to receive the highest grade (*laudatur*) for a dissertation defense (Kindleberger 1987, p. 393). Following the success of his dissertation in the academic community GM I's reputation at this early stage in his career extended well beyond Sweden. Irving Fischer wrote GM I and told him that he had been informed that Myrdal was 'one of the rising generation of economists likely to make real contributions to the subject' (Fischer 1926). The two exchanged written works, Myrdal sending his dissertation, while receiving Fischer's *Mathematical Investigations in the Theory of Value and Prices* in return.

The Political Element in the Development of Economic Theory, 1930

The focus on natural sciences while he was a *gymnasium* student contributed to Myrdal's concern with facts, and with his desire to observe facts clearly without bias. GM III credits his university mentors with encouraging original thought, open discussion, and controversy, admitting to having been inspired by the 'unquestioning appreciation of independence and originality in scientific work and their unhesitating acceptance of criticism' (Myrdal 1958a, p. 251). This independence of thought, plus some inspiration from his friend Alf Johansson, with whom he was philosophically harmonious, and the influence of Uppsala philosopher Axel Hagerstrom, who believed that no objective values exist, led to Myrdal's decision to analyze the role played by values throughout the history of economic theory.

He was seeking a solution to the problem of how to introduce valuations into economic analysis and thus to draw political conclusions on a scientific basis. Valuations, according to GM I, were established by the influential and decision-making groups in the society under study. Consequently, his method of analysis included the requirement that social psychology be relied upon for 'careful psychological stud[ies of the attitudes] of as many groups as possible' (Myrdal 1958a, p. 229). GM I argued that once these 'a priori' ideas were known to the economic researcher, the economist's role would be to 'explain the actual situation and state the effects of different possible modes of action in relation to the same initial situation' (Myrdal 1969a, p. 2).

GM I's initial attempt to resolve the value question culminated in his book *The Political Element in the Development of Economic Theory*. GM I was seeking to prove that it was possible for there to be a positive economic theory independent of all subjective valuations. However he was not able to make the contribution he intended – namely to demonstrate that it was possible for economics to be value free if the analyst's valuations were kept separate from the analysis. At the completion of this study he realized such a position was untenable. Years later he admitted to having been guilty of 'naive empiricism' for assuming that observations could be made without any preconceptions and that the facts could be organized into some system in an unbiased manner (Dykema 1980, p. 148). However, the book is considered a significant contribution to economics, 'truly a seminal work ... [which] overhauled in many ways Max Weber's notion of objectivity in the social sciences' (Balapkins 1979). According to this analyst, '[i]ts most distinctive feature is that Myrdal rejected the widely accepted doctrine of value-free economics, which most economists accepted ... [as] the brash young Myrdal bluntly told his fellow economists "don't pretend, don't play games with your value-free stance"' (Balapkins 1988, p. 100). *The Political Element* was considered by the Royal Swedish Academy to be one of Myrdal's three greatest works.[64] Another analyst argues GM I's criticism is a

particularly significant ... [contribution due to] his recognition that the assumption of interpersonal comparisons of utility had been made *implicitly*. ... With this insight, he was able to challenge the ideological character of modern economic theory in general. He argued that ... [e]conomists anticipate their ideological intentions; their choices of problem areas and explanatory variables are inevitably colored by what is anticipated (Dopfer 1988, p. 229).

Monetary Equilibrium, 1931

GM I describes *Monetary Equilibrium* as an 'essay [which] bears the mark of the time at which it was written and the background of its author. It belongs among the attempts made during the early years of the great depression to reach a basis for a deeper and more comprehensive monetary theory'. (Myrdal 1939a, p. v). In the process of writing *Monetary Equilibrium* GM I provides a new conception of monetary equilibrium in which stability occurs only when there is 'correspondence between the actual and anticipated course of events' (Seccareccia 1992, p. 159). His theory anticipated some significant aspects contained in Keynes's *General Theory of Employment, Interest, and Money*.[65] For example, GM I 'reached the eminently Keynesian conclusion that a monetary equilibrium between savings and investment is consistent with various levels of employment'.[66] He received high praise for this articulation of Wicksell's pioneering which offered his contemporaries and followers a more solid theoretical foundation to build upon. Bertil Ohlin credits Myrdal's effort for 'mapping out the paths and the results to which a consistent extension of one variety of Wicksellian thought would lead ... [thereby encouraging Swedish contemporaries] to explore alternative paths' (Ohlin 1978, p. 388).

Monetary Equilibrium has been classified as 'one of a trio[67] of fundamental contributions to monetary theory in the Wicksellian tradition' (Velupillai 1992, p. 137). Myrdal is credited with being able to 'formulate a more polished and integrated approach to monetary economics than ... Wicksell' (Seccareccia 1992, p. 144). In response to a request from Friedrich Hayek, Myrdal wrote a condensed version of the book, and it was included in a collection of essays edited by Hayek and published in 1933.[68] John Hicks claimed he was 'lucky' to have access to this book 'so early' (1934), and that this work and other Swedish contributions to economic theory influenced him more than the work of Keynes and other Cambridge economists. Hicks believed GM I (and other members of the Stockholm School) had a better understanding of anticipation than Keynes, and along with other neoclassical economists used Myrdalian concepts such as 'ex ante/ex post savings and investment, his explanation of unemployment in terms of wage rigidity, and his rationale for short-run fiscal stabilization policy ... [as] building blocks of the postwar neoclassical synthesis' (Seccareccia 1992, p. 162). This synthesis can be found in Hicks's IS-LM models and contemporary macroeconomic disequilibrium theory. Hicks also points out that in a 1934 document Myrdal appears to have anticipated Keynes by describing the multiplier process. (Dostaler 1990, pp. 210–12).

International Trade Theory

Upon his return from America in 1930 GM I accepted an offer to become Associate Professor of International Economics at the Postgraduate Institute of International Studies in Geneva. There he taught seminars on topics such as 'International Double Taxation' and 'Contemporary International Economic Questions', and did research on international trade and macroeconomic policy. A contemporary of GM I, Egon Glesinger, recalls his experience with Myrdal. Having studied international economics in Geneva, Glesinger traveled to Sweden to determine who was the Stockholm's School's 'big man' in international economics among Myrdal, Ohlin and Gösta Bagge (all students of Cassel). Glesinger offered each a look at a theory of international trade developed by one of his professors from Geneva. Bagge did not analyze it. Ohlin (who was so gifted that by age 24 he held a chair in economics in Copenhagen) analyzed the theory and, in front of business leaders and government authorities, 'suggested a campaign to which he pledged his fullest support' (Glesinger 1949). Myrdal read the theory, and rather than offer his own analysis asked one of his graduate students to evaluate the theory during a class with Glesinger present, after having first evaluated the theory with his students. The student pointed out the errors it contained. Glesinger conceded the errors, concluded who Sweden's brightest young economist was, and referred to Myrdal and his students as 'the most brilliant group'[69] of academics he had met (Glesinger 1949).

Closing Comment

Some of GM I's theoretical contributions would become the basis for Sweden's 1930s macroeconomic policies. In addition, there is evidence in his early writings that he would recommend an expansion of the state's agenda. For example, in *Monetary Equilibrium* GM I alluded to the superiority of state intervention in economic affairs over a laissez faire policy, especially the belief that business cycles could be mitigated through monetary and fiscal policy which fostered macroeconomic stability (Myrdal 1939a, pp. 178–80).

THEORETICAL MACROECONOMIST IN THE NEOCLASSICAL–WICKSELLIAN TRADITION

Pedigree

Based upon his interests, conceptualized reality, and method of analysis, GM III classified GM I as a 'pure theorist' (Appendix, Myrdal Interview 1982), a member of the 'macroeconomic neoclassical school' (Myrdal 1978a, p. 772) who was 'fascinated by abstract mathematical models of the 1920s' (Balapkins 1988, p. 100). GM III describes GM I's method of analysis as being 'focused on economic theory of the established type as it had developed in the classical and neoclassical tradition' (Myrdal 1969b, p. 10). GM 1 has been considered by others as a 'pure theorist' (Seccareccia 1992, pp. 161–2) whose scientific career was that of a 'traditional monetary economist' (Dopfer 1988, p. 227). A Swedish analyst argues that from 1925–33 GM I was a 'pure economic theorist' (Lundberg 1974, p. 473), and according to another Myrdal scholar was 'purer than the rest' (Harrison 1976).

Methodology

It has been asserted that GM I approached economics from a conventional, narrow 'isolationist' perspective (Reynolds 1974, p. 488), and that throughout GM I's written works he focused on purely economic problems and the roles played by a limited number of economic variables, although supplementing orthodox methods of analysis with his own methodology. A somewhat different appraisal of GM I's methodology claims that he deviated slightly from orthodox neoclassical economists, many of whom 'headed towards axiomatization of economic dynamics, borrowing their paradigms from classical mechanics that postulate the invariance of natural laws [whereas] Myrdal's [GM I's] analysis was, from the beginning, more *empirical* in its basic approach' (Dopfer 1988, p. 228).

In his dissertation GM I chose to depart from the partial static equilibrium approach. His method of analysis contained a dynamic theory of future prices in which risk preference as well as changes in economic variables were included in explaining the trend which future prices could be expected to follow. He rejected the notion of price determination within some partial equilibrium framework where 'static *ceteris paribus* conceptions' prevail (Lundberg 1974, p. 473), arguing that 'a]bove all, the process of price formation is dynamic and ... [s]tatic models are therefore of little use' (Myrdal 1969a, pp. 189–90). In its place he developed a dynamic theoretical structure of future price formation built around the influence of changes in economic variables anticipated by the entrepreneur as well as the same entrepreneur's attitude (whether optimistic or pessimistic) towards risk aversion.[70]

By the early 1930s GM I's interests shifted to monetary theory. He realized that the static equilibrium approach was insufficient for analyzing economic problems, and sought to define a dynamic cumulative process of change to incorporate into his method of analysis. GM I believed that the conventional approach suffered from the attempt by economists to explain equilibrium within a partial static framework. He maintained that 'the equilibrium character of a situation cannot ... be characterized sufficiently by a mere study of the general price movements' (Myrdal 1939a, p. 142). He went on to argue that as opposed to the orthodox 'highly unreal abstract concept of equilibrium', with its 'stationary [equilibrium] time period', a dynamic and cumulative process, involving the impact of entrepreneurial expectations upon the formation of prices, would generate conditions of monetary equilibrium (Myrdal 1939a, p. 23).

> The underlying idea is that one cannot assume an identity between demand and supply of consumption goods except in a state of static equilibrium. This proposition should seem obvious to the unsophisticated mind, since decisions to buy and sell a commodity are made by quite different individuals ... To treat supply and demand in ... [this case] as being identically, rather than conditionally equal, would involve a highly unreal and abstract concept of equilibrium. (Myrdal 1939a, p. 23)

As opposed to the orthodox concept of equilibrium, GM I believed that a dynamic and cumulative process, involving the impact of entrepreneurial expectations upon the formation of prices, would generate conditions of monetary equilibrium. He pointed out that

> [t]he occurrence of change is contradictory to the idea of a timeless point. At a point there are only *tendencies* which can be studied and must be studied as a preparatory step to the dynamic analysis proper which refers to the causal development in time up to the next point studied. It is the analysis of that development which gives the *raison d'etre* for introducing periods of time in economic theory. (Myrdal 1939a, pp. 44–5)

Having rejected the static equilibrium method of analysis, GM I uses Wicksell's dynamic theory that economic development occurs in a circular and cumulative direction away from equilibrium as a starting point from which to build his own framework for integrating monetary theory and price theory with the role of expectations. He begins by questioning the Wicksellian conception of a monetary equilibrium, arguing that '[t]he method of simply assuming a stationary starting point is therefore unsatisfactory. It evades the theoretical problems without solving them. In a stationary position there is equilibrium even in those relationships the stability of which would be incompatible with monetary equilibrium when primary changes occur' (Myrdal 1939a, p. 39).

GM I then sets out to 'clarify the content of this particular formulation [that is, monetary equilibrium]' (Myrdal 1939a, p. 30). He perceives the 'central problem' as follows: '[f]rom the standpoint of the fundamental ideas of Wicksell's monetary theory, what do the properties of a price situation in a non-stationary course of events [including expectations] have to be in order

that this situation can be characterized as a position of monetary equilibrium?' (Myrdal 1939a, p. 42). He sought to answer this by identifying the
formula for the condition of monetary equilibrium, the 'missing equation' –
which was 'namely the one determining the *multiplicative factor*, by which
the relative prices of equilibrium theory can be translated into absolute money
prices' (Myrdal 1939a, pp. 11–12). Although unable to complete this task,
GM I's book contains a number of theoretical contributions (see below). His
method of analysis in *Monetary Equilibrium* includes defining all 'concepts
in relation to the single *entrepreneur*, which is necessary as they include
elements of anticipations, risk valuations and capitalizations'[71] (Myrdal 1934b).
His empirical approach distinguishes his method of analysis from that of
other neoclassical economists at the time.

GM IN THE MAINSTREAM?

Narrow focus on economic theory

Throughout the formative period of GM I's intellectual development a number
of influential (albeit conflicting) factors manifested themselves in his method
of analysis. These factors include the drive to become an eminent economist,
held in high esteem by his mentors – especially Wicksell whose moral character he admired (Swedberg 1990, p. xiii); the desire to succeed Cassel as
professor at Stockholm University; the urge to rebel against his more orthodox, conservative mentors; the desire to develop economic theories superior
to these mentors; the struggle to free himself from the conventional wisdom
inherent in his graduate school education; the realization that both institutions as well as borrowing from other social science disciplines are important
in analyzing 'economic' problems; and his negative reaction against both
specialization in economics departments throughout the United States and
the rising influence of American institutional economists.

Many American economics students upon completion of their PhD degree
most likely have experienced similar conflicts.[72] However, nearly all of these
young economists choose to repress their intellectual creativity and not deviate throughout their careers from the perspective and method of analysis they
were taught in graduate school. Their reasons for behaving so can be attributed to their need to justify having made a big investment in learning (and
mastering techniques of) one perspective and methodology, being impres-
sionable, undoubtedly being caught up in the mainstream (where getting
published and promoted requires articulating the conventional wisdom while
deviation from this mainstream invites criticism and contempt), and wanting
to show they can articulate the learned perspective better than their peers.[73]

In GM I's case he was fortunate that his mentors were unlike most contemporary economists, for they encouraged criticism and open discussion of different philosophical and methodological issues raised by their graduate students and were willing to base academic appointments on quality of research rather than demonstrated willingness to accept and articulate mainstream views. This intellectual climate permitted Myrdal to vent his rebellious, inquisitive, and brilliant mind in path breaking directions.[74] GM I also believed that he and his colleagues were intellectually and morally superior, and he implored them to reject 'shallow materialism' in favor of contributing to the development of a better Swedish society (Jackson 1990, p. 46). This belief was manifested throughout Myrdal's life.[75]

While working in Geneva he became involved with the macroeconomic policy research being carried out at the University of Stockholm, especially by Erik Lindahl. This was the beginning of the Stockholm School. These young economists built upon the monetary theory and policy contributions of their mentors, particularly Knut Wicksell and David Davidson. This research, combined with his desire to rebel against the conventional wisdom – especially that of Wicksell – led GM I to seek to demonstrate that he could develop a theory superior to his politically radical but intellectually conservative mentor's pioneering efforts in monetary theory.

GM III believes this effort (*Monetary Equilibrium*) represented 'sort of an attempt ... to be a man like Wicksell ... to show what Wicksell really said ... And then I continued my speculations about what Wicksell ought to have meant. I mean, this was in immanent criticism' (Myrdal Interview, 1980). Another reason was GM I's desire to gain prestige as an economist. Referring to attitudes within the profession during the late 1920s GM III recalls that 'the highest prestige was given over to ever more esoteric theoretical constructs in terms of the "economic" factors' (Myrdal 1975b, p. 11).

Seeds of a New Perspective

There were, however, signs that GM I eventually would not find the neoclassical perspective efficacious. In his critique of the biases inherent in public finance literature he argues for an alternative to the static model for evaluating the effect of different tax policies, one which would account for factors in the 'dynamic problem of price formation'. He believed that '[r]ealistic investigations of the effects of taxes should therefore embrace the whole tax system, ... should be supported by sociological and psychological research and should be built upon a dynamic theory of price formation' (Myrdal 1969a, p. 190).

GM I came to think that a realistic conception of the economic order was possible if scientists adopted a 'common-sense element' in their research (Myrdal 1939a, p. 213). He called for economists to borrow from related sciences and inductively create a structure of an economy, urging them to reject the conventional approach which relied on abstract, metaphysical concepts in deductively constructing a picture of the community's economic affairs which did not conform to reality (Myrdal 1939a, pp. 136–46, 212–13). GM I also criticized the conventional economic perspective which held that society's interests would automatically (via market forces) be reconciled into a state of harmony. 'The idea that one can judge social policy from a "purely economic point of view" is thoroughly metaphysical. It assumes tacitly that there is such a thing as the interest of society as a whole, and that particular interests, though superficially antagonistic, are at heart reconcilable' (Myrdal 1969a, p. 195). GM I did not accept that people were motivated only by economic interests, and believed that social objectives and ideals 'to which they want their society to conform' (Myrdal 1969a, p. 93) were significant factors which shaped behavior.

GM I went on to advocate an analysis of societies' 'institutional setup' which would 'examine to what extent any groups are sufficiently powerful to bring about institutional changes' using a 'technology of economics' approach (Myrdal 1969a, pp. 196–98). One Myrdal scholar describes this technology as 'a branch of modern, psychologically-oriented sociology' (Carlson 1978). GM I recognized that the institutional set-up was dynamic and evolutionary, but argued that it was essential to 'know the distribution of power amongst social groups in order to estimate what institutional changes are feasible' (Myrdal 1969a, p. 198).

Anti-institutionalist

GM I defended the same theoretical school GM III would be so outspoken against. This defense is evident in GM I's attitude toward American institutionalists to whom he was introduced during his 1929–30 visit to the United States. As GM III recalls, '[a]t that time I was utterly critical of this new orientation of economics. I was in the "theoretical" stage of my own personal development as an economist. I even had something to do [along with Ragnar Frisch and Irving Fischer] with the initiation of the Econometric Society, which was planned as a defense organization against the advancing institutionalists'[76] (Myrdal 1975b, p. 6). His motivation was to 'defend the purity of theoretical economics against the heresy of institutionalism' (Harrison, 1976) which in 1929 was 'growing in importance' (Appendix, Myrdal Interview 1982). The Society was intended to be an international organization with the purpose of advancing economic theory in its relation to mathematics and statistics. GM I was particularly disturbed by the 'naive empiricism' (Myrdal 1958a, p. 53) of the institutionalists.[77] He felt vindicated in his attack, for as GM III recalls during the early 1930s when macroeconomic theories and policies were adopted to combat the effects of the Great Depression 'we economists of the "theoretical" school, accustomed to reason in terms of simplified macro-models, felt we were on top of the situation, while the institutionalists were left in the muddle ... [and this] gave victory much more broadly to our "theoretical" approach' (Myrdal 1975b, p. 7).

Struggle and Rebellion against his Mainstream Elders

The years 1928–31 were his 'philosophical period'. One important feature of this interval was his rebellious challenge to the prevailing conventional wisdom of his economic elders. In referring to John Maynard Keynes as someone who 'certainly enjoyed posing as a rebel' while developing his own economic theory rather than seeking the rewards received by articulators of accepted doctrines, GM III is describing his own intellectual personality throughout his career. 'Without any intention on my part, I happened to remain a rebel, following a different, and indeed a contrary, cycle to the common one' (Myrdal 1975b, p. 11).

In 1928, as a newly appointed assistant professor, GM I was asked to deliver a series of lectures. Seeking an answer to the question concerning the proper role of values in social research, he chose the title 'The Concepts of "Value" and "Utility" in Economic Theory' (Myrdal 1958a, p. 237). GM III admits that GM I's motivation for choosing this topic 'was negative – to demonstrate that certain practices of reasoning common in economics were logically defective' (Myrdal 1958a, p. 237). At the time he was a member of a group of young Swedish economists who challenged the orthodox thinking of their mentors and engaged in pioneering efforts in economic theory and policy. These young economists chose to deviate from the conventional perspective each previously had applied to the theoretical problems they dealt with while conducting their own dissertation research. Their innovative theories challenged the orthodox theory, and their 'fortitude' for doing so has been attributed to 'some fundamental insights arrived at independently from their theoretical researches' (Uhr 1951, p. 120).

Early in Myrdal's career Alf Johansson had suggested to him that he 'steal the public support from the elders' by writing a 'popular pamphlet' which was a 'carefully documented criticism of the dominant laissez-faire school' (Myrdal 1958a, p. 252). This GM I set out to do in 1928, and the effort culminated with the publication of his *The Political Element in the Development of Economic Theory* in 1929. According to GM III this

> embarkation upon the attempt at immanent criticism of economic theory ... [was] an individual manifestation of a common urge among the younger generation of Swedish economists of the 'twenties' to liberate our minds from the teaching of

the older generation. ... [He felt] the need to protest against the intellectual domination of the older generation. It led me to a critical scrutiny of the value problem, because I was aware that this was their weak spot (Myrdal 1958a, p. 239).

GM III admits that at that time he was 'angry' at the older generation of Swedish economists 'because they were explaining what is right politically from an economic point of view' (Appendix, Myrdal Interview 1980). He approached the analysis of the question of values in economic analysis by criticizing the subjective theory of value inherent in the liberal economic theory which evolved from the natural law and utilitarian philosophies. He focused on the 'normative intention' contained within the theory, arguing that orthodox economic theory did not provide a practitioner with the basis for drawing political conclusions on a scientific basis (Myrdal 1958a, p. 253). For example, he argues in *The Political Element* that

[t]he subjective theory of value, like other theories with a normative intention, makes it appear possible to deduce, by logical process, rational political principles from its analysis of social phenomena. The argument of this book is that such a deduction must involve a fallacy somewhere; some link must be omitted in the chain of reasoning from positive analysis to normative conclusions. In this case, the fallacy is the assumption of interpersonal comparisons of feelings. Analysis is based on incomparability, conclusions on comparability. The theorist is often incapable of seeing the fallacy. It is latent in ... [the theorist's] approach to the whole problem for ... [the theorist] sets out with the aim to arrive at certain conclusions which are precluded by ... [the theorist's] premises (Myrdal 1969a, p. 88).

GM III recalls that even as he wrote *The Political Element* he 'had begun to doubt the correctness of ... the critical argument in the book' (Myrdal 1958a, p. 253). GM III admitted that GM I 'was mistaken' in seeking to identify an 'objective' (in the positivist sense) economic theory, one which was independent from any normative judgments (Myrdal 1975b, p. vi). During the early 1970s he recalls that in 1929

I still believed that there was a solid and objective value-free economic theory ... Now after further studies in several fields – and particularly after my labor with the Negro problem ten years later – [I realize] that this is mistaken and that value premises are needed already in the attempt to establish facts and causal relations between facts. But this inadequacy – as I now see it – does not diminish the main content of the book which is to give a critical analysis of how economic theory has branched out from the philosophy of the eighteenth and nineteenth centuries and largely remained so influenced today (Myrdal 1972).

Following the completion of *The Political Element* Myrdal continued to ponder the problem of inserting value premises into economic analysis for over one year. Unable to recognize that values existed at every stage of analysis, he made an 'abortive' attempt to reach a solution to the problem of how first to define objective norms, and subsequently, draw political conclusions on a scientific basis in an article published in 1930, 'Ends and Means in Political Economy'.[78] GM III points out that '[t]he article elaborates the logical difficulty, not to say, impossibility, of inserting value premises into economic analysis ... To me the problem was very serious and personal. Because of my inability to find the way out of the maze, I felt a deep frustration in my scientific work and did not write much more for two years' (Myrdal 1958a, p. 255).

GM I's pioneering analysis of objectivity in economics has offended mainstream economists from his era until today. In particular, they take exception to GM I's accusation that in terms of objectivity neoclassical economics was not based on a firm foundation, and that as a result facts and values were confused while certain values were hidden in analysis purporting to be value free – especially when economists reached political conclusions based upon their analysis. In his last major work, *Hur styrs landet?* (Myrdal 1982) GM III laments that *The Political Element* is 'unfortunately as much to the point today (1982) as when it was originally published' (Swedberg 1990, p. vii).

Institutions

In evaluating the extent to which GM I belonged to the mainstream economists of that early era GM I's view regarding the importance of institutions in analysis is noteworthy. While not embodied in his early research to a significant degree, it would be fully articulated by GM III and become central to his interdisciplinary method of analysis. GM I recognized the role of conflict and institutions in social change, arguing that change was initiated by interest groups resolving conflict within society through their exercise of power. He criticized the conventional economic perspective which held one could 'judge social policy from a "purely economic point of view"', and that society's interests would automatically (through market adjustments) be reconciled into a state of harmony (Myrdal 1969a, p. 195). He advocated an analysis of society's 'institutional set-up', which he believed was 'changeable in various directions and to various degrees', so as to determine the distribution of power within the social and political structures and 'to what extent any groups are sufficiently powerful to bring about institutional changes' (Myrdal 1969a, pp. 196–8).

Throughout the 1915–33 period GM I began to recognize that the neoclassical approach was inadequate for analyzing societal problems. He concluded that there were neither universal truths for explaining human behavior nor any inherent moral order. As a result, he began to believe that it was necessary to develop a broader perspective and different method of analysis which relied more on common sense than natural law, and more on inductive than deductive reasoning.

SUMMARY – THE TRANSITION TO GM II

During the late 1920s the Rockefeller Foundation's Paris office scouted Europe for the brightest young social scientists, offering them a fellowship for study in another European country or in the United States. Having received Rockefeller Fellow awards, GM I and Alva left Sweden in 1929 and devoted one year studying and traveling in the United States while associating with many American scholars, particularly sociologists and psychologists. Some of these scholars became life-long colleagues and friends who would influence subsequent research and political activity undertaken by the Myrdals. The experience in the United States did not, however, immediately manifest itself in GM I's intellectual concerns and methods of analysis. He would remain faithful to many aspects of the neoclassical perspective for a few more years, and defend this perspective against the rising tide of institutional economics in America.

Although his first encounter with American institutionalists only served to harden GM I's faith in conventional economic theory, the year he and Alva spent in the United States was a 'very crucial period' (Appendix, Myrdal Interview 1980) in their lives. For the first time they witnessed racial tension, slums, and the dramatic effects of the stock market crash on the American society. The experience served to transform them from 'ivory tower intellectuals ... [to persons] committed to political involvement and to radical reform of the Swedish social order on the basis of a scientific sociology' (Carlson 1978). GM III said that year in the United States made him and Alva 'politically ... conscious and [they started] becoming radical' (Appendix, Myrdal Interview 1980). GM III recalls that American professors in the late 1920s 'were so good at explaining why everything was bad, but they had not practical proposals ... We [GM I and Alva] were more interested in what to do about it. And that was also why I left behind this pure economic theory because when you are dealing with the wrongs in society you don't get very far with that' (Harrison 1976, p. 5). Thereafter they 'saw politics, interference in society [that is, social engineering] as a purpose in life' (Appendix, Myrdal Interview 1980). In a letter to Cassel, GM I states that 'after this [experience in America] I am likely never in my life to write anything again on general economics. I have learned what I have wanted to learn here ... I will concern myself with something which has a more direct connection with human life' (Carlson 1978, p. 142). This he did during the 1930s as his interest in stabilization policy and transformation issues helped convert him to GM II, a political and social economist.

3. Gunnar Myrdal II: 1929–38, political and social economist

INTRODUCTION

The period 1929–38 was momentous for Myrdal's career, and over these ten years his intellectual development was protean. Following the United States experience as a Rockefeller Fellow and an academic position in Geneva he returned to Sweden in 1931 to become Acting Professor of Economics at the University of Stockholm. In 1933 he succeeded Gustav Cassel as the Lars Hierta Chair of Political Economy and Financial Science – a position he held until 1950. In 1926 the Swedish Parliament began commissioning experts to analyze the country's major social and economic problems. In the capacity of expert advisor Myrdal served on four Swedish Royal Commissions (Housing, 1932; Population, 1935; Budget, 1936; Agriculture, 1938). As a Social Democrat he was elected to the Swedish Senate to represent the district of Dalecarlia from 1935–8.

The evolution of his intellectual development is reflected in the breadth of his research. His main publications written during the 1930s included:[79]

1. *Socialism eller kapitalism i framtidens Amerika?* (Socialism or Capitalism in the United States of the Future), 1931b.
2. *Socialpolitikens Dilemma* (Dilemma of Social Welfare Policy), 1932c.
3. *Bostadsfragan sasom socialt planlaggningsproblem* (The Housing Question as a Problem of Social Planning), 1933e.
4. *The Cost of Living in Sweden 1830-1930*, 1933a.
5. *Konjunktur och offentlig hushallning* (Business Cycles and Public Finance), 1933b.
6. *Finanspolitikens ekonomiska verkningar* (The Economic Effects of Fiscal Policy), 1934d.
7. *Kris i befolkningsfragan* (The Population Problem in Crisis), 1934a.
8. *Aktuella baskattningsproblem* (Present Problems of Taxation), 1936b.
9. *Nagra metodiska anmarkningar rorande befolkningsfragans innebord och vetenskapliga behandling* (Some Methodological Notes on the Population Problem and Its Scientific Treatment), 1936a.

10. *Betankande i naringsfragan* (Report Concerning the Food Problem), 1938b.
11. *Fiscal Policy in the Business Cycle*, 1939b.
12. *Population: A Problem for Democracy*, 1940.[80]

During the late 1920s and early 1930s Myrdal's United States experience, especially the implications for his perspective and methodology, was percolating in the back of his mind. However, the Great Depression posed a crisis situation, and during such times 'there is a temporary harmony of interests in society' (Appendix, Myrdal Interview 1980). Consequently, he used the neoclassical perspective and corresponding tools at hand, with some Stockholm School modifications, to assist a Sweden in dire need of an effectual fiscal policy based on sound macroeconomic theories. It was also during this period that Myrdal began to analyze issues such as unemployment, housing, agriculture, and population. He and Alva jointly conducted a landmark population study during which his interests moved 'towards social issues, as distinct from economics' (Kindleberger 1987, p. 395).[81]

Ultimately GM II emerged as Myrdal converted from academic theoretician to political economist, then to social economist (researcher, policy maker and active public servant).[82] He became devoted to the transformation of Sweden from a predominantly market-oriented economy with a modest agenda for the state to a democratically controlled social economy (Angresano 1996b, pp. 279–328). In this respect he was influenced by Knut Wicksell whose vision for Sweden was a 'welfare state' featuring more public ownership of the means of production (especially natural monopolies); expanded social services; publicly provided health and occupational hazard protection; state-directed redistribution of income to alleviate poverty; and universal suffrage (Uhr 1951). Working within the Social Democratic Party, Myrdal was instrumental not only in promoting the macroeconomic stabilization policies he helped develop as a member of the Stockholm School of economics, but also in laying the foundation for the social insurance and welfare programs that were introduced gradually throughout Sweden after the rise to power of the Social Democrats in 1932.

THE INTELLECTUAL DEVELOPMENT OF GM II: THEORETICIAN, POLITICAL ECONOMIST, AND SOCIAL ECONOMIST

Myrdal began this period as an academic researcher examining theoretical aspects of macroeconomic stabilization, then focused on Swedish unemployment, budget, and population growth issues. As a researcher GM II was 'enormously creative in technical economics' (Kindleberger 1987, p. 402). In the early 1930s, his mentor Cassel observed that Myrdal 'has written a few remarkable books, but this is only a beginning. The world and Sweden have much more to gain from Myrdal's future findings as a scientist' (Glesinger 1949, p. 5).

Theoretician

Myrdal and his Stockholm School colleagues developed a theoretical basis for macroeconomic stabilization policy for a depressed economy based upon deficit public spending, lower taxes, and public works projects to alleviate chronic unemployment caused by a prolonged recession. In the process they anticipated Keynes.[83] According to GM III's evaluation of the Stockholm School's contributions 'we were in two ways in advance of Keynes. We were ten years older, we started here in Sweden in 1933 with an underbalanced budget ... and I wrote the theoretical motivation for it in the budget in early 1933. ... The whole theory which you call Keynesian ... was already there in [the work of] Wicksell' (Appendix, Myrdal Interview 1980). While Myrdal believed Keynes was brilliant and important, he claimed that all substantive aspects of *The General Theory* were familiar to the Stockholm School members.[84] One contemporary analyst goes further, arguing that GM II's 'description and discussions of the multiplier process ... show a very clear understanding of primary and secondary effects of exogenous impulses, with the rate of saving given its proper role ... [and that he] influenced other economists who helped build important parts of modern theory, particularly macroeconomics. Apparently even Keynes came under his influence' (Dostaler 1990, p. 212).

A famous committee on unemployment was established 1927, of which Gösta Bagge, Dag Hammarskjold and Bertil Ohlin were members (Dostaler 1990, p. 211). Myrdal joined in their efforts after returning to Sweden in 1930 from the United States. He was named executive member of the Institute for Social Sciences at the University of Stockholm, an organization sponsored by the Rockefeller Foundation. The foundation subsidized a cost of living project, the results of which were published in four volumes in *Stockholm Economic Studies*.[85] Myrdal's document was *The Cost of Living in Sweden – 1860–1930* (Myrdal 1933a), which contained important contributions to macroeconomic theory.[86] In it he attempted to rationalize the objective of budgetary disequilibrium financed through loans. He did this so convincingly that this work became the basis for the budget policies implemented in 1933 by Ernst Wigforss[87] – the Social Democrat Minister of Finance.

Following this effort GM II wrote a number of fiscal policy reports, including *Business Cycles and Public Finance – Memorandum Concerning the*

Effects of Various Measures within the Public Sector on the Business Cycles in Sweden (Myrdal 1933b). In this document he articulates the views of Wicksell by stating 'how government spending would stimulate the private sector to increase production and employment' (Dostaler 1990, p. 212). While recognizing that during a serious recession the private sector must achieve a balanced budget in the face of declining revenues, Myrdal argues the state's fiscal policy should be designed only to achieve a balanced budget over the long run. He points out that '[u]nderbalancing the budget during a depression is not primarily a deliberate policy but a practical necessity', doubting that during a depression there ever was a balanced budget (Myrdal 1939b, p. 183).

Based upon his macroeconomic research GM II recognized that deficit spending was not a panacea for macroeconomic problems, and was a 'clumsy instrument in crisis policy when utilized as the mobile factor in fighting against depressive forces which change from month to month' (Myrdal 1939a, p. 187). Instead, sound fiscal policy had to be supplemented, for if the 'more fundamental causes of maladjustment' which contributed to the deficit were not corrected, then a 'new downward turn' would ensue following re-establishment of macroeconomic stability and a balanced budget (Myrdal 1939a, p. 185). GM II demonstrated a theoretical basis for reconstructing the budget system which contained 'a new scheme of legal and institutional regulations for the fiscal households ... [which] guarantees to a satisfactory degree of the 'soundness' of public finances in the long run and allows enough flexibility from year to year for fiscal policy to serve its purpose among other measures to mitigate the fluctuations in business activity' (Myrdal 1939b, p. 186). He concluded that the system required flexibility to permit necessary deficit spending during recessions as well as to create corresponding surpluses during periods of prosperity.

Although there was a considerable decline in Sweden's unemployment during 1933 after being hit hard by the depression in 1929, 'economic stagnation' was still experienced by large segments of the Swedish population. Of the many collaborative efforts they undertook their most significant was *Kris i befolkningsfragan* (Crisis in the Population Problem), completed in 1934. In response to Sweden's declining fertility rates the Myrdals decided to examine historical trends of Sweden's birth and death rates. They determined that Sweden's 'population problem' stemmed from two sets of factors. One was a family crisis which, in turn, was caused by low wages, substandard housing, and lack of child-care facilities, among other economic factors (Myrdal 1937b). The other concerned popular attitudes toward the poor, namely a general willingness to blame this group for its own plight, coupled with a 'do-nothing' social policy on the government level. The Myrdals concluded that 'natural forces' (that is, market forces in a laissez-faire market economy) were not only incapable of rectifying Sweden's population problems, but also were lacking as a potential means for alleviating problems in the areas of housing, agriculture, international trade and poverty. One general thesis of the book is 'that a population policy can be nothing less than a social policy at large ... the population problem concerns the very foundation of the social structure and ... calls for nothing less than complete social redirection' (A. Myrdal 1941, p. 2). They subsequently proceeded to transform the population issue into an argument in favor of widespread, well planned, egalitarian reforms, using their findings to argue for 'radical changes of the whole institutional structure' (Myrdal 1939a, p. 193) of Sweden's economy.

Political Economist

Noting that his academic appointment at Stockholm University in 1933 was Chair of Political Economy and Financial Science, Myrdal considered a political economist to be one who helps to solve or ameliorate pressing social problems through analysis and the rendering of policy prescriptions, particularly those regarding distribution of income and wealth. According to GM III the political economist 'has a different fundamental approach when studying the economy' (Myrdal 1974b, p. 1). Such an economist must draw policy conclusions from research rather than provide narrow results in a 'restricted sense' (Myrdal 1974b, p. 1). The Myrdalian political economist provided both theoretical explanations of issues and offered explicit statements regarding the normative direction for society plus policies to move society in that direction. His particular normative bent was for Sweden to implement a 'thoroughly revolutionary programme' which favored greater social equality (Myrdal 1957e, p. 112). In moving in this direction he was breaking away from his mentors whom he criticized because '[t]hey were radical in a way which was not our [the younger generation of Swedish economists] type of radicalism. They were so good at explaining why everything was bad, but they had no practical proposals. ... Sure, we wanted to have the facts about how bad society is, but we were more interested in what to do about it. And that was also why I left behind this pure economic theory because when you are dealing with the wrongs in society you don't get very far with that' (Harrison 1976, p. 5). Thereafter, GM II continued working closely with Social Democratic leaders as he drew policy conclusions from his theoretical analysis, as he had done from his macroeconomic research, and became a political economist. GM III recalls that his first becoming a political economist 'was partly the result of a change in the type of practical and theoretical problems with which I became involved during my working life' (Myrdal 1969b, p. 10).

It was during the early 1930s that a unique combination of circumstances established a permanent and increasing role for Myrdal and other young

Swedish economists to shift from theoreticians to political advisors. The Great Depression forced Sweden to abandon the Gold Standard in 1931. This meant a currency devaluation, and while this stimulated demand for Swedish exports and stabilized domestic industries, a high incidence of poverty and unemployment remained a problem. The 1932–4 success of Myrdal and his Stockholm School colleagues as macroeconomic policy makers gave prestige to economists, and resulted in a permanent place being established for economists to engage in social engineering efforts (Uhr 1977, p. 117).

In 1932 the Social Democrats (with over 40% of the seats in Parliament but lacking a clear majority) formed a new coalition government after the election, with Wigforss as the Minister of Finance. An avid student of Sweden's young economists, Wigforss reacted to the *Political Element in the Development of Economic Theory* by proclaiming that Social Democratic policy makers 'need the kind of separation between science and politics that Myrdal is advocating' (Swedberg 1990, p. xxi). Further, Wigforss credited GM II for having contributed significantly to the success of Sweden's 1932–3 fiscal policies, and gave him the opportunity to apply his theories as Wigforss's fiscal policy advisor. He contacted GM II immediately after the election and solicited his advice regarding what the state should do to help Sweden overcome the depression. GM II's response was 'that the government should adopt a policy of free spending, subsidies, and other pump-priming devices, irrespective of budgetary equilibrium, and that it should restore public finances through heavier taxation later when prosperity would permit such measures' (Glesinger 1949, p. 4). Wigforss thereupon asked GM II to write down his proposals, which culminated in Myrdal's 'Business Cycles and Public Finance',[88] a condensed 45-page version of the *Cost of Living in Sweden 1860–1930* study.[89] The article contained a theoretical justification for the Social Democrat's fiscal policies and was included as an annex to Wigforss's January 3, 1933 speech on the budget. Partly due to this work GM II has been credited for being 'one of the pioneers in working out a theoretical framework of [Sweden's] economic policy' (Lundberg 1974, p. 476.)

This marked the first time the budget message of a Swedish government was presented with an official introduction signed by an individual. GM II argued that programs such as privately financed (by employer contributions), publicly distributed unemployment insurance schemes were sufficient to guarantee that the wealth created by the economy would be redistributed according to the Social Democratic ideals of integration and equality.[90] Many of those he had to convince were not members of the Social Democratic Party, and most were quite skeptical of his advocacy of a temporary expansion of public works projects which would be financed by deficit spending.

Having 'never made a secret of his conviction that *egalitarian* ideals ought to be served by public policy' (Dopfer 1990, p. 231), it is not surprising that

GM II accepted Wigforss's offer to become fiscal policy advisor. He was 'impressed with this honor and responsibility' (Glesinger 1949, p. 4) of being asked by Wigforss to recommend macroeconomic policies. He also liked the idea of switching from academic theoretician to policy maker, for he believed people would be more productive and avoid becoming stale if they changed their work and interests from time to time.[91] Having been a student and an economist 'for just as long as he wanted to stay with that trade' he accepted the proposal [from Wigforss] mainly to find out what it is like to be a politician' (Glesinger 1949, p. 5). He did not intend to abandon research. Soon after becoming advisor he confided to a colleague, 'I have been work-ing a lot on certain practical questions. ... [s]ince four months we have a socialist government: the minister of finance [Wigforss] ... has taken me into the whole business of the economic problem, especially as to financial mat-ters during the crisis ... what a delight it is for an economist to get away for some time from the class-room theories and get hold of real practical things, but naturally I am coming back to theory again sometime, and I hope that I will have gained some insight and common-sense out of this experience' (Myrdal 1932b).

Advisor to the Minster of Finance was the first public function Myrdal ever accepted, and he performed his new duties so effectively that with assistance from his 'mentor' Wigforss GM II quickly rose to prominence within the Social Democratic government. This rise coincided with Alva's and his de-sires to propose policies for Sweden based upon their main findings from the Population Study, which included that declining population would impede economic progress. The Myrdals were able to transform the population issue 'into the most effective argument for a thorough and radical socialist remodeling of society' (Carlson 1978, p. 217). They argued that since 'Swe-den was caught in a downward movement which in the thirties had become even more accentuated than in France, the ... government had to step in' (Glesinger 1949, p. 5) and make family rearing a more attractive prospect through providing a system of family benefits.

Like other Social Democratic leaders during the 1930s GM II sought a 'middle way' for the country[92] after rejecting both the laissez-faire ('do-nothing') neoclassical viewpoint and radical Marxist perspective. He consid-ered himself to be 'in line with what Marx called the utopian socialists. They were planners, which Marx was not. With Marx it should happen by itself' (Appendix, Myrdal Interview 1980). From their Population Study he and Alva endorsed the Enlightenment view that it was possible to plan society to make it a better place. GM II conceived of planning as 'changing institutions' (Appendix, Myrdal Interview 1980). He did not favor 'socio-political re-forms' that would result in 'small adjustments' to society. Instead he advo-cated 'utopian socialism [which] demands a revolutionary change of society's foundations' (Myrdal 1932c, p. 1) to be achieved through a sensible, planned, pragmatic 'social policy'. Such a process would require 'a period of leveling and compromise ... It means that the study of the socio-political ideology is really a study of liberalism and socialism as compromise and conversion' (Myrdal 1932c, p. 7). With this perspective he sought to transform the Swedish economy in a 'leftist, socialistic direction' in such a manner that 'evolution takes the place of revolution' (Myrdal 1932c, pp. 11, 14).

GM II began developing deliberate, rationally conceived policies whereby the state actively would intervene to correct pressing social and economic problems, believing that 'well-planned egalitarian reforms would be preventive, prophylactic, and thus productive' (Myrdal 1975b, p. 8). In addition to fiscal policy recommendations designed to redistribute income, the Myrdals' Population Study proposed reforms that shifted Sweden towards the 'socialisation of consumption' (Lundberg 1985, p. 14). Some family policy reforms recommended were larger tax deductions for families with children, cash grants for child allowances, subsidies for pregnant women, public housing, publicly funded health care for children, free school lunches and textbooks, free public day-care center loans to newly married couples in need, aid to orphans and children of widows and disabled men, an improved national pension scheme, publicly funded school lunches, and a national dental service. The Population Study opened an era of social reform, systematically focused on the welfare of children and the family, and resulted in the establishment of the Royal Population Commission in Sweden and in the rest of the Scandinavian nations, as well as in Britain.

In the role of advisor to the Minister of Finance as well as a member of the four Royal Commissions and Swedish parliament Myrdal was well positioned to work on the problems of national planning[93] (*'planwirtschaft'*) which focused on the interrelated problems pertaining to monetary policy, unemployment policy, and public works as related to fiscal policy, and later in the 1930s to resolve Sweden's housing and family problems. The comprehensive framework for fiscal policy he prescribed and the macroeconomic policies he championed were specified in his 'Business Cycles and Public Finance' (Myrdal 1933b). These included temporary deficit spending and publicly financed works projects which would later be phased out following economic recovery, national economic planning, currency devaluation, redistribution of income sufficient to lift the lower classes out of poverty, and publicly funded programs to create full employment. He believed deficit spending would stimulate the business sector through a multiplier effect, be feasible from a cost/benefit standpoint; not require raising taxes, and not create a debt that would jeopardize the government's fiscal soundness (Uhr 1977, pp. 103–7). To convince Parliament to adopt his policy proposal, he emphasized the multiplier effect of an expansionary fiscal policy, arguing that a cumulative growth process would ensue which would serve to alleviate involuntary unemployment while providing public goods which would be of some value to the nation. 'As workers on the public projects spend their wages, they increase demand for consumer goods. The government in placing orders for materials and equipment for its projects with private firms would little by little induce the latter to recall more and more workers, laid off earlier, to produce these goods. In their turn, workers would raise consumer demand further as they spent their wages, and so forth' (Uhr 1977, p. 102).

That GM II's recommended macroeconomic policies contributed to Sweden's post-1933 economic recovery is clear, although the extent to which he can be given credit for the recovery is subject to debate. It is generally agreed that factors contributing to improvements in performance indicators included the multiplier effects of deficit spending on public works projects (after Myrdal's proposals the percentage of previously unemployed who had jobs on public works projects rose from 25% to 63%, with the other 37% on cash relief (Uhr 1977, p. 112)), increased Swedish exports, and government price supports and subsidies for agricultural products. Some give Myrdal considerable credit, noting that '[i]n Sweden, Myrdal's budget ideas produced rapid results. Helped also by a variety of other independent events, such as the British embargo on Russian timber, Sweden was the first country to recover from the depression at a time when all others were still in the midst of it ... [Myrdal] succeeded so well that his budget theories were subsequently adopted by many governments all over Europe and even in the United States, where they became an important element of the early New Deal' (Glesinger 1949, p. 4).

However, a different view from another analyst argues that '[i]n his role as member of Parliament and in Swedish publications in the mid-1930s, Myrdal proposed all sorts of policies to moderate the effects of unemployment in Sweden. This gave him his reputation as the architect of the Swedish welfare state, and he is credited with having stimulated ... Wigforss to unbalance the budget by spending on public works. The originality of these proposals, and especially their effectiveness, have been somewhat exaggerated in world opinion' (Kindleberger 1987, pp. 394–5). Since it is not possible to separate the impact on any economy's performance of policy proposals from that of either institutions and their working rules or the external economic environment, there is no resolution to this difference of opinion. What is agreed upon is that the contributions of Myrdal (and his Stockholm School colleagues) pioneered a new area of macroeconomic theory and policy, and that their assistance to government ministers enhanced the prestige of Swedish economists (particularly members of the Stockholm School) which enabled Myrdal actively to engage in social engineering as a social economist after the mid 1930s.

Social Economist

There are five propositions which depict an approach to economics generally adopted by contemporary social economists (Angresano 1986, pp. 147–8). GM II can be considered a social economist not only because he (1) strove to convert economics into political economy, (2) emphasized an inductive approach to societal problems with a concurrent rejection of narrow, orthodox economic analysis, and (3) adopted an interdisciplinary approach to issues whereby economic and non-economic factors were included in the analysis. These are characteristics of the Myrdalian political economist. GM II eventually went beyond this and engaged in social engineering, manifested by his (4) willingly establishing social goals for Sweden, and (5) accepting the task of making policy recommendations and working to implement them not only for efficiency and stabilization problems, but for societal transformation as well.

GM II's becoming a social economist was influenced by his education in *gymnasium*, his professional relationship with Alva, contact with other intellectuals, his view concerning the role of intellectuals in society, acceptance of Social Democratic ideals, respect for the Swedish political scientist Rudolf Kjellen, and ultimately his election to the Swedish Senate as a Social Democrat. As a *gymnasium* student, GM I was introduced to the Enlightenment philosophy and adhered to its spirit throughout his career. This philosophy led GM II to see himself as a moral philosopher whose role was to help society determine its goals. The inspiration to change social institutions through education and legislation by enlightening Swedes with his research findings and policy proposals was nurtured further by his becoming familiar with 'progressive' social scientists John Dewey and John R. Commons who 'resonated to the Progressive generation's optimism, moralism, and commitment to social engineering' (Jackson 1990, p. xv).

Myrdal's professional relationship with Alva, a 'Social Democratic feminist' (Jackson 1990, p. 68), was perhaps the most significant factor not only in his becoming a social economist, but in his overall intellectual development. Both Myrdals had been appalled by the extremes in distribution of income and wealth in the United States and the extent of poverty, as well as the laissez-faire government attitude and the inability of American intellectuals to be effective as the 1929 national disaster struck. As a result they decided to do in Sweden what was not being done in the United States, namely '[t]o use social scientific knowledge to bring about social and economic reform' (Jackson 1990, p. 63). Their Population Study stimulated social and political debate throughout Sweden, and it had the effect of making unacceptable to a majority of the population any return to the liberal, 'do-nothing' laissez-faire economic policies prevalent until 1932. Alva encouraged her husband to become involved with Sweden's political life, and therefore it was natural that they joined the Social Democratic Party whose ideals were most consistent with their own.

Myrdal held an elitist view that 'intervention by intellectuals' (Jackson, 1990, p. 69) should play an important role in improving the economy, society, and the parliamentary process through social engineering – working within political parties, on special commissions, and on parliamentary committees. Some of Myrdal's published works during the early 1930s indicate that he associated himself with this elite class destined to reform Swedish society (Myrdal 1932c). At that time, he was influenced by other intellectuals from related social science disciplines, and Swedish architects and town planners. They held frequent meetings during which Myrdal was '[c]hallenged by Alva's questions and criticisms and stimulated by a brilliant circle of young Swedes who delighted in debunking the received wisdom' (Jackson 1990, p. 55). The group sought to integrate architecture with politics, economics, social psychology and ideology as they planned social and political reforms for Sweden, seeking to improve the quality of life (housing, family relations, working conditions) for all Swedish citizens. These reformers concluded that transformation of Sweden's society was necessary, and that it required state intervention through national planning – especially redistributional measures designed to create a more equitable distribution of income and higher levels of consumption of both private and public goods for all Swedish families. This experience served to transform Myrdal into a 'most unconventional economist' (Jackson 1990, p. 55).

In accepting Swedish Social Democratic ideals Myrdal committed himself to creating a more humanitarian economy capable of increasing opportunities for the poor by stimulating employment while promoting family welfare through social insurance and welfare schemes. He became instrumental within the Social Democratic Party as an advisor, planner, and Senator working to implement the transformation policies he had helped develop with his circle of intellectual reformers.[94] Their proposals would make all segments of the Swedish population the common responsibility of the state. In this regard Myrdal was influenced by Rudolf Kjellen, political science professor and member of Swedish Parliament representing the Conservative Party. Kjellen 'preached a doctrine of the subordination of the individual to the state … [arguing that] citizens had a moral duty to place the collective welfare of the nation above the pursuit of their individual or group self-interest' (Jackson 1990, p. 45).

Following the favorable effects of Sweden's 1933–4 fiscal policies and publication of the landmark Population Study in 1934, Myrdal's stature rose considerably. Concerning the study's recommendations, he was given credit for having 'not only contributed a constructive idea to his nation but … [for giving] his party a program which nobody dared oppose. When his friends in the government discovered the attractiveness of this proposal they decided to build their re-election campaign in 1936 around it. As a result, the Socialist government scored an overwhelming victory' (Glesinger 1949, p. 6). Consequently, Myrdal became a natural choice for public office. Social Democratic officials suggested that he present himself at the first opportunity for election to the Swedish Senate.

Myrdal agreed to run for election in 1935, which he won. His satisfaction with becoming a member of parliament emanated from his 'restless temperament, wide-ranging interests, practical concerns, and love of new experience and human interaction' – none of which were well suited for restricting himself to pure theoretical research' (Jackson 1990, p. 61). By the mid 1930s he had come to believe that social engineering was 'the supreme task of an accomplished social science' (Jackson 1990, p. 89).[95] Even before the election he admitted he was seeking 'to get the government [to adopt] ... some very socialistic measures of planned economy' (Myrdal 1934c). As a public servant Myrdal worked to implement the transformation policies he helped to design,[96] describing the transformation policy process and his role to a colleague: 'As to the social program of the Government, it is running more and more in the terms of the prophylactic social policy, which I have advocated as population policy. All the proposals from the population commission from last year (except the proposal for taxation reform) are laid before the Parliament this session. In the housing commission we are preparing a big scheme for the country; in the population commission we are now taking up the big families problem – free school lunch, free school shoes, cheaper education and nursery schools, etc. Just now there is no reason for extensive public works, as our unemployment is cured' (Myrdal 1937a).

Myrdal was effective in having many of his policy recommendations adopted, including those pertaining to the transformation goals he, Alva and their intellectual circle established for Sweden. As an elected Senator 'Myrdal concentrated on certain tangible results irrespective of political considerations or party interests. In accordance with Swedish parliamentary technique, ad hoc committees composed of representatives of all parties were usually entrusted with studying Myrdal's proposals and recommending the necessary action. Invariably, it happened in these committees that the bright boys from the right, center and left rallied around Myrdal' (Glesinger 1949, pp. 6–7). This meant that committee reports came to the floor of the House with strong support from all political sides.

As a social economist dedicated to the transformation of Sweden GM II was the leader of the Royal Housing Commission responsible for recommending long-time housing policy for Sweden. The commission's report provided detailed statistical analysis of the housing situation and established a program of government housing subsidies for large families and construction of planned public housing projects. As a member of Parliament Myrdal led the successful drive to alter the tax structure and provide facilities and subsidies to families as a means of combating the population growth rate problem. This culminated in the adoption of an active population policy by the Swedish government[97] which proved successful in reversing Sweden's declining population rate. Myrdal proposed and worked to have adopted other family policies such as subsidies for housing and for pregnant women, loans to newly married couples in need, aid to orphans and children of widows and disabled men, larger tax deductions to families with children, better child care facilities, free school lunches and textbooks, free health care for children. Collectively, they became one of the mainstays of the post-1932 Swedish economy.

GM II'S TRANSITION TO AN INTERDISCIPLINARY METHODOLOGY

Although he had developed an interest in broad social issues while a Rockefeller Fellow, during the early part of the 1929–38 period GM II continued to use traditional theoretical methods for his macroeconomic theory, policy, and international trade policy research. He still harbored criticism of American institutionalists, and the Great Depression necessitated pressing policy decisions. Consequently, as a member of the Stockholm School seeking quick remedies to depressed economic conditions, he adhered to and defended simple theoretical structures and a straightforward economic approach for resolving Sweden's pressing macroeconomic problems.

His method for analyzing fiscal policy issues reflected relatively little concern for related social science disciplines. On the other hand it was more practical than the 'hyper-abstract theoretical models' (Myrdal 1974b, p. 7) GM III would criticize continually, and it offered policy conclusions. GM III points out that '[u]nder the premises of crisis and depression the methodological problem of practical economic research was put into a new light' (Myrdal 1958a, p. 255). A Swedish analyst of the Stockholm School describes the work of GM II and other young Swedish economists as 'a limited suppression of period analysis' as opposed to earlier comparative static analysis of a few macroeconomic variables (Uhr 1977, p. 120).[98]

While GM II gradually changed his perspective towards what economics is and what economists should do, he knew this change would require a new methodology. Therefore, his transition to a new perspective and new methodology were reciprocal developments, as one influenced the other. Faced with contradictions between the neoclassical emphasis on laissez-faire policies and his growing desire to engage in social engineering, GM II knew a break from conventional wisdom would be necessary for solving Sweden's 1930s problems. He realized that '[e]conomists would have to "close the account books" of neoclassical economics and "cancel once and for all" the supposedly inviolable "economic principles"' (Jackson 1990, p. 70). Although he retained the traditional economist's quantitative emphasis, he came to recognize that while the macroeconomic data may look satisfactory large segments of the population may still be miserable. In response he began working simultaneously on both qualitative social concerns and quantitative macroeconomic issues. His genius was to recognize that an interdisciplinary approach was necessary to solve problems previously seen as separate but which he saw as interrelated. He believed there were no 'economic' problems, but rather that society's problems were complex and not simply economic, sociological, political or psychological. Further, he eventually was able to 'transgress the inherited boundaries among disciplines' in all his research '... by broadening the approach to all human relations' (Myrdal 1978a, p. 772).

This transition began as his interest in Social Democratic Party issues increased. GM II realized that his theoretical bent was insufficient for providing a substantive basis for radical political and egalitarian social reforms in Sweden.[99] He gradually 'found that my theory left me with tools that were inadequate for the study of social reform. Such a study could not rationally be confined to economic factors like production and distribution, but had to be conceived in terms of practically all human relations' (Myrdal 1975c, pp. 2–3). Consequently, GM II sought to develop his own method of analysis because other social scientists had failed to work out a correct methodology for the social sciences. He deviated from the 'limited area' of economic theory in the classical and neoclassical tradition as his respect diminished 'for the traditionally rigid boundary between separate disciplines of social science as they have developed pragmatically to fit teaching purposes and to meet the need for specialization' (Myrdal 1969b, p. 10). As early as 1931 Myrdal began to integrate history, sociology, politics and economics while developing an interdisciplinary viewpoint and emphasizing social reform for dealing with problems of equality in Sweden. With the publication of The Population Study it was clear that GM II was committed to engaging in practical, interdisciplinary research with an emphasis upon policy proposals. His goal became 'to use social scientific knowledge to bring about [egalitarian] social and economic reforms' (Jackson 1990, p. 63).

After returning to Sweden from the United States Myrdal retained the close association he and Alva had developed with American sociologists William and Dorothy Thomas. Influenced by Commons's idea of bringing together a multidisciplinary team of sociologists, economists and statisticians for social research, GM II proposed that the Thomases, Alva and himself undertake a joint research project to prepare the theoretical basis for Swedish social legislation, which would be called 'The Relation of Behavior to Social Structure in Scandinavia'. The study would be longitudinal with the objective of working out specific problems relating to the behavior norms and deviations developing among groups of people in a changing or varying social environment. Myrdal stressed that '[m]ost important of all ... is the growing integration of economic and social interest groups outside politics in its proper sense'. (Myrdal 1931a). Therefore, he recommended that the analysis focus 'on the deeper more sociological side of the problem' (Myrdal 1931a), particularly communications between government institutions. Myrdal also advocated studying 'the saving and consumption habits of different groups', paying attention to the 'sociological problem of social mobility' (Myrdal 1931a) as it affects consumption and savings.[100] Ultimately, he wished to determine 'the relation in Sweden between saving and largeness of income, changes in income, wealth and changes of wealth, age, number of children, social stratum, occupation, phase of the business cycles, and so on' (Myrdal 1931a). Due to an extremely heavy agenda as researcher, consultant, and public servant GM II was unable to become involved actively in the study. However, a comparable study was completed by Dorothy Thomas and published as *Social and Economic Aspects of the Swedish Population Movements 1750-1933* (Thomas 1941).

A similar multidisciplinary method of analysis characterizes the population study. There was growing concern with declining birth rates in Sweden (1930 versus 1895), particularly among poorer families (in which both husband and wife were employed) residing in industrial communities. The Myrdals were interested in determining factors causing these trends, as well as the secular trend in migration, cyclical fluctuations, and how business cycles reflect themselves in migration. They sought to 'collect, classify and analyze statistical materials on the changes in the Swedish population during the period of industrialization, with the ultimate aim of getting to know not only the interrelations between the movements of the different factors of population, but also the relations between these and all the other changes of economic and social character which, together, make up the process of industrialization' (Myrdal 1932a, p. 1). It was recognized that since 'internal migration is distinctly a phenomenon of cycles ... therefore a thorough understanding of migration cannot be arrived at by studying census figures' (Myrdal 1932a, p. 1) They also sought to comprehend the interconnections between migration and other factors in the population dynamic and between that dynamic and Sweden's overall economic development. Therefore the Myrdals believed that 'only a totally new, comprehensive, multidisciplinary vision could identify the causes lying behind the birth decline and offer possible solutions' (Carlson 1978, p. 200). GM II argued

[i]t is not possible to analyze migration as an isolated fact. It must be studied in connection with all the other factors of population ... changes and differences in age distribution are among the most important results of migration in its dynamic phase, and these changes and differences have in their turn effects upon migration, partly directly and partly indirectly through changes and differences in the relative number of births and deaths which, to a certain extent, must be supposed to influence migration. You have an interdependent mechanism of population and it is this mechanism as a whole which must be supposed to undergo changes under the influences of (or, better, in some relation to) social and economic changes of the most different kinds. This population mechanism is, in a certain sense, the smallest unit which you are allowed directly to correlate with other social phenomena, even if this unit must also be analyzed and studied, and even if you then may concentrate most of your interest on migration. These considerations have led us to incorporate in our study not only figures on migration, but also on nativity, mortality and age distribution (Myrdal 1932a, p. 2).

Using a multidisciplinary methodology, the conclusion was reached that the decline in Sweden's birth rates was not merely an economic problem, but was 'social-cultural' and 'social psychological' (Carlson 1978, p. 200). The Myrdals also discovered that Sweden's housing problem was a related issue, and the root of that problem could be found not simply in poverty, but in attitudes and institutions prevalent in Sweden.[101] Further, they argued the problem had a circular, cumulative nature so that the lack of government support for poorer families would mean further reductions in the birth rate, continuation of the poorest getting the worst homes, and reduced economic progress. On the other hand they believed state-supported family policies would be prophylactic and stimulate economic progress. The Myrdals used these findings to transform the population issue into an argument in favor of widespread, well-planned, egalitarian reforms as part of a comprehensive social reform program consistent with the Social Democratic ideals they sought to implement through social engineering.

In developing his own multidisciplinary perspective GM II formed a different conception of human behavior, and new, holistic conception of Sweden's institutions and behavior of the country's economic order that had to be transformed which influenced his method of analysis and transformation policy prescriptions. Alva convinced him 'that the ideas of "economic man" did not stand up to the results of contemporary psychological research' (Swedberg 1990, p. xii). GM II came to endorse the environmental view of human behavior held by Kjellen who argued that unlike conservatives who believed human nature was 'unchangeable', radicals perceived behavior as being environmentally determined, prompting them to believe that '[t]he individual, and thereby also society, can be improved by social reform'. (Myrdal 1957e, p. 115). This view also was consistent with Myrdal's belief in the Enlightenment which held that human beings were good and their behavior and living conditions could be improved by changing and improving social institutions.[102] The population study convinced him that most people did not have the capability to choose what was good for them. This served to justify his adopting an elitist position that social engineering directed by a small group of intellectuals would be the most effective means for transforming Swedish society in the direction he deemed most favorable.

As for the economic order, GM II recognized that neoclassical competitive market assumptions were not realistic for Sweden. Before Marquis Childs' *Sweden: The Middle Way* (Childs, 1936) demonstrated how the Swedish cooperative movement expanded to counter the economic power of entrenched industrial monopolies, GM II understood that the socioeconomic order in Sweden was not that of a Schumpeterian world. This was one reason he chose to bid the invisible hand goodbye and advocate state intervention, especially in regard to the 'population problem'. Another reason was his accepting the important influence on both macroeconomic variables and family living standards of non-economic conditions such as the nature of educational and health facilities, attitudes towards life and work, institutions (especially those which influenced economic, social and political stratification as well as the distribution of power in Swedish society), and the policies chosen by influential groups to deal with the community's social issues.

Throughout an otherwise evolving period in GM II's intellectual development he never stopped addressing the objectivity question. The constant theme, prevailing in all of his work, was 'that all economics is normative, concealing, or as in his case, exposing a value system' (Kindleberger 1987, p. 402). Reflecting back on the 1929–38 period, GM III recalls that '[l]ike the others [his Stockholm School colleagues], I was also drawn into work on all sorts of Royal Commissions and Committees and was a member of Parliament from 1935. From my philosophical period I had kept as a hobby the ambition to attempt always a clarification of the chosen value premises for practical proposals. A specimen of this type of philosophical meticulousness was an appendix to the principal report of the Population Commission' (Myrdal 1958a, p. 257).[103]

SUMMARY – THE TRANSITION TO GM III

To GM II's chagrin, the extensive package of transformation measures he proposed was not implemented in its entirety throughout Sweden. Some believe it was due to his impatient, insistent style which hindered his legislative ambitions. He wanted to reform Sweden to a degree that was too radical and too fast for either his government colleagues or the general public to accept. Eventually he became frustrated with politics, and chided interest groups for not following what he believed was in the national interest. GM II has been described as a legislator who 'was impatient with the day-to-day round of public duties, disliked the compromises necessary in parliamentary politics, and considered the Swedish bureaucracy a 'cemetery of words and deeds'" (Jackson 1990, p. 81). In addition, since GM II was very strongly opinionated and exceptionally intellectual, 'he found it unnatural to accept party discipline and to defer to older men that he regarded as intellectually inferior' (Jackson 1990, p. 86).

The Social Democrats' ability to implement radical redistributional reforms also was tempered by their having to form a coalition government, thereby necessitating that reforms proposed placate some 'non-socialist' parties. The necessity for compromise among all political parties meant that practical politics prevailed over scientific analysis and ideological conviction. The onset of World War II contributed to bringing a temporary end to what momentum there had been for introducing some of GM II's transformation policies. It was at this time GM II lost interest in and control over the Population Commission's work. Reflecting back upon his social economist period, GM III recalls that '[t]hrough the circumstances of the time and our own ambitions, several of us were brought into political life or became lost in administration ... we must now concede that it is highly questionable whether this departure from the tradition has brought advantages large enough to compensate for the disadvantages. We [the "younger generation of Swedish economists"] learned a lot ... but we also lost much valuable time and became less effective as researchers and teachers, at least for the periods when we were more fully occupied in practical and political tasks' (Myrdal 1958a, p. 246).

As GM II grew impatient with the slow pace of reform implementation he received a letter from Frederick P. Keppel of the Carnegie Foundation inviting him to undertake a comprehensive study of race relations in America. '[T]he Carnegie tradition had been to support "exceptional men", and Keppel concluded that Myrdal deserved the opportunity to write a major survey of the American "Negro problem"' (Jackson 1990, p. 35). GM II also was invited because the foundation desired a 'social scientist with broad training and acquaintance also with practical affairs from a neutral democratic country with no race prejudices – a man with a "fresh mind"' (Myrdal 1938c).

GM II's first reaction was to decline the invitation because of his responsibilities as an elected member of the upper house of the Swedish Parliament, and his belief that 'I don't know a bit about the Negro' (Myrdal 1938a). Upon further consideration the 'Negro problem' intrigued him.[104] He also was enticed by the autonomy and resources that would be made available to him for the study. Finally, GM II accepted the invitation, and resolved to be fully committed, stating that 'I shall work on the Negro – I will do nothing else: I shall think and dream of the Negro 24 hours a day, for I will really do a good job' (Myrdal 1938a). He confided in two American friends the reasons he and Alva decided to undertake the study. 'This was, after all and in spite of it all a chance to make a big move in our life. You know we like that sort of thing. We are rather tired of Sweden and everything we are mingled in here. Economic policy is a boring affair in good times and I don't believe there will be a big depression for some years' (Myrdal 1938c).

Myrdal now was free to resume his career as a researcher, 'engag[ing] in disinterested social science research and be intellectually free, neutral, and skeptical' (Jackson 1990, p. 86), and to apply his strong interdisciplinary bent to a pressing social problem. Reflecting back upon the 1929–38 period GM II told friends that 'we [he and Alva] are closing a chapter in our life, a chapter filled by work and struggle, some defects but also very much success. We have proven that things can be done in this country and have started a lot of things, which will then run by their own momentum. We are now preparing our return to the scientific convent. To leave politics we have, however, to leave the country ... So now we are making the big dramatic move in our life' (Myrdal 1938a). This move would result in Myrdal's greatest contribution to social science while serving to transform him to GM III – institutional economist.

4. Gunnar Myrdal III: 1938–87, emergence as an institutional economist

INTRODUCTION

So much has been written about the major works of Gunnar Myrdal III (GM III) that a detailed summary of the important contributions contained in each work would be redundant. Instead, this chapter focuses on his intellectual development as an institutional economist and will include: the basic characteristics of an institutional economist, what GM III means by institutional economics, how GM III conforms to the characteristics of an institutional economist in the American tradition,[105] and how and why he became an institutional economist. For the purpose of this analysis what is important about GM III's writings is not only their content, but the relationship between each work and the environment which inspired it, as well as the relationship between his different works. Consequently, emphasis is placed upon his main intellectual concerns – the landmark studies of regional, national, and global poverty and transformation – within the context of when, where and how they originated. In addition, his interdisciplinary method of analysis, conception of the socioeconomic reality, and resolute rebellion against mainstream economic thought will be described.

BIOGRAPHICAL SKETCH AND MAJOR CONTRIBUTIONS

1938–42: Landmark Study in Race Relations – Transformation of America

When the Carnegie Foundation decided to fund a landmark study of race relations in the United States the choice of project director was made by the Foundation president, Frederick Keppel. In making his choice Keppel adhered to Andrew Carnegie's maxim and set out to find the exceptional individual and, once having found someone with exemplary talent and proven ability to produce high quality work to give that person a free hand. Keppel found such an individual and, in August 1937, formally invited Myrdal to undertake a 'comprehensive Study of the Negro in the United States ... in a wholly objective and dispassionate way as a social phenomenon' (Keppel 1937). He explained to Myrdal that the Carnegie Foundation decided to choose a foreigner because 'it has seemed to us that it might be desirable to turn to someone who would approach the situation with an entirely fresh mind... [someone from] a non-imperialistic country with no background of domination of one race over another' (Keppel 1937). Myrdal was still absorbed with Swedish transformation matters, and consequently rejected the initial offer. However, upon further reflection he and Alva recognized the possibilities for their making a major contribution towards transforming America. In October of the same year he decided to accept the Carnegie Foundation's offer, informing Keppel that he believed his 'special qualification for the task is very much due to the impartiality of a social scientist having acquired no prejudices in the matter in one or the other direction' (Myrdal 1937c).

Keppel asked Myrdal to begin the study 'by traveling through the South rather than settling down to do library research on race issues... [Myrdal] soon recognized Keppel's wisdom in forcing him to confront the realities of discrimination right away, recalling that "I was shocked and scared to the bones by all the evils I saw, and by the serious political implications of the problem which I could not fail to appreciate from the beginning"' (Bok 1995, p. 2). Soon thereafter Myrdal responded to the opportunity to demonstrate his ability to put together a superior team to undertake a landmark study. Those familiar with this stage of the study argue that Myrdal was brilliant in his ability to choose the best people and organize them to produce an excellent report, a talent for which he would be praised in his subsequent transformation studies and United Nations work. He encouraged his team to recognize that the dilemma America faced was the contradiction between its egalitarian principles and prejudicial practices, always believing that such a contradiction could be overcome. To Myrdal '[t]he challenge for the nation lay in living up to its principles by altering its practices. Merely stating the dilemma, however, would do little to bring about such a change. Only by exposing the underlying conditions to full view and by exploring the details of possible remedies could the process of change be set in motion' (Bok 1995, p. 3). Among his basic hypotheses was the belief that discrimination against African-Americans was due to white prejudice, and that such prejudice was mutually interrelated to the low level of living endured by nearly all African-Americans at that time. He came to this conclusion after having focused upon institutional factors in his study of American history and an analysis of prevailing social conditions. His main policy recommendation was that radical institutional reform was necessary to alleviate the widespread poverty he observed throughout the African-American community.

The study culminated in the publication of *An American Dilemma*, considered by many social science analysts to be one of the classic contributions to social science research, partly because of Myrdal's masterful ability to integrate economics, sociology and social psychology. One analyst argued that Myrdal 'succeeded in achieving his objective. His brilliant analysis of the causes and aspects of the problem has remained unchallenged except by those who did not read the book and the solution which it advocates is typical of Myrdal's realism. He is firmly convinced that there is no ground for any discrimination. But he knows that this cannot be abolished at once. He therefore proposes a gradual evolution' (Glesinger 1949). Keppel also was lavish in his praise. In a congratulatory letter after the study had been completed he told Myrdal that '[y]ou brought to it [the study] the glorious attribute of youth, which in your case is not merely a matter of the calendar, but also of some apparently indestructible inner quality, and with youth you brought energy, initiative and resourcefulness. You brought also and retained to the end something that isn't often associated with youth, and that is magnanimity; in my pretty long experience I have never known anyone who received more advice and suggestions, and accepted them in better spirit' (Keppel 1942).

1942–7: Minister for Swedish Government – Postwar Recovery

In the fall of 1942 Myrdal returned to Sweden, and for the next five years was involved actively with Swedish economic policy making. He seemed to benefit from the 'new experiences of the political process which is part of the social reality that we are studying', but recalled that '[a]s far as scholarly writings are concerned, this period is barren' (Myrdal 1958a, pp. 258–9). His first task was participating on a government committee that was planning Sweden's post-war recovery, which included accompanying a mission to the United States in 1943 to discuss trade and other matters. That same year he returned to Parliament after being re-elected to the Swedish Senate to represent his district of Dalecarlia. The following year as Chair of the Swedish Post-War Economic Planning Commission he directed the drafting of the Social Democratic post-war program. In 1945 his responsibilities grew as he joined the Central Bank of Sweden's board of directors, and later was appointed Swedish Minister for Trade and Commerce. In this latter capacity he ,characteristically created controversy by arranging for Sweden to enter a trade agreement with the Soviet Union.

Myrdal's objective in concluding this treaty was 'to assure reasonably high levels of activity in a few important sectors of Swedish industry'[106] as well as to establish closer relations between the two nations (Balapkins 1988, p. 101). One basis for committing Sweden to enter such a pact was his belief that two of Sweden's main trading partners, the United States and the United Kingdom, would experience serious post-war recessions. Unfortunately for Myrdal, the opposite occurred as both nations' economies joined Sweden in realizing favorable economic performances after the war. Meanwhile, the terms of the trade agreement with the Soviet Union became unfavorable for Sweden, especially since the Swedish labor force lacked the labor necessary to fulfill Sweden's terms of the trade pact.[107] Myrdal was blamed, and in the face of mounting public pressure he knew his tenure as Minister would soon end.

1947–57: Executive Secretary for the United Nations Economic Commission for Europe – Transformation of East and West Europe

He may have realized that Sweden was too small for his transformation ambitions. When he was asked to assume the position of Executive Secretary of the United Nations Economic Commission of Europe (ECE) upon the recommendation of Oskar Lange, Myrdal accepted. Both the United Nations and the Soviet authorities had endorsed Lange's recommendation because Myrdal was both highly qualified in trade and transformation matters and was a person whom both sides could trust, a rare combination during the inception of the Cold War. A friend of Myrdal's describes him as a 'natural leader' who was perfect for a position which required combining international economic expertise with managerial and diplomatic skills. 'I have seen Gunnar in many situations and I have also seen other big men in similar situations. What makes Gunnar different from all others is his naive belief that one must always tell the truth and that one must always remain decent and assume that other people will act likewise. This gives Gunnar an exceptional strength and makes him a natural leader ... he never hesitates to admit his mistakes. He never tries to conceal them. He never lies' (Glesinger 1949). Myrdal's leadership skills enabled him to become deeply involved with international transformation for the next decade (and thereafter) through his United Nations directorship, and in delivering two sets of lectures which eventually would be published as *An International Economy* (Myrdal 1956a) and *Economic Theory and Under-Developed Regions* (Myrdal 1957a).

The stated objectives of the ECE were to facilitate concerted action for the economic reconstruction of Europe, to raise the level of European economic activity, and to strengthen the economic relations of European countries with each other and with other countries of the world. In joining the ECE Myrdal thereby became an international civil servant charged with directing international transformation activities. As a social scientist he was in prime position to study from within the evolving European post-war social and political process. When he assumed the executive secretary position World War II had been over less than two years, the Cold War had begun, and not only the ECE but the United Nations had been recently established.

In addition, a decision had been made by the leaders of the Western powers to have Marshall funds distributed by a different organization than the ECE, much to Myrdal's chagrin. There was a debate between the United States, United Kingdom, France and the Soviet Union regarding their position and the United Nations' position vis-à-vis the ECE. A point of contention concerned how Marshall funds were to be distributed, and it was also debated whether or not the ECE should embrace all of Europe. Myrdal feared that a 'dangerous competitor' to the ECE might be established to administer Marshall funds, and that such an institution would exacerbate tension between East and West Europe and undermine ECE efforts to foster cooperation continent wide. The term 'Western Europe' was not to Myrdal's liking since he believed it represented a forced negation of the common European heritage as well as an unfortunate effect of the Cold War. He deplored nationalism in Western Europe and the lack of East–West cooperation. He also recognized the precarious political situation he was in, noting to a colleague that 'I am running the Secretariat of a political organization, the great majority of which is Western' but that once a year the Russians criticized the ECE's work as part of its desire to drive a wedge between itself and the United States and Western Europe (Myrdal 1952). Nevertheless, one of his first tasks was to mediate between United States and Soviet authorities, encouraging broader East–West trade relations in the belief that an expansion of such trade would foster peace.

Myrdal had very high hopes for the ECE, and made it clear before accepting the position that he did 'not want to become a letterhead of an empty piece of paper' if the work of his commission were to become futile (Myrdal 1947a). Myrdal ambitiously viewed the ECE as an institution which would facilitate establishment of a complete system for international cooperation in economics. He wanted the ECE to promote closer integration of European economies and foster international cooperation – his value premise being that nationalism was not preferred to such cooperation. In choosing a staff he looked for persons who would see themselves as global representatives of the United Nations rather than considering themselves as representatives of their own country.

Quickly Myrdal surrounded himself with talented professionals as he 're-cruited an outstandingly able team' (Streeten 1992), one which would succeed in the difficult task of blending independent economic analysis of a high scientific standard with effective practical policy making. Under his guidance a Research and Planning Division of the ECE was set up which would prepare an annual series to be published as *A Survey of the Economic*

Situation and Prospects of Europe. The series guiding principle was to present analysis of the dominant features of the economic situation of Europe as a whole and to emphasize those problems which were common to the nations of post-war Europe.

Myrdal enjoyed his 'unique' ECE experience, for it afforded him as a 'social scientist to live for a while as a real insider and actually see how the mechanism of power in a democracy functions. My interests are turning more and more towards the international problems and now I have the chance to really be studying them in a way as a "participant observer"' (Myrdal 1947b). His focus turned to an analysis of Europe's economic problems and to proposing practical steps for solving them in Geneva, relying upon his on-the-spot acquaintance with the problems of reconstruction and recovery and personal contacts with government ministers and technicians in all European countries.

Being consumed with administrative duties left Myrdal little time for scholarly work. He did have time to prepare and deliver a lecture at the University of Manchester in March of 1950 which was later published as 'The Trend Towards Economic Planning' (Myrdal 1951c). In this article he argued that a different post-World War II historical context and evolving industrialized economies rendered invalid the beliefs that a laissez-faire market economy characterized by 'perfect competition' still typified the economies of Western industrial nations, and that self-regulating prices would automatically guide these economies towards some equilibrium position. He perceived such beliefs to be rooted in doctrinal positions influenced by the Cold War. His view was that the 'forces of history' led these nations to become 'centrally regulated' societies with free enterprise activities operating with an institutional framework whose working rules were established through 'state controls' (Myrdal 1951c, p. 16).

Myrdal argued that the state was therefore 'forced into taking over more and more responsibilities for the direction and control of economic life by events, not by conscious choice' (Myrdal 1951c, pp. 5, 6). Some form of economic planning had followed state intervention of the 1930s' Stockholm School variety. This planning, he believed, was not merely an alternative for industrial economies in the 1950s, but a 'destiny'. Myrdalian planning was not a command type of mechanism, but featured greater assumption of responsibility by society for the performance of the economy. In countries such as England, Sweden, Denmark, and Norway a non-ideological, pragmatic type of state economic planning and 'rational' controls were introduced 'to steer and rectify the blind workings of the price mechanism', and in the process became the 'almost generally accepted basis for economic policy' (Myrdal 1951c, p. 37). This argument impressed Paul Samuelson, who praised Myrdal for also pointing out 'that the same self-interest which drives markets inevitably leads, in the political sphere, to the use of the State to affect distribution – along with pressure-group jockeying and deadweight losses, thus echoing [Joseph] Schumpeter ... and the 1986 Nobel laureate in economics, James Buchanan' (Kindleberger 1987, p. 402).

Myrdal's reputation as a scholar remained elevated at the world's leading academic institutions. Between 1951 and 1954 he was offered academic positions at Yale University, The University of Wisconsin, King's College of Cambridge, and was encouraged by W. Arthur Lewis to submit his name as a candidate for a new chair on race relations at Oxford University. He declined these positions because the ECE was offering him 'interesting and challenging possibilities' (Myrdal 1954a), and because he felt an obligation to continue guiding the ECE's efforts towards fostering closer economic and political ties throughout Europe. He did confide to a friend and colleague at Cambridge that he wished to remain at the ECE because he felt a sense of duty, but added that he longed for a big research project so that 'his productive capacity would grow' (Myrdal 1951a). Four years later he believed he had found such a project, and decided that he would soon thereafter leave the ECE and concentrate on writing a big book on the Far-Eastern problem.[108] One inspiration for his undertaking such a study was his desire to be reunited with Alva who was in India as Sweden's Ambassador. Myrdal confided to a friend that '[w]e thought of that [type of study] already when Alva took her appointment and actually suggested it to the Swedish government' (Myrdal 1955b). In 1956 he was finalizing plans for an Asian study that he believed would take three years for the research and another half year to write. Thereafter he planned to return to Stockholm with Alva 'to settle down to a more quiet scholarly routine as professor at the University of Stockholm' (Myrdal 1956c). After receiving the necessary financial support (see below) Myrdal formally resigned from the ECE on 17 April 1957 to undertake the study of the southeast Asian region.

In the official ECE press release announcing his retirement (Myrdal 1957c) Myrdal noted that during his ten-year directorship his group's successes included helping to keep open the dialog between East and West European governments on mutual problems. He pointed with pride to his having established 'an independent research division, carrying out professional economic analyses of a high scientific standard' (ECE/Myrdal, 1957b), claiming that economic policy problems analyzed by his group were considered by the ECE member governments. In his official farewell address, Myrdal proclaimed that the 'ECE's whole history is indeed a history of a determined and not altogether unsuccessful effort to accomplish economic co-operation in spite of the political split in Europe and the tension and increased preparedness also for settlement of the political issues. In that sense, the governments in the ECE have built up a tradition which can now help to prevent a further drift towards international disintegration' (Myrdal 1957c). He noted that the ECE was not a supranational agency by itself, but an institution which provided the means to resolve European economic problems European governments chose to deal with – and that '[a]t its most effective, the ECE is an instrument for reaching multilateral inter-state agreements' (Myrdal 1957c). He praised the ECE for making positive contributions towards alleviating raw material supply bottlenecks in the immediate post-war years in 'acting as a "bourse" for coal, steel, agricultural, and timber products' (Myrdal 1957c). Finally, Myrdal gave credit to the ECE for enhancing the expansion of post-war East–West trade and exchange of technical information during a period of high political tension throughout the continent. He did allow that while he deplored the Cold War it did serve to make the ECE more effective as a link between the two sides.

Others extended lavish praise on Myrdal for the ECE's accomplishments. Lange argued that much of the success of the ECE 1947–57 'was due to the personal efforts of its Executive Secretary, Professor Myrdal' (Lange 1957). Walt Rostow, who beginning in 1949, served for two years as Myrdal's Special Assistant and Chief of the ECE Central Office. He credited his boss with establishing a viable institution in a continent racked by war and division; establishing *A Survey of the Economic Situation and Prospects of Europe* which stimulated thinking about Europe in government and intellectual circles; and originating technical committees for coal, steel, timber, transport, electric power, trade, among other areas which dealt with 'real problems' and carried out fundamental studies of the trends and problems in Europe while offering some viable solutions based on sound analysis. Finally, Rostow praised Myrdal and the entire ECE for having 'helped to keep alive the idea of a Europe' that is not divided into East and West (Rostow 1949), and for holding a bridge to Eastern Europe when no one else in a position of authority from either the United States or Western Europe was able to do so (Rostow Interview 1996).

While offering his recollections of that period as well as of the friendship he maintained with the Myrdals for decades thereafter, Rostow recalls there being very high morale within the ECE. He attributed this in part to Myrdal's excellent ability as an administrator and management philosophy. Like Keppel and Carnegie, Myrdal's approach to staffing was only to choose 'first class people', and to make the unit as small as possible since Myrdal recognized that there are not that many first class people. Myrdal followed the same hiring pattern when he set up the ECE that he had employed while working in the Swedish government. As leader of this unit Myrdal, despite being very egocentric, was also 'a charmer'. When dealing with those outside his unit Rostow described Myrdal as 'the smart alec kid who came from a farming region to Stockholm to take on the bourgeoisie'. However, Myrdal was similar to the European Coal and Steel Community's architect Jean Monnet in terms of his ability to guide conflicting interests towards a compromise solution.

In serving under Myrdal, Rostow and the rest of the ECE staff were charged with the task of finding a solution during Europe's reconstruction period to the continent's coal and steel geopolitical problems which had stimulated two world wars. Faced with the French–German and East–West issues, the ECE tackled the problem on a number of fronts. They worked with Poland to export coking coal to Western Europe. Rostow wrote a technical paper concerning the future of the coal and steel in Europe which would become the basis for the European Coal and Steel Community. The ECE, according to Rostow, also was instrumental in 'saving Yugoslavia' from Soviet domination. In 1948 the Soviets were squeezing Yugoslavia by cutting them off from coal supplied by Czechoslovakia. Myrdal and Rostow headed the ECE group which helped Marshal Tito get coal after Yugoslavia had requested coking coal from the Ruhr. Tito, having been assured of a steady supply of coal, was thus able to defy Stalin.

As the ECE gradually became more bureaucratized Myrdal became increasingly anxious to leave his position so that he could 'devote all my time to scholarly work' (Myrdal 1956b). He began to present lectures dealing with transformation issues in underdeveloped nations. In late 1955 he was invited to give a series of three lectures at the National Bank of Egypt the following year in honor of the bank's 50th anniversary. These lectures were designed to complement the material that would be published the following year in *An International Economy*.[109] For his Cairo work, Myrdal chose to present theoretical lectures titled 'Development and Under-Development – A Note on the Mechanism of National and International Economic Inequality'. He described the content of the lectures to the chief of the bank's research department (Myrdal 1955c). In the first lecture he intended to 'confront the facts of life with theory: the great and increasing inequality between developed and under-developed countries, on the one hand, and the theory of international trade, on the other'. The next lecture would introduce his notion of the 'backwash effect' as he began to 'develop more positively my theory that a stable equilibrium notion is usually a false analogy'. The final lecture would 'treat the problem of international inequality'. The lectures were published in Egypt under the same title, and an expanded version was published in Britain as *Economic Theory and Under-Developed Regions* (Myrdal 1957a), and in the United States under the title of *Rich Lands and Poor*.

The central theme of the lectures was that 'mainstream economic theory had little to offer less-developed countries to assist in their growth and that free trade hurt rather than helped' (Kindleberger 1987, p. 399). Myrdal also professed skepticism about the assumed tendency that economies tend to self stabilize and that inequality between nations tends to be reduced if economies were left to operate according to natural market forces. Rather, he argued the opposite occurred[110] and called for a new transformation perspective towards underdeveloped countries since he believed that the conventional wisdom of the time suffered from a biased, unrealistic conception of the poor nations' socioeconomic reality. He reiterated his finding from *An American Dilemma* that state intervention would be necessary to provide impetus in guiding the poor countries' economies towards being characterized by less inequality in their distribution of wealth, income, and employment opportunities.

As part of the celebration of its 200th anniversary Columbia University planned a Bicentennial Conference to which Myrdal was invited to present a paper. He chose the topic 'Towards a More Closely Integrated Free World Economy'. Myrdal confided in a friend that in this lecture he was 'attempting to do a full-scale social science approach to problems which are customarily dealt with in very old-fashioned, classical economic terms' (Myrdal 1954b). Some scholars have observed that this lecture might have forced Myrdal to present his views pertaining to an integrated world economy before he might otherwise have done. Nevertheless the paper was well received, and Myrdal decided to expand what was a 50-page paper into a 375 page manuscript (Kindleberger 1987, p. 399). Due to its length Columbia could not print the whole manuscript, so Myrdal approached Harper Brothers who agreed to print it as a book. The revised version of the paper was published as *An International Economy: Problems and Prospects.* The book focuses on problems and prospects for integrating world economies through trade and commercial policy, following Myrdal's analysis of this policy and factor mobility in both developed and underdeveloped countries.

The familiar objectivity issue is addressed explicitly in an appendix, 'Methodological Note on the Concepts and the Value Premises'. Here Myrdal argues for 'an empirical study of people's opinions on the matter under investigation' as the proper method to determine the correct value premises (Myrdal 1956a, p. 337). One value premise he chose is that international economic integration is a 'moral problem' (Myrdal 1956a, p. x). Myrdal explained his position by arguing that the Western ideology and value system of modernization had suffused much of the underdeveloped world, and that these values conflicted with the regional, tribal and religious characteristics of underdeveloped countries, as well as with their social and political structures which were neither consistent with nor conducive for Western-style modernization. Nevertheless, he believed it was morally correct and possible to introduce the underdeveloped countries to the values and politics of Western welfare states. This position followed from Myrdal's initial conception of development – that the main problem contributing to underdevelopment was international economic inequality, and that this inequality could be alleviated by 'creating an international welfare world, comparable to the Swedish welfare state' (Kindleberger 1987, pp. 400–401). However, he realized while writing *An International Economy* that the extent of the required redistributional reforms must far exceed the type of reforms he previously had advocated, and helped implement, for Sweden.

Myrdal's analysis of the interaction between rich and poor countries also led him to disagree with some basis tenets of classical trade theory, especially the factor price equalization theorem. From his point of view free trade served not to lessen international income inequality, but in fact initiated a process which 'tends to set up a [circular and] cumulative process' in the opposite direction (Myrdal 1956a, p. 340). This was a theme he would repeat in his *Economic Theory and Underdeveloped Regions*. He recognized that the same processes which contributed to economic and social dualism in rich nations through backwash effects also operated between rich and poor countries. Since the laissez-faire market mechanism was conducive to such polarization of the world economy, he argued for 'a greater degree of economic integration of the Third World into the world economy through solidarity between rich and poor countries, economic aid and foreign investment' (Chossudovsky 1992, pp. 90–91).

It was while doing research for *An International Economy* that Myrdal first conceived of the existence of 'soft states' in which political elites translated their political power into economic power, and then used their greater economic power to further enhance their political power. He also recognized that underdeveloped countries were not characterized by the social and economic features common to the Western Schumpeterian world, so that reliance upon market forces driven by entrepreneurs through supply-side innovation and high rates of reinvestment would not be an efficacious policy in nearly all of Africa, Asia or Latin America. However, Western 'predilections' towards the underdeveloped world stimulated the advocacy of conventional policies based upon both the classical and neoclassical paradigms, thereby diverting attention from what he argued was the main issue – inequality. Myrdal lamented that this diversion was caused by an unfounded faith that unregulated market forces would stimulate development and, in the process, reduce inequality, throughout the international economy. He pointed out that those who had taken the time to analyze the particular problems facing underdeveloped countries had come to a different conclusion concerning the preferred agenda for the state. 'All special advisers to underdeveloped countries who have taken the time and trouble to acquaint themselves with the problems, no matter who they are ... all recommend central planning as a first condition for progress. Implicitly they all assume a different approach to the social and economic problems of the underdeveloped countries today than that which historically was applied in the advanced countries. They all assume a very much greater role for the state' (Myrdal 1956a, p. 201).

Myrdal concluded his analysis with a warning and an appeal. He issued a warning that there was a conflict brewing between the 'white nations and the countries of color', and that the growing income gap could lead to an international catastrophe. His policy recommendation was for increased international aid directed towards alleviating the extensive inequality, and for individual rich nations to reach 'bilateral or multilateral agreements' with poor countries, with trade in industrial products established on the basis of lenient terms for the underdeveloped countries, to foster cooperation and integration (Myrdal 1956a, p. 5). Myrdal recognized that, like Sweden, most underdeveloped countries had small domestic markets, thereby necessitating close economic integration with the rest of the world so that they could achieve economies of scale. Finally, fearing that more favorable trade terms and closer integration with the rich nations would be insufficient for promoting development throughout the underdeveloped world to the extent he preferred, Myrdal appealed for equalization of opportunities, arguing that 'no economic progress is possible without vast redistributional reforms' (Myrdal 1956a, p. 180).

1957–68: Landmark Study of Asia – Transformation of Underdeveloped Countries

Myrdal spent this entire period as research director and primary author of a landmark study of the causes of poverty in Asia. In applying for financial support for the project, he stated that the main purpose of the study was to 'make a balanced appraisal of the situation in Southern and South-eastern Asia as it is developing under the influences of forces from outside and from within. ... A main emphasis of the study ... would be on the [economic] problems of the region as a whole ... both in the treatment of individual countries and in the study of their relations to each other and to the outside world the economic potentialities will be viewed in their social and political context. Thus the study will necessarily include an analysis of the new nationalism in the region, as it is conditioned by social, cultural, religious and racial conflicts' (Myrdal 1956d). He encountered some difficulty obtaining the necessary funding. The first potential source of funding he approached was the Carnegie Foundation, but they already were heavily committed to area studies. The same was true with the Ford Foundation, as they were providing financial support to numerous Asian studies projects. The Rockefeller Foundation offered no support either. He eventually was successful when the Twentieth Century Fund, a non-profit foundation for scientific research and public education on current economic and social questions, agreed to provide

$140,000 for the project in 1957. Myrdal was to receive $14,400 for 2.5 years – the length of time he anticipated it would take for the study to be completed.

He undertook the project with characteristic vigor, quickly organizing a superb research team. However, it would take him a decade to complete the landmark study. One reason for this unanticipated duration was that soon after starting the project Myrdal expanded its scope to include almost the entire social, economic and political life of nearly half the world's population. In doing so *Asian Drama* 'represents the only attempt to test ... [Myrdal's development theory] on a specific group of countries' (Ethier 1992, p. 68).

The study began in 1957 with a focus on the underdeveloped countries' colonial history and their transformation efforts following their gaining independence in the immediate post World War II period. By the spring of 1960 the research had been completed and Myrdal was ready to begin writing the report. He then left India for Europe so as to have access to a research library and better staff assistance. After a brief stay in London and Kiel he returned to Sweden in 1961 where he intended to remain until he completed the written phase of the project. That same year he was appointed to a special chair, Professor of International Economics, at Stockholm University, and also became Founder and Director of the Institute for International Economic Studies. He soon would add to his prestigious positions that of Board Chair for the Stockholm International Peace Research Institute as well as Board Chair for the Latin American Institute in Stockholm. It was late in 1961 that he realized it would take him far longer to complete his written report of the Asian study than originally anticipated. He apologized to August Heckscher of the Twentieth Century Fund for not having completed the study, noting that '[m]uch of the expenditure for collaborators in the beginning of the work was misspent ... [and that] the book developed as a "destiny", diverging from my preconceptions which I now recognize to have been conventional; after the errors and trials the study could certainly have been planned differently, and more economically, but that we could not do at that time' (Myrdal 1961).

Five years later Myrdal was still feverishly working to complete the study. In a spring correspondence with Heckscher he claimed that '[t]he book will be a melody in the big fugue of scholarly discussion that will within 10 or 15 years, as I believe, entirely change our approach to the problems of underdeveloped countries' (Myrdal 1966a). A few months later he again apologized to Heckscher for taking so long to complete the work, but emphasized that it was not due to lack of effort. 'I have been laboring harder than at any time of my life, and harder than anyone I have seen, in order to get this tremendous work out of my system: days and evenings, Saturdays and Sundays, without vacations' (Myrdal 1966b). Finally *Asian Drama: An Inquiry Into the Nature and Causes of the Poverty of Nations* was completed in 1967. It had become the comprehensive study of economic trends and policies in South Asian countries.

In describing and analyzing the neocolonial system throughout Southeast Asia and the behavior of the respective economies in the region post-independence, Myrdal became pessimistic about the possibility for these countries to realize development under the guidance of economic planning. This growing pessimism has been attributable to the important ramifications for development due to the initial conditions which characterized these countries, the modest spread effects and large backwash effects caused by these conditions (particularly the large stagnant rural sectors), and the 'institutional rigidities' created as a result of their history and culture. These conditions which handicapped development efforts included the caste system in India, corruption and 'soft' governments throughout the region, high population growth rates, a distribution of income far more highly skewed than in rich countries, entrenched political and economic power among the elites who actively resisted transformation efforts, and high rates of illiteracy among the masses. Myrdal particularly was distressed about the 'soft state' which featured an 'unwillingness to coerce in order to implement declared policy goals, and to resist the hard local power of caste, land and culture. It is not the result of gentleness or weakness but reflects the power structure and gap between real and professed intentions' (Streeten 1992, p. 126).

One regional development expert describes *Asian Drama* as 'a study in the broader, political, social and economic problems of Asia, particularly of the Indian sub-continent... [in which Myrdal provides] wide ranging references to economic history, history of economic thought and political opinions' (Myant 1968, p. 242). The same analyst praised the book for demonstrating the inappropriateness of Western economic theory in an underdeveloped world context without any knowledge or empathy towards the historical context, philosophical bases, or principal institutions upon which economies were based. 'This way of misapplying [Western] economic theory will of course lead to wrong results irrespective of whether we are applying Western economic theory to Western countries or to Asia' (Myant 1968, p. 243).

Using the same methodology he has adopted for *An American Dilemma* and *An International Economy*, Myrdal identified his set of value premises for the Asian subcontinent under study – his 'modernization ideals' (Myrdal 1968, pp. 49–70). 'The gist of these ideals is that economic development should be a conscious and deliberate effort, based on the pressing social and economic problems. There is no room in this new era for custom, tradition, or laissez-faire' (Balapkins 1988, p. 103). However, despite its comprehensive analysis of the economic, historical, social and political conditions of the region and Myrdal's articulation of what constituted development for these countries – with the corresponding barriers which needed to be overcome, the book was criticized for its absence of coherent, concrete development proposals.[111]

Myrdal was praised for recognizing the need to focus on the agricultural sector if development were to occur in the region, and for understanding that the anticipation of large-scale employment creation in the industrial sector of these Asian underdeveloped countries was ill-founded. The conclusions Myrdal did offer in *Asian Drama* were deemed more pessimistic than his earlier works, especially those contained in *An American Dilemma*. This pessimism has been attributed to Myrdal's ability to relate better to American citizens than to those of Southeast Asia (Streeten 1992, p. 113). The 'drama' Myrdal envisions was due to the conflicts throughout the region and the inevitable clash of aspirations with the unfavorable economic performance, all leading to a climax which has the potential for unleashing considerable social unrest. To head off such unrest Myrdal advocated planning to consist of 'fairly orthodox indirect controls' such as discretionary monetary and fiscal policies as well as state-directed export promotion and land reform measures (Myant 1968, p. 244). He argued that 'it would be unrealistic in the case of these Southeast Asian countries to consider a development plan based on increasing capital investment, technical modernization of the means of production, and increasing exports, as was the case in Europe in the early days of capitalism' (Ethier 1992, p. 79). Myrdal, well in anticipation of the post-1978 Chinese development experience, also believed that democracy, while highly preferable, was not necessary if an authoritarian government could provide measures to stimulate development consistent with his modernization ideals.

Myrdal's other conclusions reflected his faith in the state planning to guide the transformation of these poor countries and his disdain for orthodox economic development policies. His emphasis on a dual development strategy which included a focus on rural development was in response to the Lewis industrially oriented model which relied on 'surplus labor' from the agricultural sector. Included among his demands for international assistance was his call for aid to be 'concentrated on agricultural productivity, water, sanitation, education and similar public undertakings rather than on industrial projects' (Kindleberger 1987, p. 401). While criticizing rich nations for not providing sufficient aid to the Southeast Asian nations' transformation efforts, he was even more critical of development policies which had been adopted by these poor countries. In response, Myrdal also called for modernization of the agricultural sector through major transformation policies such as 'modification of ownership patterns, cultural adaptation to local climatic conditions, and change in the way people think' (Ethier 1992, p. 81). He stresses the importance of changing values and institutions, arguing that as these existed they constituted the primary impediments to development by maintaining the dual socioeconomic social and political structures and the corresponding skewed distributions of income, wealth, and opportunity. Such pleas for greater equality and radical land reform and his emphasis upon the ability of corrupt and privileged ruling elites to frustrate reforms designed to benefit the masses led to *Asian Drama* being banned by some Southeast Asian nations (including India and Pakistan).

1969–87: World-wide Transformation Policy and Anti-orthodox Economic Thought

Throughout the last two decades of his life Myrdal continually received international acclaim for his landmark transformation studies. Among his prizes and awards during this period were more than 30 honorary degrees, co-recipient (with Alva) of West Germany's Peace Prize (1970), the Nobel Prize in Economics (1974), and being named a Member (and the recipient of a Large Gold Medal) of the Royal Academy of Science of Sweden, and gaining membership in the British Academy and American Academy of Arts and Sciences. In addition, he held numerous visiting professorships and fellowships in the United States.

The adverse reaction of critics to the lack of positive policy measures in *Asian Drama* led to Myrdal's *The Challenge of World Poverty* which was based on a series of lectures he delivered at the Johns Hopkins School of Advanced International Studies in 1968. Myrdal told a colleague that he wrote *Challenge of World Poverty* as an attempt to provide 'the missing part of *Asian Drama* containing the policy conclusions, [however] I found that I could not account for those conclusions without giving a condensed account of the facts and factual relationships' (Myrdal 1969d). The book was a summary of each of the major problems he dealt with in *Asian Drama*, and it provided a detailed program for combating world poverty. In writing this policy manual Myrdal 'came to believe that a comprehensive policy part could be made valid for the whole underdeveloped world and not restricted to South Asia as I insisted upon doing in the factual analysis' (Myrdal 1969c). Central to the program were Myrdal's advocacy of radical, comprehensive agrarian and educational reforms as well as reform of the 'soft state' – underdeveloped country governments Myrdal described as corrupt and dominated by opportunistic upper class members who regularly practiced nepotism and favoritism while discharging their duties towards the poorer segments of their population. He also was critical of the rich countries for ignoring the plight of the poor, arguing that their neglect was for socio-political reasons.

An American Dilemma was never far from Myrdal's thoughts, and in 1974 he accepted a visiting position at the University of California, Santa Barbara's Center for the Study of Democratic Institutions. During an interview concerning why he chose to work at the Center Myrdal admitted that he wanted to 'come back and see what actually happened [to race relations in the United States]. ... I was also interested to see the changes, the trends; to go over it again' (Myrdal 1974c). He was working on *An American Dilemma Revisited*, seeking to reevaluate the original study's 'conclusions in light of how race relations in America had evolved in the ensuing decades, and "to express my worried thoughts about the future development"' (Bok 1995, p. 1). Unfortunately, health problems due to his advanced age of 87 led him to realize that he could not oversee the needed revisions, and the book never was completed. What he had completed decades earlier, however, was an intellectual transformation to GM III, institutional economist.

THE INTELLECTUAL DEVELOPMENT OF AN INSTITUTIONAL ECONOMIST

Characteristics of an Institutional Economist – the American Tradition

There is no definition of an institutional economist that is universally accepted either by practitioners who hold an institutional perspective or their orthodox counterparts. However, a review of literature written by self-proclaimed institutional economists indicates that certain propositions can be identified which, when taken together, depict an approach to broad economic issues generally adopted by institutional economists. Hence, to be considered a practitioner of institutional economics one must

1. Hold a vision of a reasonable society in which the common social will is expressed collectively, not through market forces.
2. Favor economic progress, but conceive of such progress in terms of changes in attitudes as well as in material terms.
3. Believe that society can realize progress if it adopts technological (as opposed to institutional) means for resolving its problems.
4. View social change as society resolving the inevitable conflict between technological and ceremonial forces through an instrumental valuing process.
5. Have a conception of the socioeconomic order by which the economy is submerged in, rather than separate from, a broader social order; human behavior is believed to be culturally conditioned, often irrational, and usually occurs in response to shifting non-economic forces, especially the pursuit of security – rather than being due to changes in economic factors.
6. Adopt a holistic, long run perspective towards socioeconomic change.

7. Be satisfied that while the direction of socioeconomic change can be predicted, precise and determinate conclusions cannot be drawn by relying on an 'economic' model.

What Institutional Economics Means to Myrdal

The essence of Myrdal's conception of institutional economics is his broad conception of societal issues. In his words, '[t]he most fundamental thought that holds institutional economists together ... is our recognition that even if we focus attention on specific economic problems, our study must take account of the entire social system, including everything else of importance for what comes to happen in the economic field' (Myrdal 1978c, p. 13) – especially the economic and non-economic factors which comprise a social system. The non-economic factors he emphasized include educational and health facilities and levels; distribution of power in society; economic, social and political stratification; and institutions and attitudes. In evaluating a social system Myrdal argued that all economic and non economic aspects 'must be taken into account, either when considering [development, which is] the movement [upward] of the [social] system and also when analyzing what happens to one set of conditions, for example, economic factors or one economic indicator, such as production or GNP. Only a holistic, what I call "institutional" approach is logically tenable' (Myrdal, 1974a). This approach takes into account the social reality of institutions and the attitudes formed within them, which attitudes, in turn, support them. Another 'central idea' in the Myrdalian institutional perspective is that 'history and politics, theories and ideologies, economic structures and levels, social stratification, agriculture and industry, population developments, health and education, and so on, must be studied not in isolation but in their mutual relationships' (Myrdal 1968, pp. ix–x). Another characteristic of the Myrdalian institutional economist 'is someone who does not think that the interrelating coefficients between economic factors can be measured with quantitative precision, and that we should be aware of the huge area of less reliable, complete and precise knowledge' (Myrdal 1978a, p. 775). In this regard institutionalists follow a holistic approach, being able to 'forgo much of the simplicity and precision of conventional economics' (Myrdal 1976, p. 216).

Many criticisms against the orthodox economic perspective are presented in opposition to the institutional approach. GM III harshly criticizes mainstream development economists in particular for overemphasizing economic factors, arguing that this results in 'the isolation of one part of social reality by demarcating it as "economic" [which he believes is] logically not feasible. In reality, there are no "economic", "sociological", or "psychological" problems, but just problems, and they are all complex ... . Most of the great economists in the classical and neo-classical line from Adam Smith to Alfred Marshall were vaguely aware that this was a mistaken approach. As they were prepared to include in their analyses what they saw as relevant elements of living conditions, institutions, and attitudes, they were, indeed, almost all "institutional economists" long before that term was invented' (Myrdal 1975b, pp. 142, 143). In many of his post-1970 written works, Myrdal emphasized that both theoretical and practical problems existed, and that the best way to approach them was not to rely on closed economic models, but to take an instrumental approach by choosing different methods best suited for each problem. He did not apologize for his 'negative' research approach that opposed the '"closed models" of conventional economics', believing it was necessary to be outspoken against unrealistic, inappropriate methodologies (Myrdal 1976, p. 215). He encouraged all economists to pursue a 'trans-disciplinary' approach to societal analysis by widening the scope of their research, and to become political economists while accounting for the role of human valuations in their research.

While working on the race relations problem in the United States Myrdal emerged as GM III with an institutional perspective. His brand of institutionalism has been described as 'an amalgam of facts, logical analysis and intuitional grasping of the significance of the total economic and social situation' (Gruchy 1972, p. 214). In *An American Dilemma* he was explicit that his methodology would include social psychology for an analysis of the 'doctrines and ideologies, valuations and beliefs embedded in the minds of white and Negro Americans' (Jackson 1990, pp. 189-90). GM III openly states that *Asian Drama* embodies an institutional approach as he attempted to analyze the development problems of South Asia in the manner that Adam Smith studied England's development problems two hundred years ago[112] (Myrdal 1968, pp. ix–x). He recognized the nature of attitudes and institutions which in the underdeveloped Asian nations were inhibiting the introduction of policies designed to stimulate development from having a 'circular causation' effect throughout the social system. Due to these inhibiting conditions GM III argued that social scientists analyzing underdeveloped countries needed to adopt an 'institutional approach' to focus on the inherent 'attitudinal and institutional problems' (Myrdal 1968, pp. 1863–4).

A comparison of Myrdal's contributions to those of the American institutionalists reveals that GM III is more of an institutionalist in the strict sense of the term than the American institutionalists, for he has been willing to advocate institutional reform as well as to engage in social engineering efforts (Angresano 1981). While American institutionalists emphasize the influence of technology on long term societal change, GM III focuses on immediate reform and places greater emphasis upon the role of state intervention and education for stimulating social change. His short-run view of conflict resolution through state intervention does not coincide with the American institutionalists' long-run view that technological behavior will emerge as the evolutionary outcome of conflict resolution through a learning-by-doing process of social valuing. Myrdal thereby has offered a modified version of institutionalist thought while applying his own perspective to contemporary problems. GM III believes no other contemporary institutionalist has formulated a theory, including his own methodology, as he had done (Myrdal 1978a). He further distinguishes himself from the contemporary American institutionalists by pointing out that their perspective remained somewhat static due to their heavy reliance upon the past contributors (such as Veblen, Ayres, and Commons). Unlike his American counterparts, GM III describes himself as an 'individualist' (Appendix, Myrdal Interview 1980). Overall, he believes he has broader roots than the Americans because of his individualism, the theory he developed, and because of his diverse research and social-engineering interests.

Becoming an Institutional Economist – the Emergence of GM III

Myrdal's research experience with broad transformation problems, especially the Population and United States' race relations studies, ultimately led to his abandoning the neoclassical perspective in favor of an institutionalist perspective and methodology. He recalls that by the late 1930s 'I had become an institutional economist. In Sweden I became involved in social equality problems, which I found could not be handled scientifically except by broadening the approach to all human relations' (Myrdal 1978a, p. 772). He recognized that attempting to focus only 'economic problems' and seeking to resolve them using 'economic theory of the established type as it had developed in the classical and neoclassical tradition' was inadequate when applied to the problems of poverty and societal transformation (Myrdal 1969b, p. 10). Subsequent research, especially the race relations study, led him to develop his own unorthodox methodology as he moved 'further and further away from that limited area [of neoclassical economic theory] until I became accustomed to thinking of myself as a political economist, and later, as an institutional economist ... . [Meanwhile, he developed] a growing disrespect for the traditionally rigid boundary between separate disciplines of social science as they have developed pragmatically to fit teaching purposes and to meet the need for specialization' (Myrdal 1969b, p. 10). Myrdal recalls that a major influence of the race relations study 'was to make me a full-fledged institutional economist ... . Nothing of scientific importance could be ascertained except by transgressing the boundaries between our inherited disciplines' (Myrdal 1978c, pp. 12–13).

After he completed *An American Dilemma*, his 'most important book', Myrdal did relatively little reading beyond those works directly related to the studies he undertook after 1942[113] (Appendix, Myrdal Interview 1980). He had been successful in changing his perspective because he was both willing and able to transgress related social science disciplines following his own admission that conventional economic tools were inadequate for analyzing broad social problems. In completing his landmark study of underdeveloped nations he emphasized that '[i]t is my firm conviction that social study must be comprehensive enough to be adequate to reality, and that this reality is very different in South Asia from what it is in the West ... Therefore I have rejected the "modern approach" which abstracts from modes and levels of living and attitudes and institutions, and have adopted instead an institutional approach' (Myrdal 1968, p. 1834).

A UNIQUE, HETERODOX METHOD OF ANALYSIS[114]

Although GM III has been accused of being a 'normative social scientist', one scholar familiar with his contributions to economics describes Myrdal as a 'positive economist ... [who] believes – and practices the belief – that the first necessity to understand the structure and operation' of the society he is analyzing from an interdisciplinary perspective (Reynolds 1974, p. 484). Four distinctive aspects of GM III's method of analysis can be identified, each of which contrasts sharply to aspects of the methodology practiced by neoclassical economists. These are his position regarding objectivity in the social sciences, interdisciplinary approach to analyzing issues, theory of social change, and conceptualized reality. Taken together they comprise an analytical method that contains a useful theory which can serve as a basis for transformation policy making.[115]

Objectivity

GM III believed that '[r]esearch is always and by logical necessity based on moral and political valuations, and that the researcher should be obliged to account for them explicitly (Myrdal 1969b, pp. 73–4). Consequently, the ability to hide one's ideological persuasion is something GM III argued a social scientist could not achieve. He believed the particular criteria chosen as the basis for evaluation by an analyst, the method of measuring these criteria, and the relative importance attached to each would be influenced by the analyst's viewpoint. It was, according to GM III, 'naive' to hold that social scientists were able to identify 'truth' objectively, and therefore they had 'to be as wary of all the influences that distort their own research as of the biases and rationalizations that they aim to expose among others' (Bok 1995, pp. 3–4).

GM III was fond of stating that every view (conception of the socioeconomic reality and conclusions drawn from analysis) has a viewpoint. By this he meant that results of analysis are influenced by the normative propositions held by that analyst. While analysts may purport to be engaging in value-free, positive analysis, GM III believed all have 'hidden values' which influence their conclusions and policy prescriptions.[116] This, he argued, is particularly true of neoclassical economists who seem to have a preference for free trade and laissez-faire domestic policy. Failing to state one's normative propositions explicitly leads to analysis and conclusions which GM III believed could be 'biased' – systematically twisted in an opportunistic direction. For example, recent transformation policy making throughout Central and Eastern Europe would have led GM III to argue that the goals and policy prescriptions Western advisors offered to Central and East European authorities have been ridden with the values inherent in neoclassical theory.

To reduce such bias in what is generally presented as 'objective' analysis, he proposed that analysts accept that economics is a moral science and thereby identify explicitly their viewpoint, or normative propositions. He refuted the positivist claim of neoclassical economists that economic theory can prove certain norms exist.[117] Instead he argued social scientists should accept that these normative propositions are 'extra-scientific' and do not emerge from the analysis itself, and that social laws do not exist as do physical laws of the universe. His method of analysis began with the specification of his explicit normative propositions which he believed were 'tested for relevance, significance, logical consistency, and feasibility' (Myrdal 1975a, p. 300) to the problems he analyzed.[118] Doing so, GM III argued, would allow the social scientist to combine these value premises with an 'analysis of the facts [which would] permit rational policy conclusions ... [because these conclusions] only spell out the logical policy implications of the selected value premises in a known context of reality' (Myrdal 1958a, p. 261). Therefore, in explicitly stating their value premises analysts would be able

> (1) to purge as far as possible the scientific investigation of distorting biases which are usually the result of hidden biases; (2) to determine in a rational way the statement of problems and the definitions of terms for the theoretical analysis; (3) to lay a logical basis for practical and political conclusions. (Myrdal 1975a, p. lxxviii)

Interdisciplinary Approach

GM III's analysis integrated history, politics, social psychology, and sociology with economics, for he believed that 'our traditional division of knowledge into separate and delineated social science disciplines has no correspondence in reality; concrete problems are never simply economic, sociological, psychological or political' (Myrdal 1957d, pp. 166–7). His inter-disciplinary approach to societal analysis was a departure from the tradition-ally rigid boundaries between separate social science disciplines as they had developed pragmatically to accommodate pedagogical purposes and the de-sire for research specialization. Such an approach made for a wider range of empirical observations and required common sense, rather than adherence to a strict theoretical framework, to choose or develop an appropriate theoretical framework that is the most adequate for analyzing the particular issue in question. While arguing that it would be ideal for a 'scientific solution' to the problem of poverty in a particular society to be 'postulated in the form of an inter-connected set of quantitative equations [capable of] describing the move-ment of the system studied', he recognized that doing so would result in a technically elegant description which omitted the vital non-economic aspects of the problem (Myrdal 1957d, p. 19). He believed that 'the coefficients of interrelation between all the conditions in the social system – and the inertia, time lags, or in extreme cases the total non-responsiveness of one condition to changes in other conditions or some of them – usually are unknown, or our knowledge of them is utterly imprecise' (Myrdal 1974a, p. 732). Therefore, although GM III relied upon his theory of social change to structure his thinking, his approach featured a reduced emphasis on precision and formal analysis than that which characterizes economic theory in the neoclassical tradition. He believed that his method of analysis emphasized 'logical con-sistency and realism' and was not 'model-thinking' (Myrdal 1961).

Based upon the race relations study GM III concluded that the plight of America's African-American population was 'intertwined with all other so-cial, economic, political, and cultural problems' (Myrdal 1975b, p. xxiii). The basis for his position followed from the analysis of American race, culture, population, economics, industry, agriculture, education, law, class, family, and religion – as each affected the 'Negro' population. He began the economic analysis component of his study with a historical review, then outlined this population's socioeconomic status vis-à-vis that of white Ameri-cans. In identifying causal relations among conditions, Myrdal concludes that aspects of the African-American's 'economic status' (including distribution of income and occupation, unemployment, consumption, education, and resi-dential pattern) were 'interrelated and mutually reinforcing'. For example, '[r]esidential segregation perpetuates educational disadvantages, which con-tributes to an adverse occupational distribution, which makes for low income levels, which perpetuates patterns of slum living' (Reynolds 1974, p. 480).

Myrdal also applied his interdisciplinary approach to analyze poverty in selected Asian countries, particularly India and Pakistan. Beginning with an in-depth study of each nation's colonial history, he identified the socioeco-nomic condition of each nation and the factors impeding development. A typical finding concerned the vicious, circular nature of conditions which perpetuated poverty. He concluded, for example, that poor nutrition led to low productivity of labor, which had a detrimental influence on the output of food and consequently on the level of nutrition and labor productivity. Low labor productivity and low incomes meant that savings for investment were minimal while consumption levels (particularly food) were low as well. Consequently, new equipment and other inputs (such as fertilizer) could not be introduced while people were not capable of extended periods of hard manual labor – and in response labor productivity and incomes remained low.

Theory of Social Change

Recognizing that a theory of societal change was necessary before an analyst could organize the facts observed, and finding neoclassical theories lacking as a means for analyzing the problems he chose to study, GM III devised his own theory of societal development. To him theory was a broad vision of what essential facts are (conceptualized reality) and the causal relations between the facts (theory of social change). GM III referred to his theory of social change as the principle of circular and cumulative causation which he believed had wide, if not universal, application. 'The underlying fact is the existence of such an interdependence between all the factors in a social system that any change in any one of the factors will cause changes in the others; these secondary changes are generally of a nature to support the initial change; through a process of interactions, where change in one factor continuously will be supported by reactions of the other factors, the whole system will have been given momentum to move in the direction of the primary change, though much further' (Myrdal 1956a, pp. 15–16).

This theory depicts a dynamic causation process in which GM III recognized both the interrelationship among all relevant economic and non-economic factors involved in the process of social change as well as the interlocking nature of the circular and cumulative aspects of change. The process of social change in the Myrdalian scheme stems from changes in all relevant factors necessary to induce circular causation such that a social process would tend to become cumulative and often to gather speed at an accelerating rate. First, a change in one endogenous condition will induce a response in secondary endogenous conditions. These changes, in turn, are likely over the long run to stimulate further changes in related conditions as the interrelationships among conditions and changes create a cumulative causation process with the social system continuously moving away from any equilibrium position. Myrdal argued that changes which occur stimulate social change in one direction (positive or 'spread effects', negative or 'backwash effects'), and that the ultimate resting place of the system is not easily predicted. This is because 'coefficients of interrelation between all conditions in the social system ... and time lags ... usually are unknown ... [therefore] our knowledge of them is utterly imprecise' (Myrdal 1974a, p. 730). Tendencies can be identified for the purpose of policy making, but precision in forecasts cannot be expected.

Whether a policy's impact initiates a positive or negative movement depends if its initial impact has a favorable or unfavorable effect upon development, which in the Myrdalian theory contains six key variables: production and income, conditions of production, levels of consumption, attitudes towards life and work, institutions, and public policy. To each variable he assigned an equal value so any change upwards or down in one necessarily pulls the other in the same direction. Positive changes in one condition (e.g., increased level of consumption) would result in secondary changes, thereby improving another condition (worker productivity) which, in turn, promoted greater output and income and this completed the circle by reinforcing further increased consumption, the initial condition affected.

Conceptualized Reality

GM III's theory of social change was shaped by his conception of the socio-economic reality, human behavior, and history. From his point of view the socioeconomic order consists of a wide set of social relations. There are a number of relevant, interrelated economic and non-economic conditions which constantly interact to generate social change. Included among these conditions are the level and methods of production, productivity of labor, distribution of income, and level of consumption. Important non-economic conditions he accounted for in his analysis include the nature of educational and health facilities, and attitudes towards life and work – especially as they are influenced by religion. Other conditions are social mores, principal economic, social, and political institutions – particularly those which influence the stratification of power in society, and the working rules established by authorities for these institutions.[119] Consequently, Myrdal believed 'economic' problems could not be studied in isolation but only in their demographic, social and political setting.

He was critical of narrow neoclassical conception of the socioeconomic reality, including the notion of economic determinism. This notion holds that there is one 'basic factor' which predominates to the extent that significant economic and social transformations are expected to ensue following a change in one factor – such as a change in relative prices or privatization of previously state-owned enterprises. In his words, there 'is no "basic factor." Everything is cause to everything else. It is not even feasible to define clearly this "economic factor", supposed to be basic' (Myrdal 1975c, p. 4). As a result

GM III chides most economists (both those holding a Marxist ideology and laissez-faire advocates) for failing to adequately account for non-economic factors while placing emphasis upon some basic factor to which all other economic and non-economic variables are expected to adjust once the 'basic economic factor' has been altered.

The experiences of both underdeveloped countries and post-1989 Central and East European nations, where favorable adjustments to promote growth were expected following high levels of investment or wide-scale privatization, have demonstrated the fallacy of the economic determinist view and its belief in a fatalistic tendency for society to adjust in a predictable manner to changes in economic variables without prior introduction of necessary changes in pertinent non-economic conditions. One contemporary scholar argues that the problem stemmed from the misguided perspective most conventional economists have towards transformation of a society.

> Economists have refined enormously their understanding of relatively small problems by modeling and statistically investigating them while taking the broad parameters of economic life as given. However, when it came to thinking about the huge question of how the communist countries might best make the transition towards a system that would provide a better life for their long-suffering citizens, most economists forgot how little their analysis had taught them about the large issues. Instead they plunged into advising about how best to reform the communist systems with great confidence bred from their improved understanding of relatively small problems. They leapt from the complexities of their own special fields into grand simplistic generalisations in areas about which they often had painfully limited knowledge, and for which their training had served them ill. ...
> If ever an issue called out for real political economy it was the transition from communism. (Nolan 1995, p. 312)

Those seeking to direct the transformation of an economy, GM III argues, must recognize that attitudinal and institutional change have to precede changes in economic variables. He cites the case of the Green Revolution where the introduction of hybrid wheat and rice seeds which, under ideal conditions that included large inputs of water and fertilizer, would boost the productivity of land by about two to four times as an example where his conception was ignored – with undesirable results. Technological change had preceded attitudinal and institutional change. The result was that for decades after the seeds were made available to farmers a majority of the poorer farmers realized few benefits from the introduction of the new seeds because complementary changes (such as giving them better access to water, fertilizer, or credit) were not made available to all small farmers in the area targeted for development.

GM III's conception of the socioeconomic reality in underdeveloped nations includes his belief that a 'soft state' is pervasive. Such a condition exists where political leaders are neither able nor willing to promote development efforts.[120] The characteristics of the Myrdalian soft state include social stratification, especially power vested in the upper classes whose primary interest has been to preserve the status quo, and the corrupt political structure – all of which represent remnants of a colonial heritage. He notes that 'the soft state does little to remove, and in fact helps to create, almost insurmountable obstacles and inhibitions to planning. ... [and thereby] impedes economic development (Myrdal 1968, pp. 1909–10).

Concerning his conception of human behavior, Myrdal's analysis of poverty in Sweden, the United States, and underdeveloped countries convinced him that individuals and society could be reformed through carefully planned social engineering efforts designed to alter social institutions. The primary agent for reform is education which would serve to create more rational attitudes and beliefs within people, thereby fostering higher valuations which, in turn, will 'shape' subsequent behavior (Myrdal 1975a, p. lxx). GM III recognized significant attitudinal and institutional differences among societies, and therefore argues that no single set of policies would provide a panacea for any nation.[121] He clings firmly to the optimistic elements of the Enlightenment view of behavior, namely that 'man is good and has the power of reason, he can attempt to dispel the clouds of his emotions, overcome the opportunism of his ignorance, reach a fuller and more dispassionate knowledge about himself and the world, and indeed, change his attitudes so that they become more rationally related to the existing facts and to his deepest valuations, his ideals' (Myrdal 1956a, p. 301). He also identified conflicting modes of behavior that could offset the goodness inherent in people, namely opportunistic behavior such as prejudice which he attributed to people being 'ignorant, shortsighted, and narrow-minded' (Myrdal 1975b, p. 232).

Regarding the place of history in GM III's method of analysis, he was 'not concerned with the past for its own sake, but merely in so far as important happenings in the past have influenced present situations and trends. Even in this narrower sphere we do not have the historian's interest in the 'uniquely historical datum' but the social scientist's interest in broad and general relations and main trends' (Myrdal 1975a, p. lxxix). He rejects any 'belief in a determinist philosophy of history' (Myrdal 1956a, p. 314) to explain the course of past events in either rich or poor nations. Instead he argues that the rich and poor nations' pasts, as well as the character of their societies in the future, reflect the outcome of a 'cumulative social process'. In referring to the development path followed by the modern industrialized 'welfare states', GM III maintains that 'the broad patterns of historical sequence were fundamentally similar as well as the circular causal mechanism of social economic and political factors making the process [of social change] cumulative' (Myrdal 1957d, p. 46). The development experience of rich and poor nations illustrates this view.

In rich nations during the 18th and 19th centuries there were industrial revolutions spurred on by technological innovations introduced by profit-oriented entrepreneurs within a laissez-faire socioeconomic climate. In response a cumulative process of spontaneous, rapid economic growth ensued. GM III attributes this outcome to unfettered market forces. However, in the 20th centuries a second phase occurred, with the welfare state emerging. Then in the rich nations state sanctions gradually replaced 'unhampered' market forces in shaping the social process for economic coordination. GM III attributes this transformation to the general unwillingness of people to be fatalistic and succumb to the effect of market forces plus successive international crises. The result was a growing public demand for greater coordination (planning) of social and economic affairs. The welfare states consequently emerged not merely as the outcome of a planned program of state intervention, but as the result of 'a long historical process, during which the market forces have been ever more intensely and effectively regulated by acts of public and private intervention' (Myrdal 1960, p. 79).

Concerning the poor countries, GM III does perceive of a mid-20th century economic history being characterized by a socioeconomic climate that was nearly as conducive to promoting development as the Schumpeterian world encountered by many rich countries in the 19th century. He argues that the poor countries have faced different 'initial conditions' than rich nations during the latter nations' industrial revolutions. These conditions include shortages of essential raw materials; an unfavorable climate; rapid population growth; weak bargaining power in international trade and capital markets; absence of modern technology; backward agricultural sector; tradition societies; and corrupt government where political power is concentrated within a small, elite class capable of translating political power into economic power, and vice versa.

The Myrdalian conception of history separates the path of poor countries into two phases. In the first there was the colonial era which was not conducive to widespread economic development. Rather, there was a lack of formal education provided to the masses, while those who received training were often indoctrinated with a Western mentality as well as being taught skills useful only within the colonial administrative apparatus. In addition, the colonial government served the interests of the foreign power while failing to permit the expression of any common social will on behalf of the interests of the indigenous population. Therefore, 'constructive measures' (Myrdal 1957d, p. 59) to promote widespread economic progress were never introduced. The sudden granting of independence to the colonies after 1945 was followed by the emergence of newly independent, poor nations whose political leaders were neither able nor willing to promote development efforts.

GM III AGAINST THE MAINSTREAM

Myrdal's criticism of neoclassical economics was extensive.[122] He recognized the inadequacy of its static equilibrium approach for analyzing societal problems, and derided its focus on 'economic' variables to the exclusion of non-economic factors. His response was to argue there was 'no distinction between facts corresponding to our traditional scholastic divisions of social science into separate disciplines ... The distinction between factors that are "economic" and those that are "non-economic" is, indeed, a useless and nonsensical device from the point of view of logic, and should be replaced by a distinction between "relevant" and "irrelevant" factors or "more relevant" and "less relevant"' (Myrdal 1975b, p. 142). The neoclassical emphasis on economic factors he deemed inappropriate, claiming it results in 'the isolation of one part of social reality by demarcating it as "economic" [which he believes is] logically not feasible' (Myrdal 1975b, p. 143).

GM III derides neoclassical economists' strong technical bent (to the neglect of the non-economic factors he argued were important) and policy prescriptions which had their roots in traditional neoclassical theory – both of which he argued were irrelevant for nearly all nations not belonging to the Organization for Economic Cooperation and Development. In particular, he criticizes neoclassical policy makers for reducing all problems to a matter of optimum allocation of resources and for assuming that efficiency and favorable economic growth would ensue following the establishment of competitive markets. This reductionist approach followed from what he believes was the neoclassical simplistic conception of reality, especially its monolithic, deterministic vision of the behavior of an economy. This vision viewed development as occurring in a linear, mechanical, simplified manner according to which neoclassical economists assumed that once certain economic conditions had been established (such as privatization of previously state-owned enterprises or liberalizing rules pertaining to free trade) the market mechanism would emerge and prosperity would inevitably ensue.

One-factor solutions purported to be panaceas for societal problems come under severe criticism from GM III, especially if they stress the economic factor to the exclusion of non economic variables. He was wary of simplistic answers to complex problems, arguing that '[i]n any interdependent system of dynamic causation there is no "primary cause" but everything is cause to everything else' (Myrdal 1975a, p. 1065). The tendency of some neoclassical economists to stress the predominance of one basic factor's influence through an economy represents to GM III a form of 'economic determinism' since he believes that 'the one-factor theory always implies a fatalistic tendency and prevents a rational conception of interdependence and cumulative dynamic causation' (Myrdal 1975a, pp. 1069–70).

GM III characterizes traditional economists as being 'naive empiricists', (Myrdal 1978a, p. 778), which ironically was the same judgment he had rendered against the American institutionalists in the 1930s. He is especially critical of the application of conventional economic thinking in development economics, citing as inappropriate the use of 'closed models' which he argues are characterized by 'simplicity' and 'precision' (Myrdal 1976, p. 215). Such models which purport to be able to predict the outcome of economic policy measures in poor countries contain 'not only ... [a] lack of reliable quantification of all the things that are deemed desirable or harmful, but also, more fundamentally, the almost total absence of quantitative knowledge about the coefficients of interrelations among the various factors determining the movement of the social system as a whole. This becomes particularly apparent when, as certainly we should, we include living levels, attitudes, institutions, and political forces as they operate in a circular causation with cumulative effects, which governs the movement of the social system' (Myrdal 1975b, p. 202).

That neoclassical economists advanced their theories as universal propositions valid for every time, place and culture, seeking to create 'an absolute and timeless economic theory' was 'foolish' to GM III (Myrdal, 1951b). During the mid-1970s GM III predicted that a 'more institutional approach will be winning ground, simply because it is needed for dealing in an effective way with the practical and political problems that are now towering and threatening to overwhelm us. Much of the present establishment economics is just going to be left on the wayside as irrelevant and uninteresting' (Myrdal 1974b, p. 14). One normative proposition underlying the neoclassical paradigm is a strong ideological commitment to laissez-faire policies which, Myrdal contended, was a deterrent to the establishment of rational, state-guided development policies.[123] This final criticism is the basis for some of the transformation lessons which can be drawn from analyzing Myrdal's work. These lessons are provided in the final chapter.

5. Myrdalian contributions to transformation issues

INTRODUCTION

Studying the works of Gunnar Myrdal, particularly his contributions to trans-formation issues, yields considerable benefits to social science teachers and researchers, especially those interested in Central and East European (CEE) transformation. One important benefit is that time spent analyzing his major societal studies, particularly *An American Dilemma* and *Asian Drama*, could leave the analyst with a perspective and basis from which a compelling, coherent, and useful method of socioeconomic analysis can be articulated. This Myrdalian perspective contains a holistic conception of societal devel-opment which is rooted in the history, philosophical currents, and contempo-rary socioeconomic conditions of the particular country under study. The perspective also contains a theory of social change that is based upon an experimental, pragmatic, evolutionary approach to transformation.

Predictions based upon an analysis utilizing such a theory of social change should not be expected to yield results which are as coherent and determinate as those arrived at by practitioners of neoclassical economics and its nar-rower perspective. However, given the reductionist nature of the neoclassical perspective and theories from which accurate predictions of the path and extent of societal development are uncommon – especially when CEE or underdeveloped countries are the target for analysis – Myrdalian proponents should not be deterred.[124] Evidence from the adverse impact of policies implemented throughout CEE and the underdeveloped world that were de-signed by Western economic advisors with an orthodox perspective towards societal issues lends credence to the argument that Myrdal's transformation perspective provides the means for gaining a better, more realistic under-standing of economies. Further, this evidence supports the position that his method of analysis is capable of providing a sounder basis for transformation policy formulation consistent with promoting development in the country or region in question.

In many respects Myrdal's life is both an example of and a model for transformation. He describes his intellectual capital as being 'eclectic, always changing' (Appendix, Myrdal Interview 1980) rather than having remained in a stationary state after his graduate school education. He was inspired by the particular socio-cultural environment of each society he studied and the historical context during which he carried out his broad analysis. As he moved from the problems of Sweden to those of the United States, post-war Europe, and underdeveloped countries he continually succeeded in shifting the focus of his attention and refining his perspective to best suit the unique transformation problems being faced. In each case he was willing and able to develop a new perspective and to provide policy prescriptions that in addition to having some theoretical basis, were also pragmatic and applicable to that particular society. He thereby developed eclectic policies that responded to particular institutional conditions for each of the widely diverse cases he encountered.

His theory of social change and corresponding policy prescriptions have been a source of inspiration for other social science researchers. Sissela Bok argues that '[w]ithout such a possibility of shifting the equilibrium, and without the examples of so many persons willing to break into the cycles of despair and set in motion changes for the better [as Myrdal's principle of circular and cumulative causation's "spread effect" indicates can occur], none of us might continue to work at social problems. Here again, my father saw a special role for social science in offering a systematic, rational approach to coordinate disparate efforts and to help mobilize large-scale social change. There could be little reason to attempt such change haphazardly. And those who held forth simple remedies for complex problems were not to be trusted. Interrelations are in reality much more complicated than in our abstract illustrations' (Bok 1995, p. 8).

His enormously time consuming landmark studies contained path-breaking contributions, albeit at considerable cost to himself and his family. He chose to devote an overwhelming majority of his time to transformation matters in order, as Bok recalls, 'to have a chance to produce work that truly contributed to human knowledge and to the common good' (Bok 1995, pp. 1–2). Having traced his intellectual development from neoclassical macroeconomist to his own brand of institutional economist, those transformation contributions are next summarized – abstracted from their original context in the previous chapters – in a manner that would have been unjustifiable if they had been presented without any prior analysis of this development.

This final chapter should appeal to social science teachers and researchers seeking to broaden both their perspective towards societal issues and their method of analysis. The chapter begins by summarizing and analyzing Myrdal's contributions to transformation issues and demonstrating the usefulness of these contributions for political economy purposes, especially throughout CEE. Detailed examples pertaining to CEE countries, especially Bulgaria, Hungary and Russia, as well as transformation issues concerning

Sweden, are included. Each of the countries or regions with which Myrdal worked had a common problem – widespread poverty. Seeking to alleviate that problem he developed what he believed was a more objective means for social science research which included his vision for each society, conception of the institutional conditions pervasive throughout the society being analyzed, method of analysis for explaining the society's behavior, and policy prescriptions to alleviate the pressing poverty problem faced by the country or countries in question. Each of these contributions will be presented, emphasis being placed upon features common to his major studies as they contribute to a new transformation perspective. The last section provides a critical Myrdalian evaluation of contemporary economics education, as well as an alternative education program which Myrdal would endorse.

A MORE OBJECTIVE APPROACH TO SOCIAL SCIENCE RESEARCH

Myrdal's insistence that researchers state their value premises explicitly has exposed the problem of hidden values pervasive among neoclassical economists. In refuting the conventional view that some truths could be identified objectively, he alerts students of social science and general audiences to be wary of research results which purport to be free of bias and to search for the hidden biases which undoubtedly influence the conclusions and policies drawn from such research. He also challenged researchers to state their normative propositions openly so they could be accounted for when the results of their analysis were presented. Researchers who chose to do so could combine their normative positions with empirical evidence and, in the process, draw more 'rational' conclusions. To reduce bias in his own studies Myrdal identified explicitly his own normative propositions which he believed were relevant, significant, logical, and feasible for the particular society for which they were being proposed. Doing so, he claimed, reduced his research from the 'distorting biases' so common throughout social science research.

The importance of applying Myrdalian objectivity in analysis of CEE transformation policy making is illustrated by the cases of Poland, Russia and China.[125] An evaluation of the impact of the respective 'shock therapy' cookbook transformation measures applied in Poland and Russia compared to the impact of the gradual, eclectic transformation policies implemented throughout China much as one would play a game of chess reveals hidden biases which Myrdal would have criticized. Due to rapid economic growth in Poland after 1992, much publicity has been generated concerning the efficacy of 'shock therapy' policies both there and in other Central and East European (CEE) nations. Consequently, there have been many evaluations of the Polish economy's performance since 1990. Some have been unusually biased – reflecting a strong ideological position which manifests itself by focusing only on performance indicators for which trends became positive after shock therapy was introduced, and giving the associated policies credit for this performance. On the other hand, unfavorable performance indicators are either ignored or attributed to exogenous factors. Such biased accounts have been provided by the architects of shock therapy as well as by International Monetary Fund and World Bank analysts. In one particularly egregious example of a strongly biased evaluation the study ignores certain unfavorable Polish economic indicators (such as unemployment), praises transformation policies in Poland for their effectiveness while criticizing China for adopting similar policies, and fails to recognize that certain factors that have contributed to China's rapid growth (such as investment by Chinese expatriates) have also occurred in Poland (Woo 1994).

The extent to which such an evaluation is biased is further emphasized by a recent comparison of China's and Russia's economic performances since their respective transformation programs were introduced (Nolan, 1995). Russia introduced transformation policies based upon the 'transition orthodoxy' that characterized Poland's 'shock therapy' (Nolan 1995, p. 8). Evidence indicates that while adopting a transformation strategy which 'runs counter to the transition orthodoxy', China's economy has outperformed that of Russia in every major area while not experiencing a deep recession (Nolan 1995, pp. 7–8). This comparison suggests that the contrasting outcomes in these economies' performances was due to their different transformation strategies, and that it appears the policies introduced in China were superior to those adopted in Russia.

Other analysts have taken a critical position concerning the degree of objectivity underlying the choice of shock therapy policies in CEE. In particular, they criticize shock therapy for being a social experiment 'untested beyond the economic laboratories of Cambridge, Massachusetts' (Komarek 1992), and that there was no 'analytical proof' that shock therapy would work. They take a position consistent with the Myrdalian perspective by arguing that shock therapy's neoclassical bias and its array of policy prescriptions and proscriptions offered a 'mode of proof [that] was generally "argument by assertion" – the better known the advocates of shock therapy, the less rational argument was provided, as a rule' (Amsden *et al.* 1995, p. 12). An analyst with a more objective position would have avoided any claims of being unbiased while providing a statement of normative propositions, thereby permitting those who evaluate the analyst's conclusions to test them for logical consistency. For example, any claim to be offering a more objective evaluation in the Myrdalian sense of the performance of any CEE economy compared to that of China would require a justification for the choice of performance indicators and how they were measured and weighted so as to provide an overall index of performance. These same indicators would have to be applied to both countries, and measured and weighted in a similar manner, before more objective conclusions could be drawn. The values of the analyst would be apparent from the criteria chosen and weights selected in particular, something inherent in any evaluation process, while hidden biases could be reduced.

OFFERING A VISION FOR EACH SOCIETY'S FUTURE

In offering his vision for the future of the societies he analyzed Myrdal was not dogmatic, especially in regard to the role of the state and nature of the political structure. Underlying his vision was a resolute faith in rational, moralistic behavior to stimulate social change, and the conviction that institutions could be improved and strengthened. Relying upon this vision he set out to determine practical means to transform society, arguing that despite institutional rigidities and seemingly insurmountable problems and obstacles to transformation, 'we have in social science a greater trust in the improvability of man and society than we have had since the Enlightenment' (Myrdal 1975a, p. 1024).

He remained confident throughout the GM II and GM III periods of his career that policy makers were capable of planning social reforms to guide society towards some 'middle way' state of social and economic conditions which would be achieved through evolution rather than revolution. While preferring democratic means to achieve his goals, he was willing to accept means which went 'against my grain' such as a political structure that featured an authoritarian regime if such a regime could more effectively introduce the type of radical reforms Myrdal deemed necessary to promote development, arguing that 'from the point of view of the value premises, it would then be preferable' (Myrdal 1970a, p. 436).

Myrdal was instrumental in the emergence of a vision for Swedish transformation in the early 1930s. Prior to 1932 Sweden was suffering from a number of economic and social problems. Poverty was widespread and birth rates were declining. During the 1919–23 period the economy suffered from inflation, followed by deflation and a foreign exchange crisis. Seven years later, due to the world depression, Sweden faced some problems that were similar to those plaguing CEE nations in the early 1990s. Swedish output decreased by 25%, unemployment was rising, and another foreign exchange crisis occurred. There was an absence of competition due to a highly concentrated industrial structure. Many Swedish families experienced a declining standard of living as indicated by a housing shortage and inadequate health care and education.

In the early 1930s Myrdal joined other Social Democratic Party leaders in defining a vision for Sweden that contained the informal and formal rules which would legitimize economic policies, social insurance programs, and welfare policy measures. These ideals evolved in response to a growing empathy toward the poor and disadvantaged. Each ideal, in turn, fostered a further desire to reallocate resources from a higher level (local or central government) to the level of the household, and reinforced the willingness to place the cause and responsibility for social and economic problems on the Swedish society, not on the individual. The first ideal was to relieve the poor from distress. Myrdal and other Swedish authorities accepted the view that state intervention was necessary to assist families suffering from the effects of adverse economic and social forces beyond their control.

In challenging the conventional wisdom that low wages were necessary to ensure full employment, Myrdal and other party leaders believed that redistributional measures would be necessary to alleviate poverty, arguing that poverty was inevitable given the economic and social conditions inherent under Sweden's laissez faire policies. They sought to create policy measures that would increase opportunities for the poor by stimulating employment while promoting family welfare. This humanitarian view was founded upon three basic principles:

> 1) legislation to guarantee to every Swedish citizen a simple and decent standard of living ... [Myrdal and his Social Democratic colleagues held that] it is the duty of society to provide for the needs of the aged, invalids, widows, and those who have lost their income through no fault of their own; 2) housing and child benefits for needy families so that they should not be forced to lower their standard of living because they have children to raise. The idea is to distribute the expense over the entire population as a collective responsibility; 3) social welfare to be ... the inherent right of every citizen irrespective of his [or her] financial status (Fleisher 1973, pp. 159–60).

The ideals of integration and equality became the foundation of Myrdal's Social Democratic Party platform in 1932. To Social Democrats, integration meant an end to class conflict by putting an end to labor exploitation, establishing democratic control over the economy, and reforming industrial relations to reduce labor-management conflicts through the establishment of democratic control over the workplace. The integration ideal also meant that all segments of the Swedish population would become the common responsibility of the state. Myrdal and other Social Democratic leaders emphasized the need for state-supported social and economic reform for the purpose of promoting the well-being of lower middle-income and low-income families.

Alva Myrdal contributed significantly as well to the vision of alleviating the problems of poverty and low population growth, particularly among low-income families, that were plaguing Sweden at that time. She, Gunnar, and other Social Democratic authorities believed society needed redistribution reforms to strengthen family and marriage bonds. The Myrdals argued force-fully that a family policy was necessary, and that it should be nothing less than a comprehensive social program. The importance of equality was em-phasized, the belief being that it was the state's role to create a more egalitar-ian society through an expansion of social services and welfare policies. The Myrdalian equality ideal held that all Swedish citizens regardless of social class should receive equal treatment such as universal health care and pen-sion schemes, and be able to have equal access to all resources and opportu-nities.

Myrdal retained his egalitarian ideals, nearly all of which would require redistribution measures to achieve, when he chose the 'American Creed' as his vision for the United States transformation to improve race relations. This creed, while not a 'fixed and clear-cut dogma' (Myrdal 1975a, p. 23), con-tained common democratic principles and Christian ideals 'honestly devoted to the ideals of human brotherhood and the Golden Rule' (Myrdal 1975a, p. lxx). In Myrdal's view, the creed reflected 'where the American thinks, talks, and acts under the influence of high national and Christian precepts' (Myrdal 1975a, p. lxix). Specific aspects of this creed he chose to emphasize as his value premises for the United States included liberty, equality of rights and opportunity, equalization of living and working conditions, a decent standard of living for all groups in society, a measure of economic security, compassion for the needy, and justice.

As executive director of the Economic Commission for Europe Myrdal adhered to the objectives of his organization. Foremost among these was keeping alive the idea of a Europe that is not divided into East and West, and holding a bridge to CEE when no one else in position of authority was willing and able to do so in the belief that an expansion of East–West trade would foster peace. He sought to strengthen the economic relations of Euro-pean countries with each other and with other countries of the world. To-wards this end Myrdal lobbied extensively for having Marshall Funds distributed through his organization so as to lessen tension between East and West Europe by promoting continent-wide cooperation and relations. Through-out his tenure with the Commission he expressed a strong preference for international cooperation in lieu of nationalism.

For underdeveloped countries Myrdal chose his 'modernization ideals' as his value premises, many of which became primary goals in many develop-ment plans after *Asian Drama* was published. He described these ideals as 'mainly the ideology of the politically alert, articulate, and active part of the population – particularly the intellectual elite' (Myrdal 1968, p. 55), and argued that to avoid an expansion of the crushing poverty and social upheavals pervasive throughout Southeast Asian underdeveloped countries these ideals had to be achieved rapidly. Among the main ideals he wanted these countries to realize was rationality, which meant that 'superstitious beliefs and illogical reasoning should be eradicated' (Myrdal 1968, p. 57), and increased output per capita so as to raise living standards while improving attitudes and institutions. Among the favorable effects of improved attitudes and institutions preferred by Myrdal was that labor would become more diligent, punctual, honest, efficient and productive. Consistent with his egalitarian bent he favored 'social and economic equalization' for the purposes of promoting 'equality in status, opportunities, wealth, incomes, and levels of living' (Myrdal 1968, p. 59). Two additional premises that he advocated were realization of self-reliance, and energetic enterprise, which stand in sharp contrast to the learned helplessness pervasive throughout CEE. Finally, Myrdal recognized that his ideals could be achieved by an authoritarian regime bent on development more easily than under a democratic regime, a prediction that has proven accurate when the case of China's transformation is compared to that of nearly all CEE countries.

The post-1989 CEE transformation goals and policies which have been adopted by CEE authorities and their advisors can be critiqued from a Myrdalian perspective.[126] Since goals are 'extra-scientific', Myrdal would accept existing CEE goals as given. However, he would seek to determine if they were 'opportunistic' – biased toward Western interests. Given that value premises were not stated explicitly, he would argue that objectivity problems exist and that CEE goals may be ridden with ideological assumptions inherent in neoclassical theory, such as a desire to secure markets for exports to the West and access to CEE's raw materials, and to strengthen political influence throughout the region.[127] Furthermore, their treatment of stabilization measures as ends in themselves for the short run and the claim that these are means which can be separated from the ultimate goal (namely, the specific type of economy to be established) run counter to Myrdal's belief that development should be defined by societies' needs, not by abstract targets, and that means and ends cannot be separated. Myrdal sees a continuum (that is, what is a means in one situation becomes an end in another, and vice versa) between ultimate and instrumental goals. He argues that the method chosen to satisfy a chosen goal is not neutral since it reflects the policy maker's (and perhaps the analyst's) viewpoint. Consequently, means and ends cannot be separated.

Myrdal's ultimate goal for CEE would be a society with favorable performance indicators for the following criteria: social and economic equalization (indicated by the distribution of wealth and income), rise in productivity (indicated by the percentage change in GDP per capita), rise in living standards (indicated by a reduction in poverty, unemployment, and inflation, plus rising real wages), improved institutions and attitudes (indicated by the number of new firms developed, and declining crime rates, involvement in social and uncivil economies, and tax avoidance), social discipline and rational planning (indicated by a comprehensive development plan based upon a useful transformation perspective), national independence (indicated by political stability and an ability to legislate quickly and effectively), national consolidation (indicated by an ability to enforce laws), and political democracy (indicated by the extent of democracy and public attitudes towards governing officials).

The society would be experiencing development, which to Myrdal is not unlike the vision for CEE countries prior to 1989–90. There would be an upward movement of the entire social system, including not only the 'economic factors', but also 'all non-economic factors of relevance for the movement of the system, including ... educational and health facilities ... [and] the distribution of power in society' (Myrdal 1975c, pp. 4–5). Myrdal's ideal society would be one in which all citizens would become the common responsibility of the state. Everyone would be guaranteed a modest standard of living – particularly in housing, social insurance and welfare programs such as family services (child care, home allowance, home care for the sick and elderly), health care, and pensions. Relief for the poor, particularly for economic conditions beyond their control, would be provided by the state. One Polish analyst concludes that CEE populations, influenced by the demonstration effect of the living standards and the extent of state support provided to all interest groups throughout the Organization for Economic Cooperation and Development (OECD) nations, will not tolerate the wide income disparities and reduced state responsibility for employment, education, and other social and welfare services which are inevitable under current policies. He therefore argues that Poland 'needs to modernize and develop its sociocultural institutions within the framework of a welfare state' (Kowalik 1992a, p. 13). Since the objective throughout CEE of becoming a 'free market economy' is contrary to Myrdal's opposition to laissez-faire 'do-nothing' policies and the inevitable inequality such policies would create, as compared with his egalitarian objectives for society, he would agree with Kowalik.

CONCEPTION OF INSTITUTIONAL CONDITIONS AND BEHAVIOR OF THE SOCIOECONOMIC ORDER THAT HAD TO BE TRANSFORMED

For all of his transformation projects Myrdal studied country or regional problems in their historical, social, and political as well as economic setting. He did not focus on 'economic' problems while abstracting from the cultural context in which these problems arose. The extent of his heterodox conception of the problems followed from his willingness to recognize the contributions of sociological and psychological research. In understanding that one could not judge social policy from a purely economic point of view, Myrdal advocated an analysis of the 'institutional setup' (principal institutions which influence production and distribution activities), one objective being to determine the extent to which any social groups are sufficiently powerful to bring about institutional change. By comprehending the distribution of power among social groups he argued the policy maker was then in a better position to determine what institutional changes would be feasible.

Had Myrdal's advice been followed by policy makers working with underdeveloped countries they would have recognized that the 'initial conditions' faced were so radically different from those characteristic of nearly every member of the OECD that it would not be feasible to propose policy measures that had been deemed successful throughout Europe, the United States, and Japan. The conditions prevailing in nearly every rich nation when it embarked on its development path include a favorable climate; an abundance and variety of natural resources; low population density with frontiers to absorb excess population; a stable, honest system of government; an immigrant labor force eager to work for modest wages; the establishment of land-grant institutions of higher learning (which contributed to the development of technology suitable for our own particular resource development): and an absence of foreign influence in the form of a colonial power imposing its rules and technology.

It is noteworthy that virtually all of these factors have been absent in nearly every underdeveloped country, thereby putting these countries at a significant disadvantage when they sought to promote transformation. A similar case can be made for the initial conditions faced throughout CEE, as indicated by the cases of Bulgaria, Hungary and Russia.

Bulgarian Institutional Conditions and Behavior of its Socioeconomic Order

In Bulgaria the legacy of the pre-1990 economy has impeded transformation efforts.[128] In addition to low growth, lack of domestic and foreign credit, repressed inflation – among other problems – those seeking to transform the economy inherited state-owned enterprises that were overstaffed, with an indifferent labor force, energy intensive and dependent upon cheap raw materials and energy sources from Russia; outlets for what they produced were no longer guaranteed; there was no 'business culture' among management; and institutional rigidities were pervasive throughout these enterprises. Furthermore, the extent of institutional rigidities and their crucial role in inhibiting the effectiveness of such measures has been grossly underestimated.

The emerging body of institutional theory explains that people tend to resist institutional change if 1) such change is forced before they are fully informed and trust that there will be rewards for adopting the new institutions; 2) their attitudes included 'learned helplessness' due to decades of being discouraged from taking any initiative; and 3) there exist entrenched bureaucracies (both inside and outside of government) whose members fear that they will lose jobs, income, and privileges as a result of change. All three conditions existed in Bulgaria in the early 1990s, and many continue to prevail. Institutional change does not quickly or even necessarily follow legislation. Since the desired societal transformation requires that members radically change their way of thinking, habits and work patterns, sense of duty, and values regarding self-reliance, such change will occur slowly. Public cynicism towards authorities delays the process, for any change in formal rules that are not administered by a government bureaucracy that is legitimate in the eyes of the general population will be either ignored, suppressed, violated or distorted. Another institutional legacy is the pursuit of self-interest and clientism between political authorities and enterprise managers. This condition has persisted, as does the exercise of power by the state bureaucracy. Many enterprises are still managed by poorly trained managers profiteering due to corrupt management rather than through Schumpeterian entrepreneurial behavior. Activities in such firms have contributed to growing cynicism among the public and a growing distaste for their public officials.

In order to provide useful advice a policy maker seeking to promote development during the late 1990s would need a realistic perspective that would include an understanding of Bulgaria's institutional conditions and behavior of its 1990–97 economic order. The present economic situation in Bulgaria is grim as conditions have deteriorated considerably during the late summer and fall of 1996. The situation has turned out to be much worse than Bulgarian economists and Western advisors expected. Inflation is running at a 250% annual rate for 1996 (versus the second worst rate of 122% in 1993). The lev has devaluated substantially, from $1 = lev 67 to $1 = lev 250 between February and September, 1996. There is a deficit of essential products and Bulgarian authorities expect negative economic growth to continue. There will continue to be a shortage of electricity and an electricity rationing 'regime' during the winter, with no more than three hours of electricity made available to the typical firm or household during each four hour period. The banking system is in a state of collapse partly because many Bulgarians mistrust financial institutions and have withdrawn their money from the banks.

The country's problems are attributable to a variety of causes, many of which can be traced to its particular institutional conditions. The adverse decline in gross domestic product was attributable to a number of factors.

International political events such as the Gulf War and conflict in the former Yugoslavia meant losses in trade and payments of nearly $4 billion – losses which Bulgarian authorities doubt will be compensated. Supply-side constraints arose due to the loss of economic coordination after central planning was reduced. Since 1989 Bulgaria has experienced a deterioration in its foreign trade, including trade diversion. This has been caused by the demise of the Council for Mutual Economic Assistance (CMEA) and the corresponding emergence of hard currency constraints. As the country whose intra-CMEA trade was the most integrated (about 65% of Bulgaria's pre-1990 trade was with other CMEA members, particularly the former Soviet Union) Bulgaria was the most vulnerable as these bilateral trade agreements terminated.

Monetary restraints have not prevented hyper-inflation which reached 250% in 1996, while inflationary expectations remain high. Primary causes of inflation have been price liberalization and the increased monopoly power of domestic firms. Since the state has maintained a monopoly in most industries, and enterprise management has been pressured to increase wages in the face of rapidly declining real incomes and the need to pay in hard currency for imported materials, prices have been increasing rapidly.

The low levels of investment are due to a number of reasons. The domestic depression, burdensome profits taxes, a limit of 25% on interest payments that firms are allowed to deduct from taxable profits, the undeveloped capital market, scarce and uncertain supplies of raw materials, and poor infrastructure combine to curtail domestic investment. Many Bulgarians misunderstand entrepreneurship to emphasize speculation and trade as opposed to a process of investment to create goods and services. In addition to the factors inhibiting domestic investment, foreign investment is slow due to fear of political instability, and to the fact that all CEE nations are competing to attract foreign investment. In the process they are offering large tax breaks for investing firms – thereby reducing their potential for enhancing national government revenues.

The slow pace of privatization reflects a weak government, which has succumbed to pressure from the Bulgarian Socialist party and labor unions.[129] In response to the slow pace of Bulgarian privatization between 1992–4, privatization authorities revealed serious intentions to accelerate the process in 1995. Although authorities addressed the privatization problems and proposed some measures for alleviating them, the privatization program still suffers from internal contradictions and weak points. It could be criticized particularly in two main areas. First, the attempt to combine the market and mass privatization methods has given rise to serious doubts as to the efficacy of this approach. Though both market and mass privatization can be viewed as two means to speed up the privatization process, from the point of view of other objectives such as generating revenue for the state or the interests of the main participants in the privatization process they are very much different which allows contradictions between them. For example, there already have been considerable struggles over the enterprises included on the list of those offered for privatization under both methods. These struggles further delay privatization and make the issue controversial. Bulgarian authorities responsible for privatization will have to face the problem of the extent to which market and mass privatization implemented at the same time are compatible, and if so to what extent.[130]

The second problem area includes various strategies and schemes for privatization, but disregards one basic policy – namely, to develop a coherent, national policy for restructuring and strengthening public enterprises prior to their being privatized. All previous post-1990 Bulgarian governments have been criticized for the absence of any restructuring strategy. However, it seems that the new authorities tend to ignore that criticism. The lack of restructuring is a serious omission for, as is becoming apparent throughout Central and Eastern Europe, many enterprises will remain for a long period state dominated.

It appears that the primary concern of government authorities in 1996 is to change the form of public enterprises to private enterprises as quickly as possible. Considering the progress of the economic reform in Bulgaria and the present economic situation, one can find at least two grounds to justify the official position. First, the worsening financial status of public enterprises necessitates radical measures. This is credible especially because given the absence of any industrial restructuring program the prospects for a favorable recovery of state enterprises will remain weak. Second, the ongoing process of hidden privatization, which evidence indicates has been widespread in Bulgaria, has made authorities anxious to transfer ownership to private owners by legal means.[131] 'The monumental redistribution of national wealth and incomes has turned into a sweeping spontaneous privatization. Policy makers unaware of the country's institutional conditions that foster such privatization are busily discussing 'the advantages and disadvantages of market versus mass privatization, while mobsters are quietly carrying out their own privatization, and the state looks on' (Institute of Economics 1995, p. 11).

One outside analyst of Central and East European privatization processes argues that 'mass privatization programmes ... seem less appealing now than two or three years ago ... because they do not clearly solve the problem of having well-identified private owners who actually control and govern newly privatized enterprises' (Andreff 1995). As this same analyst points out, 'if privatization was aiming to change both corporate governance and managerial behaviour, it must be assessed as a failure in the overwhelming majority of cases, due either to an insider control by former managers or a socialization of property by the work collective. This conclusion is confirmed by many enterprise surveys in ... [economies undergoing transformation] which show only very few signs of in-depth restructuring, except when the privatized enterprise has been taken over by a foreign investor or by a private domestic firm.' These kinds of problems, however, seem to be of little concern for the present Bulgarian authorities. Due to the slow process of ownership transformation in Bulgaria, the privatization is still viewed as a top priority and a kind of ultimate objective in itself. It will be the future experience, no doubt, that will have to teach the Bulgarian authorities and Western advisors that this is not the case, especially when they face the highly complicated institutional problems inherent in post-privatization management behavior.

Hungarian Institutional Conditions and Behavior of its Socioeconomic Order[132]

In 1990 Hungary faced institutional conditions and a socioeconomic order that would preclude rapid transformation without corresponding high social costs, despite the most optimistic forecasts of Hungarian authorities and Western analysts – particularly those from the International Monetary Fund and World Bank. Included among Hungary's most pressing economic problems were macroeconomic instability and the absence of a 'business culture', an active second economy notwithstanding. These economic problems aggravated Hungary's political problems, which included the absence of faith in authorities. Not only was there social unrest due to declining standards of living, especially in terms of health care, but there was considerable consternation about the adverse effects of comprehensive reform measures. Additional economic and political problems emerged due to the termination of the Council for Mutual Economic Assistance (CMEA) in 1991. These problems will be discussed in turn.

Hungary was plagued by low rates of economic growth (about 1% annual growth from 1987–90) and a lack of domestic and foreign credit. The growth problem also was attributable to an industrial structure that historically increased quantities of capital goods and services without regard for efficiency or quality of output leaving Hungary with obsolete manufacturing facilities in highly concentrated industries. These problems were exacerbated by inflation which between 1990 and 1991 exceeded 30%, and with the energy crisis faced throughout CEE after 1989 and high inflationary expectations a significant decrease in the rate of inflation was unlikely in the near future. Pensioners suffered because their income was indexed for 2% inflation while actual inflation was about 12–15 times higher.

Hungary's economy remained conducive to a wage-price spiral partly because of the extent of state support required to maintain employment in state-owned enterprises (SOEs). The 25 largest state-owned enterprises (SOEs) had been incurring huge financial losses. These SOEs exacerbated the soft budget policy by engaging in 'queuing' with one another whereby an SOE does not pay its bills and is extended credits by other SOEs, with the SOE granting credit not having to worry if the SOE extended credit repays. Only modest relief from inflation immediately following dramatic reform measures was anticipated unless Hungarian production was able to become more efficient and competitive.

Hungarians had grown accustomed to job security, and therefore considered the 1990 unemployment level of nearly 5% unacceptable. Labor market problems were fueled by the belief that unemployment levels as high as 6% would exist in late 1991, with over 10% unemployment forecast by the end of 1992, primarily due to reform measures that required additional layoffs in SOEs. There were inadequate state funds to finance support for those unemployed. The labor market suffered further from a brain drain to Western nations which, although softening the unemployment problem, cost Hungary valuable researchers – especially in the natural sciences and mathematics.

Hungary was experiencing double deficit problems. Public debt doubled in the decade of the 1980s primarily due to housing subsidies, subsidized consumer prices, subsidies to SOEs, low savings, tax evidence, and growing foreign debt. Housing subsidies were the largest single item in the state budget, with 75% of such expenditures for interest subsidies. Hungary's financial system did not increase interest rates to reflect rising prices, thereby exacerbating the budget deficit. Not only did this affect housing subsidies, but SOEs as well. These firms paid 3% interest on borrowed money, but depositors received 20% in the state financial institutions (the difference being subsidized by the state). While the propensity to save in Hungary was very low, the propensity to cheat the state led to widespread tax avoidance. It has been estimated that about 17 billion forints in taxes due were not collected in 1990, compared to the state budget of about 54 billion forints.

The foreign debt problem was serious, for Hungary's $20 billion debt gave it the dubious distinction of having the highest debt per capita in Europe. Hungary borrowed abroad when interest rates were 5%, but rising interest rates (to over 15%) by the early 1990s meant the nation was trapped and forced to pay high debt service charges (about 13% of Hungary's GNP) – thereby limiting the state's ability to fund pressing domestic needs. The high interest rates coincided with a drastic deterioration in the nation's terms of trade in 1989, resulting in a declining demand for Hungarian exports and a negative balance of payments. The source of this deficit was dynamic mistakes made over the past decade. Hungary did not pursue policies designed to balance trade with Western nations. Rather, its first concern had been in meeting its quotas for trade within the CMEA-quotas determined through bilateral trade agreements. Inertia inhibiting the adoption of new technology to meet consumer demand was pervasive. Efficiency was not a criterion for evaluating trade performance. Unfortunately for Hungary, the incentives inherent in its procedures for making foreign-trade decisions both preserved its pre-1990 institutional conditions and exacerbated its trade balance.

As with Bulgaria and Russia, Hungarian industry was highly energy intensive, relying upon inexpensive fuel and raw materials from the former Soviet Union. Low input costs made some Hungarian industrial goods competitive in Western markets, and enabled the nation to realize approximately a $1 billion trade surplus in 1990. However, the 'price gap' due to low fuel and raw material costs ended with the dissolution of the CMEA. Hungary was faced with having to restructure its industry to reflect higher costs. Beginning in 1991 Hungary began to shift the focus of its trade from the CMEA to the rest of the world. The cost of Hungarian inputs rose considerably because it no longer was able to purchase raw materials, especially petroleum, from the Soviet Union at subsidized prices. Rather, Hungary was required to pay the world price using hard currency. Before the country could attempt to earn such currency through exporting it had to import inputs (with scarce hard currency), modernize its production facilities, and seek markets for the higher quality exports that it needed to produce.

This course of action was imperative, as it was for Japan in the 1950s and 1960s, for about half of Hungary's national income was due to foreign trade. While Hungarians were anxious to purchase Western goods, a corresponding growth in demand for Hungarian exports was not likely to occur in the absence of a favorable trade agreement with the European Union under which the Union would reduce tariffs against Hungarian agricultural and light industrial goods (e.g. shoes and textiles) substantially. In addition, the need to look towards Western markets increased due to the disintegration of the former Soviet Union economy which resulted in a dramatic reduction in Soviet demand for Hungarian agricultural and industrial products beyond what was expected following the end of the CMEA's bilateral trade agreements.

The absence of what Hungarians call a 'business culture' reinforces many of the problems already discussed. Under the pre-1990 economy there was little interest in efficiency, so SOE managers were not concerned with showing a positive balance between receipts and expenditures. The lack of financial discipline at the SOE level meant considerable overstaffing. A related problem with Hungary's SOEs was that, in the Stalinist spirit of industrial concentration, individual SOEs were very large relative to the size of Hungary's economy. As of 1990 Hungary had one of the most concentrated industrial structures in CEE. Meanwhile, there was a noticeable absence of medium-sized firms in all industries, including agriculture. Since in SOEs there are no owners accountable for losses, the countervailing interest between managers and workers was missing and consequently there was no discipline to hold back nominal wage increases. Managers generally granted workers high wage increases or permitted them to rest while on the job, conserving energy for working another job in the second economy. In this manner the Hungarian economic culture eroded the work ethic. Workers put forth little effort in their secure SOE job, and many of them allocated much of their time to a second job to supplement their income, or used equipment at their SOE of employment or office to produce a good or service for their second job. It was not uncommon for employees to steal from the state, and even take pride in doing so. Janos Kornai pointed out that people generally considered it a laudable act, rather than something to be ashamed of, when someone defrauded the state, appropriated its wealth, or shunned their own employment-related or citizen-related obligations. Those who refrained from this kind of behavior were considered to be dupes by other Hungarians (Kornai 1990).

Hungary faced the problem of introducing a 'business culture' which would include changing incentives for management and attitudes towards individual profit in an economic environment in which there was insufficient competitiveness, and where people were used to doing things informally (e.g. through the black market or bureaucracy) with trusted personal contacts. There was neither a history of private ownership, even of land, nor of entrepreneurial activity. In fact, the informal rules are the opposite. Kornai argued that Hungarians were imbued with the fallacy that if someone was earning an income above the national norm it would have to be attributable to their taking away from other Hungarians – that prosperity for some came at the cost of putting down others. Hungarians further believed such a state of affairs was a national disgrace and that wealthier individuals either had willingly to redistribute some of their wealth or the state needed to intervene and introduce radical redistributional measures (Kornai 1990).

In 1990 Hungarian institutional conditions also included many political features that were problematic. Hungary's newly elected authorities from a three-party coalition saw their popularity declining. While the results of the first elections (March and April 1990) reflected the external appearance of candidates to voters, results of subsequent elections (on the municipal level) were an indication of the voters' positions on substantive positions. In addition, voter turnout fell dramatically in 1991 with only about 30% of the electorate voting in the municipal elections. The poor turnout was attributed to the decline in economic conditions following the political revolution. Hungarians, including leading authorities, and many Western advisors imbued with the neoclassical perspective suffered from the demonstration effect of Western affluence, associating the achievement of political democracy with the easy realization of economic prosperity.

In 1990 nearly all Hungarian authorities lacked governing experience, were not enlightened regarding economic matters, and had few qualified experts with a realistic, useful transformation perspective as their advisors. There was much discussion of establishing a 'free market economy' without substantive explanations of what the nature of the principal institutions and rules regarding ownership of private property should be. It appears that many Hungarian authorities still preferred old privileges and were clinging to old attitudes, and while they were outwardly committed to transforming their economy they were not then willing to put liberalization of Hungary's economy at the center of their agenda. There had been relatively little turnover at middle and upper bureaucratic levels in 1990. This presented a serious institutional rigidity, for the ability of these bureaucrats to manage an enterprise efficiently so that it could compete on world markets was highly questionable. Those bureaucrats, conditioned to research allocation out of planned economic activities under a pre-1990 economy in which politics was dominant were not well suited to perform efficiently in a competitive environment with working rules that required competitive oriented decision making. Further, the Hungarian people had little faith in the state's ability to manage the economy. The uncertain transformation process generated resentment and cynicism within the population. Hungarian authorities suffered from the lack of an organizing principle upon which Hungarians could organize their thoughts about how a freer economy that would function to a large degree according to competitive market rules would behave.

There were considerable cleavages between political parties concerning the future of Hungary's economy and society. Significant differences existed concerning matters of collectivism versus individualism, a strong role for the church versus secularism, a social democracy versus a 'free market economy', a homogeneous culture versus a diversified society, centralized political power and maintenance of 'client' relationships versus decentralized power, and Hungarian nationalism versus Hungarian membership in the European Union. These cleavages exacerbated the intrigue and strategies of politics driven by special interests, so that coalitions such as one between SOE managers and state bureaucrats could exploit the situation and create conflicts between groups throughout Hungary. An in-depth study of Hungarian economic history would have revealed the historical legacy of atomized special interests characterized by informal bargaining between special interest representatives and members of the bureaucracy for the benefit of the parties involved rather than the Hungarian economy.

Authorities expressed their commitment to attain the unattainable – namely, introduction of genuine transformation measures in a painless manner. They diverted their attention from seeking solutions to real problems to focusing on scapegoats such as former communist party authorities and their policies.

One egregious example of political grandstanding was the proposal introduced by some members of Parliament to restore ownership of farmland according to the 1947 distribution of land. Such a policy would have created many small (about 15 acre) plots, too small for economic efficiency to be achieved, allocated among children of previous owners. Since most of these children currently reside in urban areas and have little knowledge of or interest in farming, many would be likely to sell their land – boosting land prices by an estimated 30% while exacerbating Hungary's inflation problem in the process.

There were other economic and political problems. Foreign investment had to be attracted (and with it Western products and management practices) without stimulating a loss of cultural identity. Austerity measures by the International Monetary Fund, given Hungary's debt situation, were certain to inflate existing economic problems. Hungary faced the need to develop new political and economic relationships with other East European nations following the breakup of the CMEA. Unfortunately, there remained many obstacles rooted in the institutional conditions that inhibited the introduction of effective transformation measures.

Hungary had to embark on the transformation path without the benefit of any historical examples of comprehensive reform of an economy featuring the institutions and working rules of the type of economy prevalent throughout CEE prior to 1990. In the face of mounting social tension the government, which needed public cooperation for the sequencing of reforms, needed to convince the public that the transformation process would be long and painful for some. Receiving such cooperation was problematic because there was widespread public skepticism regarding the authorities' ability to find their way through the maze of economic and political difficulties that obstruct the formulation of coherent, long-term programs to improve economic conditions. Unfortunately, authorities faced considerable obstacles to the establishment of desired, basic conditions such as macroeconomic stabilization.

Hungarian authorities recognized that comprehensive transformation measures were certain to exacerbate inflation, unemployment, and trade balance problems, as well as the country's ability to provide public assistance to those who become dependent upon assistance as a result of reforms. Any abolition of price controls (such as those exercised over rent) would result in dramatic price and rent increases while driving down real wages, especially for the lowest income groups – including pensioners. It was predicted that a sudden move to full convertibility of the forint would likely be followed by rising inflation and interest rates.

It was also forecast that following the introduction of the type of transformation measures advocated by Western agencies such as the International Monetary Fund and World Bank a substantial portion of Hungary's society would become impoverished while income inequalities between groups would increase. The modest liberalization measures introduced in early 1990 coincided with rising rates of inflation. The inflationary process was fueled by the demand for additional state subsidies to support the many SOEs that were unable to cover operating expenses. Rising unemployment was inevitable after a rapid privatization movement due to overstaffing in state-owned economic institutions. It was estimated that about 30% of the workers in SOEs, and nearly all of the managers, would become redundant after meaningful market reforms were introduced. Such unemployment was bound to be widely unpopular, and social unrest inevitable, unless there were adequate funds to finance needed compensation – which Hungarian authorities predicted would not be the case. Unemployment funds were not sufficient to finance unemployment benefits, job counseling, job search assistance, or retraining for those who become structurally unemployed or for those who need to become acquainted with the main features of a business culture (e.g. accounting, marketing, finance).

Another factor exacerbating the unemployment problem was Hungary's opening up to the West, which exposed its vulnerability to the inflow of Western goods. Consumers had greater opportunities to purchase higher quality Western goods, creating a leakage in Hungary's income stream while reducing demand for poor quality Hungarian-produced goods that previously were guaranteed an export outlet – usually the Soviet Union. It was hoped, and even expected by some economists, that many workers who left SOEs would be absorbed by the growing private sector so that the net effect would be little or no increase in the unemployment rate. However, due to the inability of output levels in Hungary (as well as quality of goods) to increase sufficiently so as to absorb SOE workers who become laid off, unemployment increased.

Funds for a safety net (which could reduce social tension during the reform process) were lacking, and the current energy crisis will only make matters worse. Beginning in January 1991, Hungary had to purchase its petroleum at world market prices using hard currency (rather than from the Soviet Union at subsidized rates), and hard currency was difficult to acquire in light of Hungary's modest export level (about $6 billion) and large foreign debt (which meant the nation could borrow little additional hard currency from abroad). Unfortunately the austerity program adversely impacted the greatest on the poorest segment of Hungarian society – particularly the elderly – while raising social tension. In July of 1990 there were price increases (between 20% and 45%) for gasoline, heating fuel, tobacco, and alcohol. After a few days of nationwide protests led by taxi and truck drivers (which included a blockade of major transportation routes) the authorities scaled back the prices.

Many institutional conditions served as obstacles to successful transformation when the attempt was made to limit the state's role over the economy. It was feared (and in retrospect this fear was well founded) that if the early transformation measures did not have a widespread favorable impact throughout Hungary there would be a subsequent gradual build-up of power by previous Communist party members who would maintain client relationships by aligning with bureaucrats to regain their lofty position within Hungary's political and social structures. These party members and bureaucrats had learned prior to 1990 that their status, power and wealth was dependent upon their ability to influence the wealth-creation process rather than their contributions to the creation of that wealth. Therefore, they sought to position themselves in the economy so that they could retain their ability to direct a favorable share of the wealth in their own direction. The evidence not only in Hungary but throughout all of CEE is that the former communist party elite were able to preserve their privileged positions and the power of economic and political institutions which they had helped to hold a monopoly position prior to 1990. Thus, the inability of Hungarian authorities to implement meaningful transformation measures was inhibited by the lack of legitimacy for the political structure. This situation affected privatization efforts. The pace of privatization efforts was inhibited not only by the lack of investment funds, but by negative Hungarian attitudes towards the pursuit of profit by individuals. People associated private enterprise with exploitation of workers and co-workers, and were jealous of other people's success in private economic ventures. Some even responded by encouraging bureaucratic intervention to prevent such private 'profiteering'.

Another institutional condition serving as an obstacle to transformation was the absence of entrepreneurial talent. While some optimistically hold that Hungary's second economy has been a breeding ground for entrepreneurs, others believe that people engaged in second economy activity have not developed Schumpeterian-type entrepreneurial skills, for they engage in much rent-seeking behavior and are very risk averse. Many of these people were reluctant to pursue large-scale business ventures, being cautious about investing their capital. Kornai believed that such people may hamper privatization efforts by actively resisting any move to make the forint freely convertible (which would thereby remove one source of their income).

The replacement of state-owned and controlled institutions by private institutions was further hindered by high interest rates and taxes, and by a shortage of funds for investment and for importing inputs. Private owners lacked the capital to finance the imports and a capital market had not been developed. Western firms with ample capital were cautious about investing in Hungary, and those willing to invest faced obstacles such as obsolete manufacturing facilities; unusual and thereby difficult to understand (for Westerners) Hungarian accounting practices; a lack of reliable parts and domestically supplied raw materials; inadequate infrastructure; slow systemic changes in the commercial legal system regarding foreign capital (although the extent of such changes is greater than in most other East European nations); and a less than enthusiastic reception from some members of society. Hungarians were wary of foreign investors, fearing a loss of identity as the East Germans experienced following German reunification. In addition, some foreign investors face resistance (e.g. slow approval of documents necessary to begin manufacturing) from governmental bureaucrats. Finally due to the regional concentration of Hungarian industry, there are mono-culture areas whose workers have developed many firm-specific skills (mostly for the coal and steel industries which employ about 3% of Hungary's workers). These people are committed to remaining where they live, fearing high housing prices after being forced to relocate in search of another job. Nearly all these institutional conditions and problems inhibiting transformation efforts were present in Russia to an even greater extent.[133]

Russian Institutional Conditions and Behavior of its Socioeconomic Order

The legacy of Czarist and Communist party rule meant that Russia was a country whose institutional conditions could be considered a greater obstacle than in either Bulgaria or Hungary. One scholar observes that '[b]ecause a large portion of the population has lived under authoritarian regimes for so much of its history, resistance to Westernization is deeply imbedded. Thus it is not surprising that Russians feel relatively comfortable with more central-ized [authoritarian] control, rather than with a freer market economy' (Goldman 1994, p. 237). The political regime in 1990 featured a firmly entrenched, very conservative centralized bureaucracy with no history of democratic institu-tions who not only would resist aggressively any transformation policy that would reduce their power, but given the experience of Lenin's New Eco-nomic Policy and subsequent 'scissors crisis', were highly distrustful of unregulated market forces. It is argued that 'Russia's delayed and sometimes negative responses to reform have little to do with conspiracies, however, and much to do with its legacies, particularly its lack of experience with the market. It is also a consequence of the fact that many of the reforms were ill conceived, not least for their assumption was just like any Western country' (Goldman 1994, p. 255).

There was political chaos throughout Russia in 1990 which one analyst argues 'creates the worst possible conditions' for establishing a stable demo-cratic regime which can transform a planned economy into one that relies much more heavily on market institutions and rules (Nolan 1995, p. 301).

There was a failure to recognize that the country was experiencing three revolutions simultaneously: one was political – democracy vs. totalitarianism, another economic – market rules and institutions replacing those characteristic of a planned economy, and international, given the breakup of the Soviet empire. The chaos which followed the dissolution of a large portion of the state apparatus coincided with the prevalence of the attitude that transformation was primarily an economic problem without understanding the close interrelationship between economic, political and social forces in society. The advice Russia received from Western 'experts' did nothing to correct this faulty transformation perspective. It was not recognized by policy makers that before the state's role was reduced many inherited institutions had to be transformed through the assertion of strong public authority control over economic activity to guide the economy in a more market-oriented direction as well as to provide social insurance and welfare programs to protect those adversely affected by transformation policies.

The Russian legacy also included the absence of entrepreneurship and any other form of non-public economic activity (relative to the rest of CEE). As a result, Russians would be slower to respond to changes in economic incentives, for these incentives would require far longer than in Asia 'to penetrate the incentive-resistant barriers erected during the seventy years of Russian communism' (Goldman 1994, p. 188). This resistance was contained in economic institutions that structurally were a half century behind the rest of Europe. This structure featured over-industrialization, with large SOEs dominating the economy, a large portion of which emphasized military production. The agricultural sector was highly inefficient as indicated by high ratios of capital, land and labor to the level of output. The pervasive large collective farms meant that it would be more difficult to transform a sector with virtually no history of private ownership and control and individual initiative, especially compared to the case of China. Russia also featured other initial conditions that generally were not faced by wealthy Western nations. The combination of the CMEA breakup and slow growth throughout Europe in the late 1980s/early 1990s meant a sudden loss of demand for Russian exports, especially those of a non-primary nature. The pervasive crime has inhibited foreign investment significantly, even though the country has a large pool of well-trained, educated workers many of whom are well suited for technical or scientific employment.

It should be noted that some believe China faced even worse initial conditions in 1978 than Russia did in 1990.[134] This implies that it was not only Russia's institutional conditions and behavior of its pre-1990 economy that account for the very poor performance of its economy over the past seven years. Instead, it can be forcefully argued that since China faced more difficult initial conditions but has developed in a Myrdalian sense far more rapidly than Russia and more than nearly every other CEE nation, the problem must lie in the method of analysis and theories relied upon to explain the Russian economy's behavior, and policy prescriptions of the Russian policy makers and their Western advisors holding a neoclassical perspective towards transformation.

METHOD OF ANALYSIS AND THEORIES TO EXPLAIN BEHAVIOR OF THE SOCIOECONOMIC ORDER

Myrdal changed his perspective and developed his own method of analysis and theories to explain the societies he studied because he was both willing and able to transgress related social science disciplines following his own admission that the economic perspective and tools he acquired in graduate school were inadequate for analyzing broad, social problems. Influential factors in his adopting a new approach to social science research included the philosophy of Enlightenment, extensive travel, collaboration with Alva, transformation work with Sweden, USA, Europe, and UDCs. However, it was his willingness to recognize the inhibiting effect posed by the artificial boundaries erected around each social science discipline, and his subsequent ability to transgress these disciplines while developing his own methodology and then transcend this analysis to formulate and implement transformation policies which enabled him to become a unique social scientist. Part of his uniqueness was his method of analysis which, while comprehensive, was sufficiently structured to become useful in transformation analysis.

To broaden his analysis of societies Myrdal worked with scholars from other social science disciplines. He recognized that only a comprehensive interdisciplinary vision could identify the causes lying behind the pressing transformation issues. He emphasized the importance of not analyzing societal problems as isolated economic facts, but to evaluate them in their dynamic relationship with other aspects (such as cultural, historical, political) of society. Having assumed this heterodox position Myrdal developed a method of analysis which both avoided being doctrinaire and included a common sense, open-minded approach to social problems.

For social scientists engaged in transformation analysis of CEE, among other regions, it would be useful to adopt a Myrdalian method of analysis with both formal models to structure one's thinking, reducing the emphasis on precision, and relying upon 'informal tests, [thereby] making a wider range of empirical observations play a role in deciding among theories' (Klamer and Colander 1990, p. 193). Following Myrdal's example, the shift would include studying the principal institutions of the society being analyzed, as well as understanding the literature of economic history and economic

thought. Such a study will enable a social scientist to understand all paradigms and 'use common sense in choosing which approach sheds most light
on a particular issue' (Klamer and Colander 1990, p. 193). Myrdal argues that
'[i]nstead of chewing over our old doctrines and doctrinal controversies,
many of them a hundred years old or more, they [young economists] should
take their pick of what is really practical and useful in our tradition and then
proceed to make their own theoretical constructions to suit their problems.
They would then find that many old and familiar arguments and theorems
become useful when adjusted to fit into a new frame' (Myrdal 1957a, p. 104).

Like Myrdal, those seeking to analyze and develop policies in different
cultures may already recognize the limitations of pure economic theory as a
methodological tool for societal analysis. Those interested in developing a
new perspective for their analysis could begin by following Myrdal's example of critically examining the conventional economic perspective. Such an
examination would reveal that most economists tend to arrive at general
propositions and postulate them as valid for every time, place and culture.
Unfortunately, adopting such propositions and one method of analysis, then
seeking to apply it throughout the world has numerous pitfalls. This problem
was summarized succinctly by one economist who criticized the 'canonical
five-point plan for stabilization' developed by shock therapy's Western architects, chiding these economists for seeking to apply this recipe 'everywhere
from Azerbaijan to Zaire' (Fischer 1992, p. 117). The Myrdalian alternative
would be to adopt a broader method of analysis and theories and treat transformation as an iterative process played like a game of chess rather than a
problem which has a universal solution in the form of a standard policy
package.

POLICY PRESCRIPTIONS TO TRANSFORM TROUBLED SOCIETIES

Myrdal would have agreed with the analyst who evaluated the transformation advice given to Russia and concluded that 'Western social science
failed badly in this period. ... It was deeply flawed. The advice which
flowed from this orthodoxy contributed substantially to the Soviet disaster'
(Nolan 1995, p. 9). Nolan goes on to identify the source of the misguided
advice. He argues that the perspective of Western advisors 'formed the
intellectual foundation of the advice given the Bretton Woods organisa-
tions, and it played a large role also through the myriad of contacts that
developed between the Russian and Western intellectual communities. The
transition orthodoxy quickly and confidently built up in the 1980s. It had a
profound impact upon the way the "transition" problem was viewed within

the reforming countries themselves. However, it was deeply flawed.' (Nolan 1995, p. 9).

Myrdal's perspective towards transformation provided the intellectual foundation for his policy prescriptions. He was a strong proponent of co-operation between the state and private sector, and held that once a society believes social engineering will be beneficial the state must initiate a system of planning to promote gradually the social will through intelligent, 'cautious', and 'foresighted' reforms (Myrdal 1975a, p. 519). Thus, Myrdalian planning was intended for 'establishing goals, choosing means, fixing targets and implementing policies' (Myrdal 1960, p. vi). Such planning was intended to be pragmatic and non-ideological – developed from common sense and experience – rather than being dogmatic and based upon sophisticated, but abstract, economic theory. Myrdal believes that each nation should determine the extent of its state's agenda, devising their own 'elaborate variations of the theme' (Myrdal 1957a, p. 42), based upon differences in resource endowments, relations with other nations, history, religion, economic and other social factors. He admits that a country's ultimate goals and the means for achieving them ought to remain flexible, determined through a process of conflict resolution rather than adherence to absolute rules or authority. As he argues '[t]he plan is itself an evolving process. Planning cannot aim at an optimum, but at improvements. It is guided by vision, but the vision is open-ended and flexible, not closed and rigid. It contains a rough perception of the connections between conditions prevailing over a period of time and the possibilities of moving, through rationally coordinated policies, in the direction of development' (Myrdal 1968, p. 1884).

The Myrdals argued in their collaborative and individual studies that what needed to follow a planning system was an educational program. Their firm belief was that a precondition for progress is attitudinal change, and that such changes can be influenced by educating the entire population, not a selected few. Another justification for education was that '[i]f this educational effort meets with success, the illogicalities involving valuations become exposed to the people who hold them. They are then pressed to change their valuations to some degree or other ... This is the reason, and the only reason why we generally assume that improved knowledge will make for "better" citizens. Facts by themselves do not improve anything' (Myrdal 1975a, p. 68).

As he grew older Myrdal claimed he was better able to 'see the truth, and the truth lay ... with radicalism' (Streeten 1992, p. 114). Consequently, he advocated radical redistributional reforms through legislation such as fiscal policy measures (public works projects, land tenure, improved access to job opportunities, legislation and institutions which promote equal justice, enforcement of the right to vote, and assurance for the poor of equal access to social benefits). Further, legislation combined with attitudinal change through education could serve to initiate comprehensive institutional and administrative reforms to break up the non-egalitarian and rigid economic and social stratification characteristic of underdeveloped countries (and throughout CEE as well).

Myrdalian Policies to Transform Sweden

In prescribing policies to transform Sweden Myrdal addressed the following questions, all of which are pertinent throughout CEE today. How could the country achieve macroeconomic stabilization, especially high rates of economic growth? How could the country increase the competitiveness of goods it produces (both for domestic and international markets)? How could unemployment and its associated social and economic costs be minimized? How could all Swedish families (especially the disadvantaged) realize a higher material standard of living? In their policy making Myrdal and his Social Democratic colleagues adopted an approach which would later prove efficacious for Chinese policy makers. That is, '[i]n analyzing large issues of system change, in which all the parameters of socio-economic life are altering, [both Swedish and Chinese policy makers recognized that] proper policy requires political economy, not merely the separate "sciences" of economics, politics or sociology. It is their interaction in a complex, indeed, organic structure that is the key to devising correct policies' (Nolan 1995, p. 5).

The measures Myrdal and his Social Democratic colleagues developed and implemented to satisfy the popular ideals contained in their vision were designed to meet specific problems as they arose, with protective and redistributive measures designed to appeal to all social classes. There was no specific dogma to fulfill. Instead, authorities relied upon Swedes to be pragmatic, sensible, and responsible when faced with choosing specific redistribution measures. Socialization measures were the means toward the pursuit of a classless society, achieved through measures designed to create greater equality of living standards. The intent was to banish poverty and to provide all Swedes with a decent standard of living. Therefore, the Social Democratic transformation policies created a comprehensive economic security system that would reach all Swedes. Programs were available on a general basis to the whole population, with the general population contributing toward paying for these programs – many of which (including child allowances) every Swede was entitled to benefit from regardless of their household income.

The Myrdalian policies stimulated the transformation of Sweden's economy from a laissez-faire market economy to a democratically controlled social economy, popularly referred to as the Swedish 'welfare state'. This transformed economy would feature an active, interventionist fiscal policy which emphasized maintenance of a high level of aggregate demand to minimize the severity of business cycles and unemployment. There were redistribution measures proposed that were designed to offset factors causing sub-standard levels of living experienced by many Swedish families. The problems encountered by poor families stimulated Myrdal and other Social Democrats to propose a 'family policy' that became the basis for extending social insurance and welfare benefits to the entire Swedish population. A third policy pertained to measures provided by the public sector. Myrdal and his colleagues were committed to socializing important functions of the family which led to a state monopoly over child care and education services.

Another feature of the transformed economy was a wage policy that was designed to reduce wage differentials and provide job security. The intent of this Myrdalian policy was to coordinate industrial relations so as to reduce uncertainty among managers and laborers by channeling market competition to areas where such forces are most likely to promote productivity. Meanwhile, measures to foster relations of social solidarity to complement that productivity were also introduced. A related Myrdalian feature advocated was active labor market measures designed to promote full employment and to increase the mobility of labor. These types of labor market measures have been noticeably absent throughout CEE.

CEE Transformation Policies: A Myrdalian Critique

Concerning transformation policies which have been implemented throughout CEE since 1989, there are five areas in which Myrdalian criticisms of such policies are pertinent. The first concerns the uniformity of the policy measures introduced throughout the region. Myrdal would agree that no single set of 'economic' policies can serve as a universal panacea for CEE. Shock therapy transformation policies would be a prime target since they 'make no allowances for cultural and historical differences between the countries and ethnic groups ... [Western experts have] been advising' (Pejovich 1993, p. 76). Myrdal would lament that the 'arrogant messianism of shock therapy' was accepted throughout CEE as a 'sweeping prescription' (Koves 1992, pp. 17, 29). A contemporary scholar of the Russian economy criticizes the shock plan introduced in Russia as being a similar remedy as that prescribed for Latin American nations. 'The key [to shock therapy] was an assumption that higher prices or market-determined prices are a panacea for a basic economic malaise. In that sense, shock therapy was like an over-the-counter drug – good for any ailment regardless of preconditions, ideology, or institutions. There was no need for a fancy prescription – brand X would do as well' (Goldman 1994, p. 100).

Based upon his approach to Swedish, United States, post-war European and underdeveloped countries' transformation, Myrdal would urge contemporary analysts and policy makers to begin with an in-depth analysis of each CEE country's history, attitudes and institutions before proposing any policies.[135] He would seek to identify the causal relations between social facts, particularly the impact of non-economic variables on development, an analysis of which 'opens up the possibility of numerous cumulative processes to which conventional economic analysis is blind' (Streeten 1992, p. 125). Once this analysis is complete, he would advocate a nationwide study of his research findings to enable the citizens to understand their unique legacy and problems. These findings would be presented in layman's terms and intended to 'free the minds of the people and the government from many popular preconceptions, often originating from their envious comparisons with the highly developed countries which otherwise are certain to dominate the economic policies' (Myrdal 1957d, p. 94). Rather than suggesting that high level authorities should introduce by fiat policies untested outside the economic laboratories of Western advisors, interest group representatives from labor, management, farmers, and consumers would be encouraged to engage in debate and negotiations concerning alternative goals and policies and 'to make their pick of what is really practical and useful in [their nation's] tradition' (Myrdal 1957d, p. 105). The state would coordinate this process whereby ultimate instrumental goals would be selected to provide the basis for a national development plan, and throughout Myrdal would cite the experiences of Asian and West European nations to impress upon CEE citizens that development is a slow, gradual process, and that they need to avoid the 'big illusion' that a 'cookbook recipe' of free market economy reforms will 'benefit everybody and hurt nobody' (Rosati 1993, p. vi).

Myrdal's criticism is echoed by others who emphasize the need for transformation policy to be eclectic, introduced in a gradual manner after policy makers in a particular country have developed their own theory of societal change appropriate for the institutional conditions existing at the onset of the transformation program. 'A policy of attempting to achieve a comprehensive revolution in all the parameters of socio-economic life is a risky method of trying to improve the performance of economic systems. The Popperian principle of experimentation is much sounder ... [and is consistent with a desired] evolutionary approach towards economic policy' (Nolan 1995, p. 311). Myrdal recognized the importance of such an approach for underdeveloped countries, arguing that they needed 'to organize their own affairs and, in particular, to control and steer their internal economic development' (Myrdal 1956a, p. 71). China exemplifies a successful case of a country adopting an eclectic approach which differed dramatically from the approach advocated in CEE by those holding the neoclassical perspective, and which has outperformed CEE countries such as Russia in terms of nearly every conceivable performance criteria. 'In every major area, China pursued a ... [transformation] strategy which ran counter to the transition orthodoxy. ... yet it was the world's most dynamic economy in [its transformation] period' (Nolan 1995, p. 7).

Myrdal's second criticism would be that the strong technical bent of Western advisors, combined with behavioral assumptions and policy prescriptions rooted in traditional neoclassical theory is at best questionable and at worst completely inappropriate for CEE. The neoclassical perspective, which is both 'simplistic' in its formulation of policies and representative of a 'revival of a monolithic and deterministic vision of the economic system and the way it works' (Dallago 1992, p. 268), leads to policies which seek to introduce institutions common to the textbook free-market economy model. In the process all economic problems would be reduced to a matter of optimum allocation of resources, and it would be assumed that efficiency would be established once perfectly competitive markets and free individuals aiming to maximize utility are created or emerge.

One egregious assumption concerns the belief that Schumpeterian-type entrepreneurs will emerge to provide the supply-side creation of new processes to simulate economic recovery. Myrdal would endorse Alec Nove's claim that it is incorrect to assume that a latent 'capitalist' class exists throughout CEE which will respond spontaneously and 'rationally to investment opportunities' (Nove 1992, pp. 6–7). Instead, the richest segments of CEE societies – the political authorities, the *nomenklatura*, and the leaders of organized crime – are attracted by opportunities for profit through short-term deals, due to the retention of their monopoly position by many state-owned enterprises even if they are privatized.[136] A Myrdalian study of each pre-1989 CEE society similar in depth and scope to those transformation studies he carried out in Sweden, the United States, and Asia would have made that outcome easy to predict, for 'the whole economic system of central planning ... [was] based on power relations and on distribution of power. And all this complex system of inequalities of agents was not at all broken in the transition process – rather it was enforced' (Klusak and Mertlik 1992, pp. 11–12).

In lieu of narrow economic models which emphasize 'easily quantifiable variables' to the neglect of 'all matters relating to differences in incomes and levels of living' such as health, education and social services (Myrdal 1970a, p. 409), Myrdal would endorse the argument some contemporary analysts have made that the transition process has political, social, legal, international, as well as economic components which must somehow be coordinated since they are mutually reinforcing. This follows from the Myrdal view that societal problems, and transformation issues in particular, are mixed and complex. All aspects of these problems are interrelated and 'must be studied not in isolation but in their mutual relationship' (Myrdal 1968, p. x) in order to predict relationships between relevant factors, so that a simultaneous, coordinated set of policy measures to engender development could be elaborated. For example, Myrdal argues that health and education reforms would have a 'double purpose of directly raising the productivity of the population and at the same time reconditioning the individuals and society so that rational motives become of greater consequence' (Myrdal 1960, p. 84).

Third, Myrdal would agree that CEE policy makers were 'naive to expect economic rationality to be the only guiding force of the transition' (Koves 1992, p. 14), an assumption which followed from their 'underestimat[ing] what de Tocqueville called] the "soft" factors of habits, mentalities, cultural routines' (Sztompka 1992). From the historical legacy of CEE many values, norms, and behavioral standards persist – aspects which Myrdal believes are the primary impediment to development. Among them is the inhibition of behavioral responses on the part of management and labor to changes in economic variables from duplicating what would be expected in a competitive market type of economy environment. Further habits and routines include the absence of individualistic, achievement-oriented competitiveness, of a civic culture whereby people willingly adhere to the rule of law, and of a business culture whereby members of firms are clean, orderly, neat, and eager to satisfy consumers. Where legislation was implemented with the intention of creating the desired free market institutions, policy makers failed to take into account the institutional legacy of a 'distributive economic system' whose participants continue to defend themselves from the threat of market forces by means of lobbying efforts to obtain state support (Mokrzycki 1993, pp. 29–30).

The CEE legacy of 'behavioral shortcomings' and 'economic incompetence' (including inept managerial and marketing skills) means that a long learning process is necessary to develop skills that will enable CEE firms to become competitive in the international economy (Swaan and Lissowska 1992, p. 94). The evidence indicates that manager and worker behavior in CEE institutions will adapt slowly when confronted with the rapid implementation of market reforms. Myrdal's policies would emphasize changing attitudes and institutions in order to enable society to escape from 'civil incompetence', overcoming 'the legacy of past attitudes through education', and focusing on bright 'young educated cosmopolitans' (Sztompka 1992, p. 9).

The decision to reduce rapidly the role of the state in the transformation process would be Myrdal's fourth criticism. He would classify as simplistic the policy makers' conception that, since the CEE political structure caused the economic conditions prevailing in 1989, its removal would 'open the road to prosperity' (Mokrzycki 1993, p. 30). Nove's argument that 'ideological commitment to laissez faire stands in the way of devising, let alone implementing an investment [and overall industrial development] policy' (Nove

1992, p. 3) would receive Myrdal's endorsement. The belief that state involvement in economic development is always counterproductive contradicts the experience of almost every OECD nation, and contradicts what Myrdal concluded in each of his transformation studies.

The position advocated by one contemporary analyst that the state should assume a prominent role in the transformation by 'taking active responsibility' for development in each CEE economy, with privatization being considered only later in the transformation process (Kregel *et al.* 1992, pp. 43–4) is Myrdalian in nature. Myrdal's policies tended to favor a 'third way' rather than either traditional command or laissez-faire market policies. Such an approach uses prices, subsidies, and public planning to alter attitudes and institutions to make them 'the instruments of reform' (Streeten 1992, p. 127). He would endorse promotion of the 'third sector' throughout CEE, particularly cooperatives, to provide some services in a manner more acceptable to the public than either the state or the private sector.[137] Development planning would be advocated whereby the state would initiate, stimulate, and steer policies by means of decentralized control (Myrdal 1968, p. 709). Myrdal planning is not centralized in the pre-1989 CEE sense, but is an evolving process through which policies to move society in the direction of development are based upon an evaluation of existing conditions. In this respect Myrdal would agree with the assessment that transformation policies should be developed in an on-going instrumental process, similar to playing a game of chess rather than following a 'cookbook recipe' compatible with International Monetary Fund and World Bank interests (Fischer 1992, pp. 116, 117). For example, based upon recent experience in CEE and China, state measures to restructure industries would be recommended to precede privatization.

Myrdal would propose state activity in redistributing opportunities and incomes to reduce poverty and to promote security, as well as to equalize living standards among all citizens. His research convinced him that there is no contradiction between the achievement of economic efficiency and an egalitarian distribution of income induced through government redistribution measures (up to a point), and that greater equality will therefore make workers more productive. He favors socialization of consumption rather than production, including offering benefits in kind and extensive state investment in health and education. Among the Keynesian measures he would endorse are state-sponsored labor market programs to maintain high employment, and the socialization of investment. He recognizes that '[t]here is no other road to economic development than a forceful rise in the share of national income which is withheld from consumption and devoted to investment' (Myrdal 1960, pp. 84–5).

Purposeful government action to reduce the corruption inherent in CEE 'soft states' would also be a Myrdal policy prescription. He believes the state needs to enforce 'greater social discipline' to overcome 'strong vested interests', whose members continue to use their power to pursue private gain, and that sweeping legislative reforms are usually inadequate (Myrdal 1970a, pp. 216, 227–8). If 'large-scale administrative reform' designed to place into high positions people with 'competence and integrity' fails (Myrdal 1970a, p. 243), then he would argue that authoritarian measures are justified – if they contribute to reducing corruption while promoting realization of development as he conceives it.

The fifth area of criticism concerns the neoclassical conception that development occurs in a mechanical and simplified way – a linear process by which it is 'assumed that once certain conditions are fulfilled [particularly privatization], the market mechanism will emerge like a Deus ex machina' (Hausner and Wojtyna 1992, p. 3). Myrdal would blame CEE policy makers for contributing to their respective countries' poor economic performance by failing to take into account the circular and cumulative causation pattern of development. For example, their stabilization policies initiated a vicious circle (especially in Russia), with restrictive monetary and fiscal policies leading to high inflation and reductions in output and unemployment, which created political and social unrest (Moskoff and Nazmi 1992, p. 78). Inflation also led to decreases in output which exceeded the decrease in employment, thereby reducing productivity and raising costs. Real wages declined, reducing consumer demand, while state investment fell in the attempt to balance budgets. With profits falling and restrictive monetary policy raising interest rates, CEE firms carried out little investment. Attempts to stabilize led to overvalued currencies, thus reducing exports. The cumulative effect has been a 'low level equilibrium trap' with slow supply-side responses (Kregel and Matzner 1992, p. 35). This contrasts with the spread effect in China in a circular and cumulative causation manner[138] stemming from the transformation strategy which initiated 'a whole sequence of virtuous and vicious circles of politics and economics ... which helped to reinforce the [country's development] path' (Nolan 1995, p. 314).

Myrdalian Policies to Transform CEE

Before prescribing transformation policies for CEE Myrdal would articulate the lessons from other transformation experiences which might be applicable to CEE nations. Lessons from Sweden's experience would be that (1) reconciliation of political cleavages, perhaps through a coalition government, is necessary before a philosophical basis and transformation measures which have broad public support can be adopted and implemented effectively; (2) establishing political democracy does not mean rapid realization of economic prosperity. Nearly all OECD nations, facing 'initial conditions' less unfavorable than CEE nations, took decades to achieve comprehensive transformation of their economies; (3) if maintenance of state-funded social insurance and welfare measures is desired, then macroeconomic stability, improved competitive conditions, and faith in public authorities are prerequisites; and (4) cooperatives can be viable, attainable institutions for increasing the transforming economy's competitiveness (Angresano 1992b, pp. 51–2).

The contemporary Scandinavian 'negotiated economy' represents an alternative type of economy whose institutions and working rules might be consistent with the type of economy open-minded CEE authorities would consider striving to establish in lieu of the 'free market economy' model towards which they have restricted their focus.[139] A number of characteristics of the Scandinavian economies distinguish them from economies of other OECD nations. These characteristics include an active interventionist fiscal policy, redistribution measures designed to offset factors causing sub-standard levels of living, extensive services provided by the public sector (such as education and child care), an institutionalized wage policy, active labor market measures to promote full employment and increase labor mobility, and cooperatives.

Another distinctive characteristic is the degree to which interest groups resolve conflicts through negotiations. The method of conflict resolution features institutionalized class cooperation through negotiation and formulation of common interests and strategies – thereby the term 'negotiated economies'. It is recognized throughout Scandinavia that '[a]n essential and even a growing part of the allocation of the productive resources as well as the (re)distribution of the output is determined neither on the market ... nor by ... public authorities. Instead, the decision-making process is conducted via institutionalized negotiations between the relevant interested agents, who reach binding decisions typically based on discursive, political and moral imperatives rather than the threats and economic incentives' (Nielsen and Pedersen 1990).

Scandinavian economies have developed social contracts based on a number of negotiated agreements pertaining to the direction and shape of socioeconomic policy as well as to the method of conflict resolution. These agreements require that competing interest groups with conflicting objectives achieve a broad consensus. In Scandinavian economies there is much interaction between representatives from the public, private and 'third sector' which includes cooperatives, voluntary associations, non-government organizations, popular movements and non-profit organizations. Institutions have evolved, particularly in Denmark, through which representatives from these sectors engage in negotiation. These institutions can be classified as public, campaign, discourse, negotiation, and arbitration and sanction institutions. It is not the mere existence of these institutions that is significant, but rather 'their elaboration and their complementariness which have made possible a specific institutional process, the negotiated economy' (Nielsen and Pedersen 1990). The organization of much decision making is 'neo-corporatist', a curious blend of popular decisions, arrived at democratically on a decentralized basis, and highly centralized decisions, made by the national government and national associations of interest group representatives. The state's role has not been authoritative, but rather that of an active participant in the decisions made by 'multi-centered structures' (Nielsen 1992).

While prices established in unregulated and regulated markets, and state intervention measures for stabilization and redistribution purposes, serve as coordinating mechanisms, conscious interaction and negotiation among interest group representatives also play a role. Negotiations are particularly significant to: redistribution measures; some interest rates and profit rates; many large investment projects; consumer policy regarding cooperatives, housing cooperatives and rental agreements; industrial relations, including centralized collective bargaining, whereby an institutionalized system of wage and price determinants is regulated by export market prices and productivity levels; and industrial policy. The Scandinavian states recognize the need for their small, open economies to maintain international competitiveness, and negotiate competition and industrial policy with interest group representatives. In Denmark the focus is on supply-side adaptations, especially stimulation of investment, where automatic adjustment will not occur; promotion of a private–public third sector mix to make a more competitive economy; identification of market, state or third sector failures and negotiation to introduce alternatives; encouragement of strategic alliances to produce favorable externalities; and active negotiation with regional trading partners with complementary economies.

Concerning the relevance of the negotiated type of economy for CEE, some Polish economists have argued that in CEE the framework for social participation and social activism should be broadened. They deem it essential for an active role to be played by both the state and interest groups, and for them to engage in public dialogue to develop goals and policy measures appropriate for their own conditions. These groups would negotiate, viewing it as an active learning process, for the purposes of forming social and political institutions and framing their respective working rules.

For CEE decision makers who develop rules and policies pertaining to transformation, the following lessons from the Scandinavian negotiated economies could be helpful. First, there is no necessary contradiction between the achievement of economic efficiency and an egalitarian distribution of income induced through state redistribution measures. Second, state intervention through a negotiation process with representatives from labor, manufacturing, commercial and consumer interest groups can be effective as a means both to reduce corruption and to develop active labor market, wage and industrial policies. These policies will facilitate the restructuring of industry and the developing of infrastructures for transport, communication and tele-communications, as well as for research, education and training institutions. Third, macroeconomic stability and improved competitiveness of industry are the prerequisites for extensive state-funded social insurance and welfare measures. Fourth, the third sector, particularly cooperatives, can provide some services in a manner more acceptable to the public than can either the state or private sectors.

Some critics argue that the CEE countries should not consider the Scandinavian 'model', particularly that of Sweden, claiming that these econo-mies have failed because of recent economic performance and the lack of public support for the Social Democrats. To dismiss the Scandinavian econo-mies on these grounds, however, is to ignore their development experience over the 1930–80 period. In the early 1930s, problems similar to those of CEE (widespread poverty, declining birth rates, inflation followed by defla-tion and a foreign exchange crisis, falling output and high unemployment) existed in Scandinavia. The success of these countries in alleviating these problems (by adopting Myrdalian transformation policies in the case of Swe-den) argues strongly that Scandinavian measures merit consideration by CEE interest group representatives.

It is conceivable that Myrdalian transformation policies intended to estab-lish a negotiated type of economy could be more efficacious for developing CEE than the currently implemented orthodox transformation measures de-signed to establish a 'free market economy'. There is growing opposition from many social groups throughout CEE disenchanted with rising unem-ployment and declining real wages. One Polish analyst argued during the early 1990s that the double distress of macroeconomic and political instabil-ity plaguing his country has been aggravated by the fact that the shock therapy approach was not 'negotiated with the representatives of the most important social groups ... [and therefore it has been] difficult to regain society's support for necessary reforms' (Kowalik 1992b). This view is not confined to Poland. To varying degrees, the state has lost its legitimacy in most CEE nations, and now must seek the support of interest groups. Some believe that the state must 'organize social consensus which aims at broad social co-operation ... [and] in doing so, both the State and the political parties comprising it would gradually gain legitimacy and political authority' (Kregel, Matzner, and Grabher 1992). Such organization is necessary be-cause currently there is no 'neutral' third party involved with negotiations in CEE nations.

New working rules for institutions trigger processes of adaptation as well as processes of resistance. Since results from early transformation based on orthodox theory in countries such as Russia were much worse than expectations, behavioral rigidity against change can be expected to increase. However, other analysts contributing to the growing body of institutional theory have argued that a negotiation process can counter this problem. 'If some basic institutions ... facilitate class- and interest-group communication and compromising, then employee resistance to organizational change may be turned into active cooperation' (Johnson and Lundvall 1992).

Another factor which inhibits the transformation of CEE economies is a cognitive restraint which puts limits on the speed of behavioral change. Economic behavior evolves as a result of a learning process. Human beings require time to absorb new information, technology and forms of organization. Open dialogue and negotiation among interest groups stimulate learning and can increase the speed with which behavioral change occurs. The state also needs to educate interest groups, particularly labor representatives, as to how to participate in a creative negotiation process.

Support and evidence, some based on comparative performances of economies, are growing in favor of active state involvement in the transformation process. One CEE analyst argues that 'during the transition there might be a case for direct controls on state enterprises to promote macroeconomic stability, rather than relying upon solely market-based measures ... for the state sector, price and wage controls, direct credit for use by macroeconomic policy makers' (Murrell 1992). Others believe that for economies that seek to become competitive on international markets the state will be the gatekeeper between the domestic and international economies in seeking to increase the market share of its corporations on the international market (Porter 1990). There is evidence that the total growth of fast-growing East Asian economies was 'highest where the growth sectors received both subsidies and demanding performance targets, especially in export markets' (Clayton 1992). Another study indicates that countries with many negotiated and other forms of 'market plus' co-ordinating mechanisms performed better than countries with heavy reliance on unregulated market mechanisms (Campbell 1992b). Many economic historians understand that 'the possession of an effective, competent state bureaucracy is a central element in explaining the rise of almost every successful industrialising country since Britain' (Nolan 1995, p. 156). This is consistent with one analyst's findings that '[macroeconomic] stabilisation strategy was most likely to work when there was "hands-on management" of a mixed economic system, and not wholesale liberalisation' (Taylor 1988, p. 168). An active third sector is another aspect of the negotiated economy which can enhance alleviation of CEE problems. One Scandinavian scholar concludes that alternatives such as cooperatives and non-profit organizations are effective in providing social services and health care. Cooperatives and non-profit organizations 'empower' their clients by providing them with an 'institutionalized voice' and an enriched working life, while non-profit organizations also 'enhanc[e] ... the effectiveness and goal fulfillment of the public sector' (Pestoff 1992).

Some analysts believe that the negotiated economy, while efficacious for the long term, is not a preferred choice for the early stage of transformation. They fear that in the absence of strong authoritarian leadership throughout CEE that is capable of withstanding contrary social pressures (such as exists in contemporary China and as prevailed in Japan throughout the 1952–80 period), negotiations may actually slow down transformation. They believe that for the time being CEE managers of state-owned enterprises and local government would feel so empowered by a negotiation process that they would actually hinder implementation of changes that would threaten their present status. The same analysts believe that prerequisites for an effective negotiation process are the stabilization of unemployment and inflation, the establishment of a system of labor bargaining, arbitration laws and proce-dures, favorable economic growth and rising labor productivity – so that higher tax rates would become unnecessary to fund the desired social insur-ance and welfare programs. It is argued that higher taxes, in particular, will inhibit economic growth in the early stages of transformation by hampering aggregate demand – thereby reducing society's discretionary income which is necessary to support the emerging private sector.

These criticisms, while raising serious questions about the efficacy of a negotiated economy for CEE countries, do not refute the need for, and the potential of, negotiation. Key issues are how authoritative and centralized state decision making needs to be, who should be involved in a negotiation process, and how to achieve macroeconomic stabilization. There is evidence that interest group leaders can obstruct necessary reforms so that in the absence of widespread support for public leaders there may be justification for more authoritarian state leadership during the early stages of the transfor-mation. It may be necessary for state authorities to replace recalcitrant enter-prise and labor leaders (while reducing the power of local government authorities) with interest group leaders who have been educated concerning the need for, and the process of, negotiation. A similar process occurred in Japan after World War II, when the Occupation Authority replaced govern-ment authorities and *zaibatsu* management with a younger generation of leaders. An increase in state authority over economic policy (preferably only until macroeconomic stability can be established) strengthens the case for dialogue and negotiation, if a return to permanent, state-dominated economic decision making is to be avoided.

Concerning the critics' defense of existing policies and the emphasis on the need to achieve macroeconomic stabilization – with favorable growth, pro-ductivity and personal income trends – before negotiated processes can be effective, the painful experience of CEE nations under current transformation policies and the Scandinavian experience after the 1930s, lead one to question the strength of that argument. Based upon the experience of Scandinavian and Asian countries it appears that active state intervention, including negotiated policies, is conducive to favorable macroeconomic performance. Political cleavages throughout CEE, exacerbated by the original transformation policies, constitute a serious obstacle, but one which the process of negotiation itself may be the most effective way of healing. Therefore, while implementing a negotiated process under strong state supervision is not claimed to be a panacea for CEE problems, Myrdal would argue that this alternative merits serious consideration, given the performance of the region's economies under the existing policies. Perhaps policy makers would enjoy more success in CEE if the policies they formulated were the result of a negotiation process which included representatives of key interest groups. If they, as well as Western social scientists, chose to adopt a Myrdalian transformation perspective that includes a multi-disciplinary approach to broad social problems, they would be likelier to avoid offering inadequate, inappropriate policies to foreign countries, especially in CEE. The likelihood of this choice being made will depend upon the type of economics education they receive and with which teach their students.

A MYRDALIAN VIEW OF ECONOMICS EDUCATION AND A PROPOSAL FOR REFORM[140]

Some observations about economics education in Russia and Bulgaria indicate the need for economics education reform that would extend well beyond including a study of Myrdal and his transformation contributions in undergraduate and graduate economics programs. When Russia embarked on its transformation path during the mid-1980s 'few, if any, of Mikhail Gorbachev's advisors had formal schooling in market economics, [so] their commitment to the market was impressive. Yet it was also clear that most of them did not fully understand what was involved in introducing the market' (Goldman 1994, p. 69). Eventually, Russian authorities sought Western advice, and the resulting surge of interested parties resembled the response of avid shoppers rushing to a going-out-of-business sale at an upscale retail establishment. As one Russian analyst describes the ensuing stampede, '[a] number of Western economists and analysts responded to this sudden overt interest in Western remedies for the Soviet economy with great enthusiasm. One after another they set off (some on their own, some invited) to Moscow to prescribe economic medicine. Nobel Prize winners like Wassily Leontief, with his input–output analysis, and Milton Friedman, with his emphasis on increasing the role of money and reducing economic fine-tuning by the government, arrived with their own brand of miracle remedies; a younger generation of highly respected economists also offered their particular remedies' (Goldman 1994, p. 79).

After arriving in CEE the Western economic advisors appeared to ignore 'how little their analysis had taught them about the larger issues. Instead they plunged into advising about how to best reform the communist systems with great confidence bred from their improved knowledge of relatively small [microeconomic] problems. They leapt from the complexities of their own special fields into grand simplistic generalisations in areas about which they often had painfully limited knowledge, and for which their training had served them ill' (Nolan 1995, p. 312). The ideological, narrow perspective led to the application of microeconomic theory rules for economizing to broad transformation issues in a simplistic manner. One recurrent theme from those partaking in the 'cavalry charge' to CEE was that rapid privatization was *the* prerequisite for the establishment of a 'free market economy'.

The academics were joined by United States Agency for International Development sponsored 'beltway bandits', consultants whose knowledge of the Russian economy and society was minimal at best. Nevertheless, despite the fact that they lacked knowledge of, or experience in, CEE the ability of these consultants to prepare convincing proposals won them lucrative contracts.[141] Thereafter they recruited other 'consultants', many of whom were academic economists imbued with the neoclassical perspective, to teach the Russians (and the rest of CEE) how to establish a 'free market economy'. Unfortunately, the plethora of conflicting remedies confused the Russian experts while their lack of awareness of other transformation perspectives precluded their considering any alternatives to the shock therapy policies to establish a 'free market economy' fostered on them by Western advisors and the international aid agencies.

In Bulgaria all universities that teach economics must offer three subjects designated as 'fundamental' by the Bulgarian Ministry of Education: Microeconomics, Macroeconomics and History of Economic Theory. Unfortunately, only full and associate professors are permitted to teach these subjects, few of whom have been retrained or received any economics education outside of what was offered in Bulgaria (and the rest of CEE) prior to 1990. Although many assistant professors in Bulgaria initiated efforts to reform the economic theory courses after having been retrained either in Bulgaria or sent abroad specifically to retrain, they are not permitted to teach these 'fundamental' courses. It is primarily the assistant professors who have a reading knowledge of the languages in which most economics books are written, who introduced the first revised courses in economics throughout Bulgaria after 1990, and who wrote the first textbooks and study guides using non-CEE economic theory. After these materials were translated into Bulgarian the old *nomenklatura* have decided they wanted to monopolize the lecturing of economics despite widespread awareness that many assistant professors are far more competent than their older colleagues. It is likely that the lectures presented will be directly from textbooks translated, nearly all of which are based upon the neoclassical perspective, or from exposure to Western advisors or consultants with a narrow, unrealistic perspective of both CEE and transformation reality.

Myrdal would attribute the perspective held by Western CEE advisors to the nature of the academic training contemporary economists receive.[142] As he noted, '[t]he result is that a student has been able to become a professor of economics while having only the most fragmentary knowledge about the society he [or she] is studying' (Myrdal 1970a, pp. 21–2). This narrow education also has been the basis for criticism leveled at Western economic advisors who proposed policies for underdeveloped nations. 'Contemporary theories of economic development are highly critical of development models implemented during the 1960s which involved the imposition from above of economic programs thought up by experts – usually Western experts' (Kowalik 1992, p. 15). The ensuing generation of underdeveloped country economists, having been trained in rich, Western nations, attempted to apply narrow Western 'economic' models to deal with their problems of poverty without having a realistic conception of the institutional conditions of their own country. Myrdal argues that '[t]his lacuna in their understanding of social problems has in recent decades been fortified by the way in which economists are being trained. Up until around the First World War, practically nobody began his scholarly career as an economist. He either, in former times, was a man of practical affairs who at a mature age turned to economics, or he had a previous training as a mathematician, moral philosopher, lawyer, [or] historian. Economists never started out as economists, which has now for about half a century been the common pattern. The result is that a student has been able to become a professor of economics while having only the most fragmentary knowledge about the society he [or she] is studying' (Myrdal 1970a, pp. 21–2).

Myrdal has been adamant in his denunciation of international assistance concerning education in underdeveloped countries, and would have applied this criticism towards education policies recommended for CEE as well. This was especially true when it is in the form of 'expert advice which stresses investment in human capital (i.e., western-style education) or in capital equipment to the neglect of institutional factors' (Myrdal 1968, p. 1540). What he most disliked about the 'investment approach' to education was that such a perspective 'entirely ignores the fact that institutional and attitudinal reforms, which depend on political decisions rather than budgetary considerations, are needed to make investments in education "pay off," and the broader consideration that the success of education depends on the policies pursued in all other fields as well as the direction of the education programs themselves' (Myrdal 1968, p. 1540).

Economics education throughout CEE prior to 1989 focused on techniques of central planning and enterprise management. Stale Marxism-Leninism served as the philosophical basis for the economic curriculum, elevated by professors, or 'mandarins', of the Soviet Union to the level of state religion in order to indoctrinate students with a 'strictly conformist way of thinking' (Myrdal 1957d). The result of conformity was a lack of real stringency, learnedness, and logic – particularly when comparisons with alternative, Western economies were made. Consequently, after 1989 many Western economists received funding to teach undergraduate and graduate students, professors, and policy makers throughout the CEE region. These economists were imbued with the Cold War mentality, caught up in the euphoria of the 1989–90 political revolutions, with a majority adhering to the neoclassical perspective and the belief in the universal validity of orthodox economic theory. Consequently, CEE authorities, faculty and students were introduced to the neoclassical perspective towards transformation. In all but a few isolated cases no other perspective which differed substantively from the orthodox view was taught.

A large majority of these teachers came from the United States. While some had prior teaching experience, most lacked experience or familiarity with CEE. Regardless of experience, these teachers generally spent no more than one academic year teaching at a CEE university before returning to their home institutions. Typically, the visiting professors reproduced the course syllabi and notes they used in classes at their home institutions (or their own notes from classes they were taught in the case of those without prior teaching experience). The overwhelming majority of economics classes taught made use of textbooks reflecting the neoclassical perspective.[143] Inherent in this perspective, as presented to the CEE audience, were four basic views. The first was that a strict dichotomy characterizes alternative economies, namely that economies are either centrally planned or free market. When challenged about their dichotomous views nearly all economists were unable to conceive of any alternative for transformation in CEE other than their abstract notion of a 'free-market economy', a notion few were able or willing to articulate.

Second, transformation from a centrally planned economy to a free market economy was perceived as being relatively easy, and not too costly, once the right prerequisites (such as liberalized prices, free markets, and privatized enterprises) were met. Third, human behavior was presented as being characterized by the actions of rational, profit-making economic agents who respond to changes in economic variables in a universal, predictable manner.

Finally, the focus on economic theories taught was on movement toward, or attainment of, equilibrium rather than on an evolutionary process of societal change within an historical context.

The pervasive emphasis was on 'mathematical formalism and obscurantist terminology ... [into which students were initiated] in progressive but somewhat repetitive stages. The whole process has the aura of a protracted initiation ceremony, in which future priests overcome their inclination to get involved in the grubby complexities of the outside world ... [Others, however,] have been all too keen to use their economic theory as a weapon in an ideological crusade' (Hodgson 1988, p. xi). Therein lie the roots of another problem, namely the hidden values contained in the neoclassical perspective, which include a strong preference for unfettered domestic and international markets, private ownership, and the absence of state intervention regarding income redistribution.

Such values are inherent throughout the reading material which has been assigned to CEE students since 1989. Nearly all textbooks recently introduced in the region have been written from the orthodox neoclassical perspective. Western teachers and textbooks are depositing information within students much as money is deposited into a bank, while student creativity in terms of evaluating alternative paradigms of economic thought or types of economies usually is not encouraged.

Myrdal would argue that the narrow perspective held by most Western economists, particularly the tendency to arrive at theoretical conclusions and to postulate them as valid for every time, place and culture, is attributable to the particularly rigorous training provided by their own undergraduate and graduate economics programs. An examination of most graduate programs in economics reveals that there is little in the training of contemporary Western economists that encourages reading in other areas such as economic development and the history of economic thought, or in the literature of comparative economics (Klamer and Colander 1990). Economics education has squeezed out sociology and has also eliminated most teaching of institutional material, shifting nearly all emphasis upon orthodox economic theory and the acquisition of technical skills with which to analyze 'economic problems', thus reducing societal problems to only their economic components. As one scholar argues '[t]he deep questions about the way in which the parameters of economic life impact upon economic performance are outside the scope of most economics courses. They involve attempting to understand the way in which culture, politics, psychology and social structure interact with the economy. This branch of the subject has been steadily squeezed out of economics. It is the stuff of political economy in the sense in which the term was understood by the classical economists. If ever an issue called out for real political economy it was the transition from communism' (Nolan 1995, p. 312).

The emphasis upon technical skills and the strong belief that natural laws typify the socioeconomic reality have resulted in a fund of knowledge and an orientation that inhibits a more innovative pragmatic perspective towards transformation issues. Since this is the perspective that is being introduced throughout CEE, economics educators (both Western and regional) are impressing upon their students in CEE that economics consists of 'devising models that ... [are] analytically neat [or technically elegant as Myrdal would argue]; the facade, not the depth of knowledge [being] important' (Klamer and Colander 1990, p. 18).

Many problems have ensued from teaching predominantly the neoclassical perspective to economic students throughout CEE. First, the only alternative paradigm and transformation model taught is that of a free-market economy, the type that only exists in orthodox textbooks and cannot be found anywhere in the real world. Alternative types of economies, such as the Chinese, Japanese, German, or Danish are not evaluated. Teaching such a narrow view follows from the dichotomous viewpoint of conventional economists – namely that they perceive a free-market economy as the only alternative to the pre-1989 economy of CEE.

Second, believing that the neoclassical theories are universal, economics teachers imbue their students with the belief that a cookbook solution in the form of certain macroeconomic policies is efficacious for transformation throughout CEE. In the process students may become dogmatic and 'blind ... to the realities of local conditions' in their respective countries (Todaro 1989, p. 11). The third problem, which follows from the doctrinaire liberalism inherent in the neoclassical perspective, contributes to ideological indoctrination in the classroom as well as throughout the economics curriculum. Having recognized the relative poverty of their countries vis-à-vis the OECD nations, students from CEE have a tendency to engage in self-deprecation. Consequently, they strive to conform to the new rules and attitudes that they are taught, adopting the perspective of foreign teachers without questioning the basis of the perspective presented.

A related problem concerns the choices made by CEE authorities about the content of the post-1989–90 economics curriculum. These choices, or lack of a choice, are influenced by the desire of CEE authorities to please Western donors upon whom they are heavily dependent for credit and trade agreements. During a 1992 teaching workshop in Krakow, which focused on what type of economics should be taught in CEE, a Hungarian official responsible for negotiating the entry of his country into the European Union remarked that Hungary wanted to teach the 'true economics'. When challenged to explain, he stated that 'we want to be just like all European Union nations'. He, along with leading authorities throughout CEE, are falling victim to coercive isomorphic pressure whereby the recipient of aid feels obligated (and perhaps pressured) to conform to the values of the donor so as to increase the likelihood that further aid will be forthcoming (Campbell 1992a).

A fifth problem is that students are presented with the fallacious perspective towards economic development which holds that a 'linear adjustment path' (Kregel *et al.* 1992, p. 37) exists between the planned economies and free market economies. This dichotomous perspective reinforces the problem of doctrine. Having begun from a position that allowed for no alternative transformation policy, supporters of the neoclassical perspective became 'hostages to this thesis', discouraging any discourse regarding 'third way' alternatives (Hausner 1992, pp. 2–3). This process has occurred despite mounting evidence that transformation policies based upon this perspective have exacerbated social and economic problems in many CEE nations.

Some illusions held by Western economics teachers visiting CEE are the fifth problem. These illusions, which include the belief that macroeconomic stabilization and institutional reform could be achieved in CEE within a few years, were passed along to their students. To many it seemed obvious that if only certain sets of assumptions contained in the neoclassical perspective were met, transformation to a free-market economy would be realized throughout these countries. They failed to recognize that in economics, as Myrdal concluded in his transformation studies, there can only be tendencies, not scientific laws of universal truths no matter how many technically elegant macroeconomic models are produced. Their assumptions were due, in part, to the fact that many general models in economics are based upon the presupposition of a particular pattern of behavior by economic actors that is not relevant for most economies, particularly those of CEE and the underdeveloped world.

Another illusion was the belief that the transformation could be achieved without a dramatic reduction in living standards for most social groups. Related to this was the illusion that a vibrant private sector would follow the destruction of the public sector. Here economists misinterpret economic history and assume that a development path similar to that which evolved in the United States in the late 19th and early 20th centuries will be repeated in CEE. Finally, it was an illusion to believe that management behavior would change quickly following privatization.

That students are not being taught the lessons of economic history, including that many countries have experienced problems when inappropriate economic models based upon unrealistic neoclassical assumptions of behavior are introduced is the final problem. The fact that economies are constantly changing their working rules and institutions is not made explicit. Perhaps most significant is that CEE authorities, faculty and students are not being taught that China has been able to implement significant, alternative transformation policies while experiencing positive changes in the same economics and welfare indicators that have been negative for much of CEE since 1989.

Myrdalian Proposals for Economic Education Reform

Myrdal would agree that the CEE education system, particularly the teaching of social science at the university level, requires radical, fundamental reform. Examples of reforms he has advocated in other transformation studies include teacher training, raising teacher salaries and social status, and introducing adult education through a university-directed outreach program (Myrdal 1970a, pp. 181–2, 187, 207). With regard to the attitudes of enterprise managers, he might endorse the introduction of a 'management contract' whereby a foreign firm would contract with a CEE government to manage an enterprise, receiving a fee (perhaps subsidized by an international agency) and a percentage of the profits in return for providing technology, training, and management expertise (Myrdal 1970a, pp. 330–31).

Myrdal would argue that economics education in CEE should serve the purpose of enabling students and policy makers to become re-educated, to deal constructively with reality, and to transform reality in a direction consistent with societal desires. A reformed economics curriculum would make these individuals more aware of the complex manner in which economies develop and of the many potential alternatives for reform. In teaching students to question their societies, relevant problems can be presented to them, and they can be urged to search for alternative solutions based upon competing paradigms of thought and working rules for their evolving institutions. Rather than feeling pressure to conform to the values inherent in the neoclassical perspective, students in CEE who receive a broad economics education can engage in an open dialogue regarding alternative solutions to the transformation problems of their respective countries. Myrdal's mentors, unlike many contemporary economists, encouraged criticism and open discussion of different philosophical and methodological issues raised by their graduate students, and were receptive to challenges of mainstream views.

To alleviate the problems resulting from the current form of economics education, education authorities in both the Western and CEE countries can adopt a broader approach to the teaching of economics. These authorities must first accept that the problems of transformation 'cannot be tackled or understood within the neoclassical paradigm ... The essentially incremental, non-institutional, timeless equilibrium-oriented neoclassical mainstream, with its methodological individualism, is largely irrelevant' (Nove 1992, p. 14). Once this is accepted, they can commit themselves to reforming the undergraduate and graduate education programs to current and future economic policy makers in their respective countries.

Second, the revised economics curriculum should include an in-depth study of the historical development experiences of other nations. Such exposure will demonstrate to students that a plurality of historically possible development models exists, especially given the Chinese experience. It will enable them to recognize that economic development is a slow process with high social costs likely if privatization is implemented too rapidly. A study of Myrdal would teach students that many possible concrete solutions to transformation problems are possible within many institutional and attitudinal frameworks, and that both economies and economics must be perceived in a much broader perspective than that postulated by traditional economics. Myrdal would encourage students to draw from historical examples to devise imaginative, innovative goals and policies with their own blend of state, private, and cooperative activity appropriate for the economic, historical, political, and social conditions in their countries. Third, Myrdal would emphasize to students the importance of understanding and integrating sociological methodology into their analyses, having both formal models and informal preferences in which a wide range of empirical observations play a role in selecting a perspective and theories. For this to be accomplished, Myrdal argues that students need to study the history and principal institutions of their own (and other) country and not be 'manhandled' into the limited scope of economic theory or any other particular discipline (Gibbs 1977).

Myrdal emphasized that studying the economic history of nations will enable students to develop a sense of how principal institutions came into being in the first place. Gradually, they will come to view present problems as an outgrowth of the past, much as he did with his population, race relations, and underdeveloped country studies. Students will gain an improved perspective on the problems of the present and those that will emerge in the future. They will learn that gradual reform can be productive and sustained, and that pragmatism can be more efficacious than dogmatism. These students should be encouraged to work co-operatively to define their own world and not let foreigners define and regulate what their lifestyles and aspirations ought to be.

Fourth, the study of economic thought would be advocated by Myrdal to become an important component of the reformed economics curricula. Such study will enable students to become familiar with all paradigms and to use common sense in choosing the paradigms or in developing new ones that are most appropriate for particular problems. Students will only learn that alternatives to the neoclassical perspective exist if they are required to study heterodox economists. There are a number of alternative schools of thought to the neoclassical paradigm as well as professional associations that challenge the neoclassical perspective, but very few of the economist students in CEE countries are being introduced to them.

Contemporary social scientists who endorse Myrdalian education proposals have offered their views on the scope and technical focus of contemporary economics education. One Swedish scholar advocates that '[e]conomics should leave all of this mathematical scholasticism behind ... and go back to its original status as a "moral science"' (Swedberg 1990, p. xxix). Walt Rostow describes today's economics as 'bad arithmetic', lamenting that in narrowing the focus of economics today's economists have 'sold their souls to differential calculus' (Rostow Interview 1996) while losing the grand tradition contained in the works of the classical economists. Myrdal would agree.

CONCLUSIONS

A more in-depth study of Myrdal's political economy which is contained in his specific works may stimulate those who have become favorably inclined towards him to evaluate their own professional lives and contemplate the possibility of developing their own Myrdalian perspective for societal analysis and policy prescription, as well as to consider promoting reform of economics education. Studying Myrdal's contributions to transformation issues in particular will yield considerable benefits to social science teachers and researchers, especially those interested in Central and East European (CEE) transformation, for the analyst could be left with a new perspective and basis from which a compelling, coherent, and useful method of socioeconomic analysis can be articulated.

Teaching students about Myrdal's transformation contributions will benefit economists and their students, for he serves as an example of someone trained in the neoclassical perspective who realized that this perspective was inadequate for transformation analysis and policy making. Students can learn how and why he developed his own method of analysis and conception of the socioeconomic reality. It will be informative for them to see how he was willing and able to transgress related social science disciplines with his eclectic perspective. Further, studying Myrdal's intellectual development is significant not only because it provides a basis for a useful transformation policy, but because it demonstrates the possibility for economists to shift successfully from the perspective they learned in graduate school to another perspective. Those choosing to adopt a different perspective that includes an interdisciplinary approach to broad social problems are more likely to avoid adhering to theories and policy measures which purport to be universal, and thus would be far less likely to advocate inadequate, inappropriate policies to transforming societies.

It is unfortunate that Myrdal is ignored by most economists in the classroom. For anyone interested in reforming an economics education program

Myrdal serves as an example for those seeking to introduce their students to an alternative to the neoclassical perspective. Changing perspectives is conceivable, and is necessary for transformation analysis and policy making. Myrdal demonstrated this is possible, and that personal, professional, and societal benefits could be realized in the process.

Appendix: two interviews with Gunnar Myrdal

FIRST INTERVIEW – JULY, 1980

Could you please discuss the main features of your intellectual development as an institutional economist?

Let me start with me as a schoolboy. I happened to go through a gymnasium in Sweden which was on a very high level. It was a Royal Gymnasium directed at natural science and mathematics, and my whole beginning of life was in that direction. Also my students and friends (I mean later at the university) were natural scientists. But in a funny way I had decided, whether you believe it or not, to actually study law. Which I did. Law takes in Sweden five years and it's just hellish. I succeeded [in doing] it in three years [just] to get out of it and I was absolutely crushed when I [finished]. The reason why I studied law was, believe it or not, that just like a boy looks at a watch (I mean, in pieces to see what's in it), I wanted to see how society functioned. My reading during my gymnasium was not only natural science – that was the main thing – [but also] policy questions and various things [like that], so I was rather an educated young man at that time.

Nevertheless, and I think I should say that I do believe that my law studies, though horrible and terrible and not very well planned in Sweden at that time, gave me two things [now] I think it over which point in the institutional direction. One thing is that a lawyer is trained, however badly his teaching is, to what I call mark words, [that is], to be clear about the meaning of words. And this I think is a very important thing. When I'm sometimes not very interested in reading reviews of my books and articles it's because I have a feeling that so many people just can't read. They just don't understand what I mean. That's one thing which you get from law studies. The second thing which you get from those studies, however bad they are, is to get hold of what is the central problem. You see, it's just that the way you put the legal analysis is always that you [start with] a complex situation and then you [take] away piece after piece in order to get [at] the crucial question. And that is also rather a good thing which you get from law studies and perhaps I shouldn't be altogether dissatisfied with this horrible mistake in my life – as a natural scientist studying law.

Well now I was, as I said, almost crushed after that experience, and it was Alva as a matter of fact who said to me that [I] should study economics. Economics is much more like mathematics and natural sciences. That was her feeling and that of course is rather natural when you think about the standard economy. At that time I had various jobs: I was judge burghmeister which [perhaps] I should describe in [a little more] detail. See, I was commander-in-chief of the whole police system in another city... But, nevertheless, I succeeded in four years – this is from 1923 to 1927 – to write a doctoral thesis which got Laudater, that's the highest mark. And then I became docent [sic] in economics and started to teach. Before that I had not written anything about policy affairs and various things, [and] I just concentrated on this book [his doctoral thesis concerning price formations] which [has] not [been] translated which is a mistake. It should have been translated but I was never very interested. [Once] I finished the thing, it was finished ... and I didn't care about what happened.

So [unfortunately] this book is not translated. It is a very highly theoretical study which I hardly understand now [since] I have been working with other problems, on the importance of risk and uncertainty it's called the *Pricing Problem Under Dynamic Conditions* which played a rather large role when we started the Stockholm School. As you know we were in two ways in advance of Keynes. We're ten years older, and we started earlier here in Sweden in 33 with an underbalanced budget and I wrote the theoretical motivation for it in the budget in early 1933. You know Hitler started similar policies, and Roosevelt's policies were never clear. It was [we in] Sweden who were in advance actually and politically but also theoretically. I do believe that our approach which was partly dependent upon this doctoral thesis of mine is [the reason] we put much more emphasis upon expectations than you get in Keynes's book.

And furthermore we were not one-sided. He calls his book *The General Theory of Employment* and God knows what. But it is not general at all – it is a depression theory. While we're concentrating on this, this comes out in my book too, on equilibrium and on the moment or what happens when you make decisions, and we [Stockholm School economists] were general. It was not only a theory to cure a depression, it was also to keep down inflation and high unemployment. We made studies of how the budget should be constructed; I wrote a book about that which is not translated – about the effects of fiscal policy.

But let's see now. Then I did a lot of things. During that time I wrote the *Political Element in the Development of Economic Theory*. And I did other things but then I [became a] Rockefeller fellow in 1929 in America and this was a very crucial period in our [he and Alva's] life. You see the Rockefeller foundation, they don't know what they did at that time. I think it's one of the most glorious things they did; you see, it was not a question then of underdeveloped countries – they were all colonial and we didn't touch them. It was Europe [that interested them] and here the Rockefeller foundation decided to get hold of the brightest kids in Europe and give them the opportunity to come to not only America, but they could [also] go to England. Some came to Sweden. But the idea was to move around and you can say that all good social scientists five years younger than me and five years older [than] me have been Rockefeller fellows. These Rockefeller fellows had an office in Paris and came up here and looked around and found that Alva and I were obviously bright people and should be given a fellowship. Then I went to America.

When I came to America the social science research council was then quite a different institution. They guided us [as to] where we should go and study, and most of the time we were together but we were also divided and I for instance was advised to go to Madison, Wisconsin in order to meet John R. Commons. I didn't understand a word of his books and I don't still but he was a very kindly fellow and taught me bowling. But I did not become an institutional economist [then]. Now you should [note] that institutionalism at that period, 1929–30, was on the upswing. They were tremendously aggressive and they talked about the new economics. The new economics was developed in line with the three big men [Thorstein] Veblen, Commons, and [Wesley] Mitchell [who], of course, called themselves institutionalist economists. It was a new kind of economics and [you] should get hold of the book the new economics [though] I don't remember who in the hell wrote it.

But anyhow I with my background in spite of having touched upon certain institutionalist elements, I was very theoretical and I was very much against it and, as I noted in some of my articles, it was at the luncheon which [Irving] Fischer gave (whom of course I knew through his books and he was as great as Ragnar Frisch, my old friend) [where] I think the idea of forming the Econometrics Society [began]. The Econometrics Society was unusual: remember that it was thought and planned as a fighting organization against these god damn institutionalists who were getting so mighty in America. So then I was very theoretical and at the same time I must say that I was disturbed, scientifically, by that year in America [when] for two years I didn't write anything except a popular article [for] *Tiden* about socialism and capitalism in America.

But for the rest I was rather crushed. It was the specialization of economics in America. You know specialization, you had so many professorships in various directions which disturbed me because to me, as a theoretical economist, economics was a very unified, technical thing. So I was rather disturbed and disturbed of course by the institutional economists. I had already at that time developed not the idea about value premises, but nevertheless that valuations play a role. That was what I criticized in political elements but I found that Mitchell who was nevertheless teaching economic history [but] he didn't understand what I was talking about and [when] I tried to tell him that economics is biased and he didn't know what I was talking about.

And so I was not very happy there but I have of course many more other experiences which were very nice. However, politically that year was very important in Alva's and my life, because when we [went to] America [we] saw all the horrors in America at that time – you know the race questions, slums and all of that. At that time we became politically conscious. This was the time when we saw political interference in society is a purpose of life. That happened in America. America was at that time even more generous to foreigners than it is now. Everybody said you should stay here with my relatives in Minnesota, you know, they always pay you when you come from Sweden. But you will see they will help you. They want us to stay. And we had to formalize why we did not want to have our future life in America. And the formula was this that these Americans – they're so god damn bright – you know, a new nation and new republic. I mean to analyze and show what's wrong. And they have so little idea of what we more naively wanted to lay the main emphasis on I mean, this was our understanding of the Americas.

Incidentally I think this is a trait which I [saw] later on. My friend Mike Harrington became very political, very famous because he wrote that book [*The Other America*]. Well it's a very famous book before [Lyndon] Johnson wrote into the field of – what did Johnson call it – poverty and all of that. But his book is very fine. The difference with us is what is in the book you should take it out because this has to do with how I look [at] America, that it is just excellent in describing how hellish the situation is. [Then] I wrote the book mainly against Galbraith a little later (I'm talking now about what's called *Challenge of Affluence*). Well, the book is mostly full of what in hell I thought at that time – not always what I think now should be done. It was this question, that we coming from farming societies in Sweden could admire the Americans – how very cute they were in describing how hellish everything was, but I remember that I said one time something to them "Why don't you do anything about that?" And they said what [should we] do. Shall I stand up in the street corner and talk? Nobody will listen to me. Yes, exactly, you have to get people to listen to you.

I mean that was our fundamental reaction to America at that time. On one hand I was theoretical like hell continuously, although I didn't produce much I was shocked by all this diversification of economics in America. We were made politically conscious and becoming radical and so on. The question to continue just a little here I would say that we had one year [1931] in Geneva, where I had my first professorship, and there we got the idea that it's not very possible to do very much by this international organization which nevertheless worked much better than the one we have now. So what one should do without some vague idea that you should try to change and reform your own country and perhaps then some international thing could be done later.

You must remember however that at that time nobody thought such a crazy thing as a second World War should come. I am now in 1929–30. There are many things to be mentioned here. We came very near World War Two in Sweden. You know we made various plans and took them to Sweden. I felt very strange to them because World War Two had no interest how to change things. An American, [sociologist Dorothy Thomas] said once that you had best work together with some friends. She and her husband William, social scientists they were but they were our friends and belong to my intellectual development. When I came home [to] Sweden then of course I got involved in political work. And I was also in a Royal Commission, and from 1935 I was member of Parliament and later we wrote the book *Crisis in the Population Problem* which played a tremendous role. Allan Carlson wrote a dissertation about that period of my life. It's not perhaps exact in everything but this was a very big thing and there you formulated what actually became of the welfare state. Although right now I don't remember it because we have been away.

In reading that thesis by Carlson today, I got the feeling that when you and Alva made the policy proposals through the labor party it was almost as if the population issue was, if I may, a pawn and that the greater issue of course was to reform the Swedish society which you favored.

All right. That was a field. And I was in all these committees in agriculture and all that and in Parliament and I was very busy and at the same time of course we [founded] the Stockholm school. It was [Eric] Lindahl that inspired me and already in Geneva my lectures were on these new ideas which later [were] connected with Keynes. Even in Sweden they talked about Keynes, about what we needed at that time. We [Stockholm School] were much earlier, much better fundamentally. And this was the life I lived and then I got this letter [from] Frederick Keppel whom I said is the greatest, in my opinion, the greatest man you [America] have had. Morally, intellectually, morally even more than intellectually because he was not a great thinker, but [he] was a head of a great foundation. It was at that time the biggest foundation and I could tell you much about that. But he wrote me a letter [from] the board.

But anyhow, I told you Alva and I were up one night looking [at] a film about doctors in white [coats] who were working with the bad health of people in poor countries. We thought that perhaps the board of the foundation must know what they are asking me to do. Of course, I knew nothing whatsoever about the Negro problem in America, nothing whatsoever. This was not the main problem in the northern universities which I visited [in 1929–30], you know, all of it was on the corner, a little vague. I had no previous experience. I remember writing a telegram to Keppel [saying] that I was ready to reconsider the situation and was prepared to discuss undertaking the project. And he was very happy and said come along and I [went] along to America. [There] I gave the Godkin lectures and got [a] doctoral degree at Harvard and you know, it was very [exciting] and at that time I [talked] with various people. I had a lot of experiences.

But the telegram I got on the boat [to America in 1938] was from Keppel asking whether I would be prepared to steer out on a journey to the South together with Jackson Davis who was the man in the Rockefeller foundation responsible for, God knows what it was called, but it was an organization to help the Negro kids in the South. And I answered from the boat that shouldn't I read something, and Keppel wrote back and said it's all biased [I] should see it with [my] own eyes. And so we toured the South and the doctor took us to college presidents and various men who worked with the good and so on. I and Richard Sterner, my very best friend with me in all my adventures, went [in] to joints [where] people were drinking beer and we went to churches and you know I [was] really trying to live there.

Oh, I could tell you the [funniest] stories although we have not time now, but I must tell you one story. It ended up, was it in Birmingham, it was a horrible place anyhow – and I was taken around by the white officials issued to take care of me and they took me to a Booker T. Washington High School which was the biggest school then in the South. And there I was sitting and listening to the Negro kids singing songs to me and behind me I had all these white officials, before me I had the Negro kids and then the president or director of the school came and asked me if I would say a few words to the Negro kids, and I have always been prepared to say a few words. So I stood up and I said this: You know you are getting an education that's very important. You know they recently had a big celebration in Delaware because there [used to be] a Swedish colony but you should know that no decent Swede went to America. At that time they had to go out on the streets and take drunkards and also prostitutes… etc., and pack them in a boat and bring them over to Delaware to work and, as I said, you find that just as there are other Americans who are very proud about having ancestors who came with the Mayflower, so there are many Swedes who are tremendously proud of having ancestors going back to that place in Delaware. And they were just the scum of the earth in the beginning but here now they are fine people, high up in Northern universities, businessmen and bankers and, you know, great people here in America who just came out of that scum.

And what's the explanation, I said. The explanation is education. So you've got education here in America and then you've got these fine people and so it's with you too, I said. When I had [spoken] so far I felt that there was [a] cold behind me ... you know, I was speaking to two audiences – these white officials and these Negro people, so I stopped and I didn't know what to do. I just didn't do anything [for] several seconds and then I got an idea and I said you have been singing to me I'm going to sing to you – spirituals; I'm going to sing to you songs which are much older and then I started singing, and when that happened every order was broken and the Negro kids stormed the platform to embrace me. And when the whole thing was over I stood there with Richard Sterner and he said [they had been] very kind and now we must go back to the hotel. But that incident was in every Negro newspaper [in] the country. And the story was this: the Swedish educator had been singing to the Negro kids. Well I really lived what this country was [going through] in the South at that time. [I] made up my mind that this is a horrible problem and I cannot do anything about it. What in hell should I do? So I proposed to Keppel ... that we should form a political committee. I've after all had the political experience. I've been in Parliament and I can be chairman. I'll even appoint [Negro] members from the South and fine southern white men. One was a big Negro who later become president of the big Negro university in Atlanta. Fisk University. You can see what I mean.

... But [let us] now talk about institutionalism. As I said I started as a pure theoretician and I was against it when I came over to America when [it] [was] really very popular. And I kept to it. I was brought, however, into social problems and the equality problem [in Sweden and the United States], and when I wrote the book which came before I went to America [*The Political Element*] you see certain touches of the institutionalist in it.

But you see here I was up to something. I thought clearly, I didn't know anything about the Negro problem but it was clear to me from my very first idea I had of it that this is not the economic problem. What in God is the economic problem? And I was finding out that what I was doing was studying American civilization from the least advantaged group, which I say in the book somewhere. So I became institutional in that sense because I was brought into a problem which I could not master as an economist and gradually of course I came into all these things, cumulative causation, [which made] [*An American Dilemma*] an institutional book.

My other [main] books are *Asian Drama* which is also institutional in exactly the same sense except that you can always count myself an institutional economist and not just a social scientist because I am most of the time working not only on economic problems but in their connection with all other problems. You see I am stressing economics, but that's not true about the book I'm writing now [*Hyr styrs landet*] because several chapters I think should be classified as political science. [Here] you see I was brought into the problem [of how Sweden is governed]. I have to deal with it as an institutionalist, I mean that's just clear. And then I had to write my god damn methodological appendices to understand it. I did not get my method from philosophy. I had to make my own philosophy and I'll always have a bad feeling for philosophers. They are not doing what I would like philosophers to do [which] is to work out the methodology for the social sciences. Later on, of course, I formulated this much [more sharply] by saying that there is no economic problem, only social problems and they are just problems and they are complex. And that's of course my fundamental creed.

But the main thing that I want to stress was [that] this happened to me starting out as the most pure theoretician you can imagine. Because of the problems I had solving the problems I had to work on and then later as a consequence of my experience, as an institutionalist, you might say I tried to formulate and [will] continue to formulate until my death what I mean by institutional economics. This is really very true that it was [because of the] tremendous experience writing *An American Dilemma* [that I became an institutionalist].

I must confess that we had no idea when we went in 1938 that there should be a war. In the spring I had been together with Joseph Schumpeter and we (Hitler had then marched into Austria) said to each other that Hitler can get anything he wants, colonies and everything – I mean, there is not going to be a war because he can get everything. And at the same time a little later I was in Chicago University, and there Lord Layton who was the famous publisher of *The Economist* at that time gave a lecture to a little group where he proved that there would not be a war because Hitler could get anything he wanted. This was quite true. He'd be a god damn fool to wage, risk, a war when he could have got whatever he wanted and he could devote himself for the rest of his life to building good roads and houses for the German people. And explore colonies, as many as he wanted.

So we did not believe in a war when we went off, but very soon of course it developed. The situation developed already on the way out on the boat. You had I think the invasion of Czechoslovakia and then the one thing after the other came and, you know, we followed this very carefully and even [up] to the very outbreak of the war I did not really believe that something so absolutely crazy could happen as a second World War. Then of course, as you know, Hitler went to Denmark and Norway in 1940, spring, May or sometime. Then I was in Washington and when I opened the newspapers that morning in the hotel I read Hitler had invaded Norway. And then we [he and Alva] decided that we should go home and there were more diplomatic things to [deal with] because it was not possible [but] we came home [and took] our children with us. Alva had been in America and taken a position publicly against all the English men sending their children to America. She [felt] whatever happens in life the family should stick together. I mean this was the idea, so we took our children home and here I wrote the end of *An American Dilemma*. Then the bombing in England happened and it was a horrible thing.

... About Institutionalism I would further say this: I've always felt myself as a sort of individual. Sure, I'm for the institutionalists because they usually take up things from a broader viewpoint – although nobody has ever formulated a theory of institutionalism as I have done in my Madison lecture [Myrdal, 1978a]. Nobody among the Americans was an individual, and they are all tied up with four men: Veblen, whom I of course read to my amusement but was not influenced by except that I became radical and he was radical; and Commons whom I never understood; [Clarence] Ayres [whom] I have not understood very much either. And Mitchell, of course, whom I understood but was a little particular with his statistics and so on.

But I've always the feeling that in a way I am lonely. I am alone. The American institutionalists gave me the [Veblen–Commons] Award. I am recognized as an institutionalist in America. But I always feel that I have broader roots for my theory when I sort them out as I have to do when I had these research experiences. Adam Smith was in many ways rather general. He took many other things into account and [Alfred] Marshall and all of them. The German school of course which I had despised very much during my theoretical days. You see it in the *Political Element*. And there are also some people, I mean the whole history of economics. [Karl] Marx in his way, I have never been a Marxist but surely I have noted certain things there which I have added to my general background. That is what I think is so funny. The American institutionalists, in explaining what they are, always come back to these few chaps which I can have [great] respect for in many ways but there are many others. In that sense there I'm the only American institutionalist who is not just American.

I believe it was 1925 when you and Alva went to England, and I'm wondering during your time in England at Cambridge University, if that had an influence on you then or soon thereafter? I'm thinking of Beatrice and Sydney Webb and Joan Robinson or anyone else.

You see, I didn't meet very many people there. We spent most of our time in the British Museum reading, which I love. You know it is a place where there is no ventilation, so you could say it was the same atmosphere in which Marx had worked. I had no connection with the London School of Economics. And when I came to Cambridge [naturally] I went to see Dennis Robertson. And when I told him I was working on a theory about pricing in a system of uncertainty he said that was what [A.C.] Pigou had written about. And then I said, yes, that is the worst of Pigou's books, and there was this sort of silence. I had no influences whatsoever. I was in the British Museum library on this theoretical book of mine, and Alva worked on her things and that was our life. We were together. Concerning the Englishmen, we were very happy to see them but it did not concern us very much.

I remember, who was that Marxist Communist, who is just dead now? at Cambridge? You know who I mean. Maurice Dobbs. And at that time there was a tremendous formalism there. You know the book about Cambridge where it said that there should always be a sugar tongue, but that a Cambridge student should never use that tongue but his finger. You know, elements of that thing. I wanted to talk to Dobbs because Dobbs had written about enterprise. And I succeeded in having lunch with him. We had lunch. I was very eager to talk to him. I don't think you could [call me] influential at all, anytime we were in England. O.K.

Why did you select as your dissertation topic, 'The Problem of Price Formation Under Economic Change'?
I will tell you where that comes from. There are three parts. The third part deals with the influence on the construction of real capital of the uncertainty factor. And you have beautiful diagrams which I and my natural science friends have constructed. It is from then I move to the earlier things; but my original idea was that I [wondered] what influence the risk element had on the construction of real capital – houses and machines and so on. And then I had to think more carefully about the whole risk situation.

When you wrote *The Political Element* were you being critical of Adam Smith and Alfred Marshall or of John Stuart Mill?
Oh sure. I was angry at the Swedish government [policies]. But you will find that in the preface which I am going to send you. It was originally supposed to be a pamphlet against these goddamn mighty odd friends we had here. The glorious people. Heckscher, Cassel, because they were explaining what is right from a political [and] from an economic point of view. You know that it was all that humbug I should crush. And then instead of the pamphlet I worked two years and wrote this book which contains the History of Economics from that point of view.

During the period 1927–1932, from the time you finished your dissertation until you began working on the population problem, did you have any vision for a future society as to how you would like to see the Swedish society become, and also what sort of instrumental goals did you have?
Well, my life was full, in '27 when I became a university teacher at the same time. I was then filled by what was coming out in the theoretical, in the economic, in *The Political Element in the Development of Economic Theory*. I was filled by that. And I don't think I was very much in anything else. And

then in '29, as I said, I came to America and it was there I had my political consciousness increased.

But it is true. The *Crisis in the Population Problem* where you have the whole welfare system we did when we came from America and we were in Geneva. Alva and I wrote two articles, I think we did it together and sent it to *Tiden*, the Social Democratic periodical. But then ... a mighty man whom I had much to do with later did not accept it. He was real neo Malthusian in the old fashioned sense, as was the whole intelligentsia in the labor party. But we had that formulated. Unfortunately these articles are not preserved. But Alva and I did not agree. I think I was more nationalistic for the Swedish people. Anyhow we talked about it.

But then in 1934 in spring we started to write *The Crisis in the Population Problem*, and then we were up on a high mountain in Norway where we had a little party for a friend. And there we wrote that book, and immediately it exploded [in popularity] ... of course we write very well ... But here in Sweden it was never even reviewed and I had the feeling that it is not for the Swedes. You see I have never gone around with the feeling that Sweden is a model. On one hand I am very proud of Sweden. I have a Swedish passport. But when I have been in [a particular country] I've been using the traditional value systems, I have been working in them ... I was working in America on the Negro problem. It's not a book for the Swedes. And this is the reason why [my books sell so few in Sweden] because I have always followed where my books are sold. We are very small in Sweden. They are not selling in Sweden. They are selling tremendously in other countries. Why in *Asian Drama*, the 10th edition in Japan I think it was.

And once, I think I told you the story, Ramon Aron the French author, [when] we were lecturing in Berkeley, said to me you are the only public person in Europe who speaks as a natural fellow here in America. I've always been on theoretical grounds against this silly idea of models. I mean, for Lord's sake, if you take any American problem, the problem of health, hospitals and all of that, you have quite different history, quite different established situations – you can borrow details, we can borrow certain apparatus or medical instruments, but you can't borrow any model. I've never had that idea. I've never thought of the Swedish model abroad. And I've never talked of a Sweden abroad. Now as I told you I am coming back and I'm writing a book about Sweden, fifty years of my life and my memory and what I see around me now.

In the Postscript of *Value in Social Theory* you talked about how after you had finished writing the *Political Element* and later wrote the article 'Ends and Means', you felt a frustration because you couldn't work out the value problem. Then you said that you didn't write very much for

two years. Did you question the adequacy of orthodox economic theory for dealing with social issues?

It was not so much, I think I was crushed by my experience, with the diversification, the many professors in various schools and all of that where I had much more unified ideas of a theoretician for one thing I think. That was an important [reason] why I felt frustrated. And secondly, because our experience in America was so tremendously big. When I came to Chicago there was a murder on the campus and Alva and I went to the place where they put dead bodies which they can't identify. We had such a tremendously wide [perspective]. Alva was family sociologist and all of that, and we had a very broad experience. Even scientifically and intellectually. That is what we had. And that probably is part of the establishment of me as an institutional economist before I knew it, because theoretically I was on the theory against institutionalism, but my experience was that I lived through this horribly big diversified America. You see what I mean?

Now concerning *Monetary Equilibrium*, what factors influenced you to undertake your attempt to integrate monetary and price theory at the time that you began to write this?

Well, you see I had already in Geneva where I was assistant professor (it was my first job) already then inspired by [Eric] Lindahl who had written about means of monetary policies. You had the whole theory which you call Keynesian which was in Wicksell, of course, and Wicksell's great thing is that he saw that this common idea that total demand and total supply are always equal. You know Say's Law, is just phony. And that is the main thing in Wicksell. Wicksell otherwise is politically tremendously radical. But scientifically he was the most conservative man you can imagine. So you can, as they do now in Sweden where they don't understand much of reality they make him a quantity theorist, almost like Milton Friedman. Now the explanation of that is that Wicksell was so conservative. When he made his capital theory tied to Bohm-Bawerk he was reading old pamphlets in England to find out if people had said something sensible before. You see he was very different from Galbraith who starts out, you know, from conventional economics and even Keynes. There is this story about Keynes, incidentally in this book which is called *Economic Theory in Underdeveloped Regions*. The story there in a footnote which is true about Keynes. Wicksell was the opposite. He was tremendously conservative, always looking for who had said something before, and always trying to get even a place for quantity theory. And my model of monetary equilibrium was sort of an attempt, the only one I've done in my life, to be like a man like Wicksell. And find out what the hell Wicksell meant. And what he should mean if he knew so much more about the subject than I did. You see what I mean.

So would you say it is almost an attempt to be a theorist, I mean more of a theorist in that you were trying to make a breakthrough in trying to integrate the monetary and price theory?
No I mean I was just writing a book and I knew everything was coming from Wicksell. And then I wanted to show what Wicksell really said, what he meant. And then I continued my speculations about what Wicksell ought to have meant – I mean this was an immanent criticism.

When did you begin to apply the ideals embodied in the philosophy of Enlightenment in writings? Also, why did you adopt these ideals?
You see I had an excellent gymnasium, very much higher than you can get now, and we had a teacher there John Lundquist, our teacher in history and Swedish who was very conservative but who gave me the essence of Enlightenment philosophy and the understanding that this was an optimistic philosophy. It had the idea that you can improve man and society by reforms, you know – this is how I understood it. And if you go through *An American Dilemma* the book ends by the word Enlightenment with a big 'E'. That is why I gave you that rather important thing about [the American Creed].

And that was our creed. Of course the tragic thing in our life, Alva's and mine, is that we began life very optimistic, I mean I've drawn the optimism out of the Enlightenment philosophy and now we end our life when the world is just going to hell. It is a question of whether or not humanity will last until the end of this century. I mean, we always kept to these fundamental values which we got from the Enlightenment. And they fitted so god damn good in the American Negro problem you know you can read the beginning of it. You know, in America what I found out very soon when I should make my value premises is that they are the only country in the world which has the most elaborate and most commonly agreed system of values and they have used hundreds of books and go through everybody. You know even this, even the Negroes think they are free. You have it in the beginning of the book [*An American Dilemma*]. And incidentally, that played a large [part] in making the book popular in America because the whole man in America wants to be a good man and here a stranger comes to him and says that here we have all that in our state religion.

When did you first begin to believe that attitudinal change through education programs would serve as a stimulus to social change?
Well, I suppose we had it all the time. Alva was the one especially who had that. We always work together you know. I look more on institutions [for] my part, that you can change institutions. That you have in last few pages of *American Dilemma*, and those pages in that sense are very important. Although education was never a very big part of my thinking – that was Alva's field.

Going back to your work with the population crisis during the 1930s, was the debate about changing the Swedish social and economic system away from 'capitalism' towards, if I may, 'democratic socialism'?

Well, I was not thinking so much about Socialism. You see I was not so much a Marxist, and as I said in this Preface that you will get Heckscher said I was unfair because here I had written an outstanding criticism of [classical economic] Liberalism, Liberal economics, and I should do the same with the Marxist economics. You see Marx has never been a personal problem for me. Liberalism has been a personal problem. I had to work myself out of the liberal economic theory I had to work myself out of it. You see that book – Marxism has never been a personal problem. Of course, the book [*The Political Element*] doesn't go so much into it, but the assumption is there that it is possible to plan society so that it became a better place. You see what I mean? That was the fundamental valuation we have gotten from Enlightenment theory. That is where you have the beginning. And I've always felt myself in line with what Marx called the utopian socialists. They were planners, which Marx was not. With Marx it should happen by itself.

Would you attribute your feeling of planning to your study of the Enlightenment philosophy or did it come more from your work with the population problem?

Yes I had it earlier. It comes out of the Enlightenment theory. You see these things in America, and they are not necessary, you can change it in that way. My friends in America could only tell how bad it was and had no ideas that they should do anything about it. I think Harrington's book is a very good book which is rightly given the credit of having been behind the whole model of Johnson (what did he call it [Lyndon's Johnson's Great Society]). There is a story I can tell you about Daniel Moynihan whom of course I've known all the time. He got Alva's book *Nation and Family* translated which was what Alva worked on there [in the United States], that's about how we looked upon the population problem. But, Moynihan told me that when [John F.] Kennedy was killed, he was on his way to the White House on some business, not with Kennedy, you know the White House is a big place. And when he [went] there he was told about Kennedy. And he walked about semi-conscious and he walked into the Oval room and in the Oval room Kennedy had two things: a vase with red roses and my book *Challenge of Affluence* [Myrdal 1963] which I wrote against Galbraith, a very close friend. So Kennedy was on his way, this was one of the things which Johnson took over from Kennedy that something should be done.

Was the notion of planning strong within you from gymnasium?

What do you mean by planning? Planning is changing institutions.

How did you feel in studying under some conservative mentors which you had in your study of economics in Stockholm?
You see at that time, we youngsters felt something should be done about unemployment and so on. Oh yes we challenged them. Change everything. Planning was not very exciting for me. Sure planning was just that you should improve society. One criticism of institutionalists is their vagueness regarding the word technology. Well, it has never played the same role as in Ayres. Technology has never played a fundamental role in my thinking. Of course, behind it all, improvement of productivity, investment and all of that but it's not the fundamental concept as it is for Ayres. Technology has never been a large part of my theory.

In *Economic Theory and Underdeveloped Regions* you talk about the liberal, radical versus conservative conception of human behavior. Today do you still hold that conception?
The debate in America today is whether or not people have enough sense to choose what is good for them or is social engineering, especially education, necessary. That's why I refer to these very last pages in *American Dilemma*. I mean I'm not giving up. I am a fundamentalist. There are fundamental things which go through my whole life, and those fundamental things are the ones which come together in Enlightenment. And you have it in the second part of *Economic Theory in Underdeveloped Countries*.

Concerning the Enlightenment philosophy and the optimism which you have held through your life, are you now pessimistic or do you feel that we've come to where we are today in the industrial and the poor nations because the institutions, proper institutional change has not come about?
Yes, and of course the tremendous thing there is the lack of cooperation – more and more international interrelations and less and less cooperation. Of course, now the world is going to hell. That is what I am writing about. In the world and in Sweden. And this is a real tragic situation. Alva has much more kindness, much more romantic idea about what can be done; she sees good things in everything, and I think pessimistic and optimistic, you know, is nonsense. I am a realist. Nevertheless you should not give up. And that is the reason, I mean why in the hell should I sit and work hard and write books when I could have a good time with my economic situation with girls and wine, you have to have some sort of belief that it matters.

This question refers to growing bureaucracies. In the United States in some institutions where there have been social engineering efforts to counteract undesirable effects of market forces, we have now these growing bureaucracies such as the Tennessee Valley Authority and the United

States Department of Energy. Do you see this as an inevitable by-product of social engineering efforts?

Well I mean – that it happens everywhere, which I am writing about in my book in Sweden, self-governing bureaucracy. It is worse here where we have officials in the people's representatives which you don't have in Anglo-Saxon countries. Inevitably, of course, it's nothing, I mean there is an institution and I want to change it, I can be pessimistic and then you can't change it but pessimistic I am not. But now everything goes to hell, which I feel about most problems in the world today.

In *Objectivity and Social Research* [page 36] you mention that higher valuations are more likely to be adhered to when people act through orderly collective bodies. And then you go on to say that people act 'more as an American, as a Christian, and as a humanitarian...' To what extent have the teachings of Christianity influenced your work? Do you consider yourself to be a Christian?

No, I am like Cassel. My friend and teacher, was a rationalist, an atheist. When he was very old he said he wanted to run me over to religion but I am withstanding that. I am not religious. Alva might be a little more. She was chosen at least to keep up with. Nevertheless, someone dubbed me as a Lutheran social scientist. When I was in school we read Luther.

In what area over the last 40 years do you feel you have made the most influence – economic thought or in economic policy?

I don't know. I never think about that. The most important book in my life was *An American Dilemma*. I think it has tremendous influence still, and to me it was a very pathetic experience. You see, I felt as I was sitting in Princeton, very beautiful, working very hard, even after dinner and I felt that my type of people in Europe were either in prison or were dying. This was my war work. So it was a tremendously important thing for me. The funny thing I remember, we went up [by] train, Alva and I, to Washington with our friend from Howard University and I had the manuscript of the book in my hand. This was 1942. And I knew that I had a great book. I knew it. And it was. It is. It is my best book. And Arnold Rose contributed very much to the book. Of course I am, you see, grateful to all these collaborators. This meant much because I got in touch in a friendly way with people who knew something about various things.

If you were your grandson's age [18] right now, what would you do if you were to study economics?

Well in economics, of course, I would now, having [the] experience which I've been through, having formed my own philosophy which I did not get from any philosophers I would, of course, work just the same as I am doing now. It might be that I would lay a main emphasis on economic problems, but it would always be that all the other things would be part of the picture. That's [what] I would do. And am doing now, and I'm writing a book about the Swedish government. I feel no hesitation [about] discuss[ing] how they have made a new constitution which I think is very foolish of them, a very bad one. I'm criticizing it very hard. I've no inhibitions of going into outside areas, none whatsoever.

Do you feel in a sense that you came too early and that there is now a lot more sympathy for interdisciplinary approaches to problems today?
Let me say one thing first – I worked on hundreds of books that were interdisciplinary as such. Mostly they were conferences with hundreds of people from different disciplines talking, and they are regularly alone or together not of the quality of what the scholar has done in their own field. I mean they don't integrate. This interdisciplinary thing doesn't solve very much. I mean you have to go deeper. You have to really apply it. It is not just coming together and saying we should learn from each other. I prefer that one individual should do their own research and then you know what you are doing. From my point – I have no respect whatsoever [for] the boundaries between the disciplines. None whatsoever.

I feel that I talk to anybody. I have no feeling whatsoever. These disciplines are, after all, the result of practical frustration considerations for teaching and research. And I don't think they are very practical because, as I said, problems are complex. And I don't know. I have some ideas about that somewhere that I thought we should have in the future. It's this organization according to problems.

Do you feel lonely in the sense throughout your career that there have been so few people who not only have attempted but have been able to deal with a number of areas, to deal with a number of problems from a social science perspective. Has that throughout your career made you feel lonely?
Yes, I feel lonely. Ordinary economists do not even review my books. It is a [testimony to the] tremendous power in the establishment and part of that power is the power of periodicals. That's the real problem.

SECOND INTERVIEW – JULY, 1982

Could you discuss the influence your experience in the United States during the late 1930s had on your becoming an institutionalist?

Very rapidly I came to understand that I was put to study the whole American civilization, so to speak, from the point of view of the least advantage group. That's quite clear and I just went ahead. It's now I came to be an institutionalist and it's also now I came to my ideas about valuations – that you must work with value premises, this is the big change in my whole life as a scholar. This [is] well formulated in the Appendices to *An American Dilemma* and of course in the whole book, and I would say that my first outline showed that now I was that and I [remained so]. This was not under the influence of American, so-called institutionalist, whom I never have been very near, you know. It's not from them. After all Adam Smith was much more an institutionalist than ones who follow. I did not follow or come from in any way a member of the institutionalists and even during that whole book I had no relations with American institutionalists.

And it was just that this is a very complicated business. I got the feeling, which I almost formulated, that all new economic problems were also sociological, political, cultural, historical problems. Problems, involved and complex as life itself, and so that was when I came innocent to this thing, I had no idea what [the] Negro problem was. It is that confrontation with this task, which ... became the *American Dilemma*. It was at this time I became an institutionalist and from the general, methodological ideas I got there, to be an institutionalist, to work with valued premises, I've continued all my life. But that was the big break in my life, and it had nothing to do with American Institutionalists. And as a matter of fact I don't even now feel very much in it. I'm just my own institutionalist in way, it's just developed from my experiences in life. Incidentally I am rather critical [of] the philosophers, because the philosophers should be responsible for research methods in Social Sciences ... Instead they work on some way usually to construct something which is very much more irrational.

From the 1930's, what were some of the subjects, reforms, the goals, and the means, which you discussed in Sweden during the 1930's, with meetings that were attended, by of course, Alva and the Thomas's, and other sociologists and architects with whom you talked?
Early in the 1930s, of course, I was mostly involved in policy and the general stuff from the Stockholm School where we were of course ten years ahead of Keynes, and I think that link is, in many respects, fundamental. But otherwise, of course, it was of social questions. We had in America become radicalized, I say, before that we [had] never taken part [in] politics and now we were in politics, and our life was filled by meetings and things like that. When we came home we became politically active in the social democratic party. Alva was of course more responsible for these practical issues, social reforms of various types which we argued for.

What role do you believe you and Alva personally had in the evolution of what we call in America the Swedish welfare state?
In our book *The Crisis of the Population* you had a catalog of welfare reforms which we wanted to make family welfare reforms and that of course has had great influence, much greater than you find in present literature, because we left the country and had been living in other places. You see the year we spent in Geneva rather immediately after [the] First World War we became rather skeptical [about] the international organizations and had a feeling that what should be done were reforms in the individual countries.

In Marquis Childs' *Sweden: the Middle Way* he talks a great deal about the cooperative movement. How did you feel about his explanation?
I think it was a friendly book. Of course it was a main element which is correct, but it places very much, too much importance on the cooperative movement in my opinion. It's not really a very good guide book to the beginning of the Swedish welfare state as we saw it at that time. Cooperatives were not the very important element in our social economic activity.

While you were a member of Swedish Parliament given that you had your objectives and that you and Alva stated them in your book about the population crisis, how did you go about trying to introduce the change, now that you were involved in politics?
Most of my time was actually taken as a member of the population commission. Alva was an expert and was interested in social reforms and I merely wrote it, but later on I wrote full time and I wrote a great number of the reports on [topics including] abortion. And I didn't like it, when I had tried to be out of it [government] I said I am a theoretical economist and I have my plans for research, then I was taken away from that, and this is one of the ways I felt a little dissatisfied and was happy to accept then the invitation from Keppel to go to the United States to study the Negro problem. But I was working full time on the population issue, that was most of my activity in these years '35–38, when we left.

Why did you accept the executive secretary position for the Economic Commission for Europe?
Well, I was a little sick and tired at that time of this work in the population commission, which [was] concerned about social reform policy, and wanted to back something else. When I took over the Economic Commission for Europe the idea was that we should be a commission of anti-communist members Canada, Europe and France, and so on and coming from Europe I should be Chairman. When I took over the European Commission of course it was just in the beginning of the Cold War, and there was an opportunity to

keep some sort of unity of Europe. That was broken off of course, because of the way in which the Russians obtained from the beginning the Marshall Plan funds.

When did you first believe in the need for an integrated world economy?
Here in Europe after World War Two some of our countries were of course underdeveloped. The south Italy, Yugoslavia and so on. And gradually that meant that I came to consider the whole, the whole world economic problem. Yeah, it was during that time and under these experiences.

What role do you feel that you and the ECE played in the development of the European coal and steel community and ultimately the European Economic Community?
Well, you see I could not be an enemy to ECE and (what was the name of the chief, he was my good friend) ... Marshall Land. Monnet [the planner] wrote to me and said [would] I help them to plan a steel community. And Tony Rose my steel director and I weren't sure he felt that we should help any government. So we made the first outline of the steel community in ECE.

Regarding the United Nations experience just in general, early in the 1950s you mentioned to friends you were longing to return to scholarly life and to do another study, what ... and you had job offers, oh my goodness, Cambridge, Yale, Wisconsin, I could go on, why did you stay until 1957?
I was just thinking I do believe that I've been rather faithful in my life. You know and I was in the Population Commission and I stayed to stick to full time work far away from my scientific interests until I was fed up. I think I can say the same in many other aspects.

Concerning underdeveloped countries, when did you first become interested in studying underdeveloped countries?
Well, that was of course during that time [1950s]. Our knowledge about the conflict in India was mostly due to pictures of campuses and dresses and dances – that happened during my work in Asia. And in writing *Asian Drama* I was of course very much influenced by my work on *An American Dilemma*. You know that even I couldn't be so faithful to the book. You know that the whole layout for *Asian Drama* is copied from *An American Dilemma*. [The perspective is] institutional, I have it in the preface.

Could you elaborate about your theory of Circular Cumulative Causation?

The cumulative position – that's a very very important thing. This is one very important methodological insight which I reached during my work. And this cumulative association I got from Wicksell. He had it in the monetary field. This is a very important thing. It's cumulative because this is a third element. You see this means that I could never as an economist talk about equilibrium. To me it was that as soon as you got a little out of equilibrium then you run off in one direction or another. And that's a very important change in my whole attitude and it's a thing which is not very commonly observed.

How did you arrive at the title, *An American Dilemma*?
But this whole idea of looking upon the Negro problem as a dilemma where you [have] higher ideals came very early on me. When you start to read it you see some American ideals. You remember the first introduction I go through. And here was a sort of difference between the recognized ideals and the reality. That I think came very early in my work. And the title which symbolizes that came once when I was working at Princeton.

In writing *Asian Drama* why did it take much longer than you originally had anticipated?
It took a tremendous time. I wondered about my whole approach, if I should start it while I remembered it in India. It took a long time before I could really start writing it. Then I worked very very hard. Then, too, of course I had collaborators, more than in *An American Dilemma*. Nevertheless, every word is written by me. You know when I worked on 'Dilemma' Richard Sterner, my friend (he's dead now, all my friends are dead) he all the time said it was becoming too big. And then when he delivered what he was preparing on economics it was so big I had to shorten it. I trimmed it down.

Just looking ahead, the future of what we call Soviet type or centrally planned economies, what do you see happening?
What's happening of course is what you know from the newspapers. It's not going very well in the Soviet Union. I mean the biggest thing economically was immediately after the war when so many people were killed, so much was destroyed and Stalin had his Iron Hand [over] Europe. Stopped it with his plans, you know his five-year plans. And now it's rather bad in Central and Eastern Europe as well.

Do you consider yourself to be an economist, sociologist, or a social scientist?
Social scientist. That's the essence of my institutionalism.

What advice would you give me in writing the book about you? What advice could I ask you [regarding] the book about your life, about your works, about the many contributions you have made?

Well, I'm typical of one long old generation. I offer an outsider's view. This is really what I tried to do. And in all my life and the writings, too. And it's an insider who had this, you can say, optimistic view which I tried to describe to you. We certainly are not leftists in the American sense but not Marxist although I read Marx. He was in one way one of the early institutionalists.

Are you still optimistic about societies?

Yes, people are taught to be optimistic. You shouldn't forget that in *An American Dilemma*. In the end I mean with all these horrors which I've described more faithfully than I would have done earlier. Hopefulness ... that is I think a very important thing. And I think a thing which was very good for publication because the good American could read it.

Notes

PREFACE

1. For biographical sketches of Myrdal see Balapkins (1988), Dopfer (1988), and Kindleberger (1987). Detailed biographical information and considerable insight into Myrdal's intellectual development and study of race relations in the United States is contained in Jackson (1990).
2. The author will adhere to the methodology of Samuel Hollander who stated, 'Textual interpretation is no easy matter ... For this reason I shall avoid mere assertion by use of direct quotation as far as practicable' (Hollander 1987, p. 12).
3. Those who have written about Myrdal have failed to understand this aspect of his intellectual development. For example, Gilles Dostaler (1990) states 'Thus the oft-mentioned so-called, clear-cut dividing line in Myrdal's intellectual development does not exist'. This is not correct. It will be demonstrated that not only does such a dividing line exist, but that there were three distinct stages of Myrdal's intellectual development. This issue is significant. Very few economists have shifted their conception of economics, economies, and what economists should do as dramatically as Myrdal. Many contemporary economists have been imbued with the orthodox conception of economics and economies, with its emphasis upon narrowly focused economic models. For those who find this conception both irrelevant and inappropriate for analyzing and recommending policies for broad issues, a study of Myrdal offers an alternative conception as well as an example of how someone with similar graduate school training was able to develop a more holistic, transdisciplinary conception.
4. Galbraith offered this assertion in one segment of *The Age of Uncertainty* series (produced by the Public Broadcasting System, and which he narrated) focusing on contributions by economic philosophers. He noted that not only do economists take this perspective to the grave, but that some take it beyond there as well.
5. Few economists besides Myrdal who were trained in the neoclassical tradition have abandoned this paradigm entirely – John Gurley, Robert F. Hoxie, and Kenneth Boulding being notable exceptions.
6. The term 'conceptualized reality' is used to represent the idealized image of the socio-economic order as perceived by an economist, an image conditioned by the cultural patterns of the society within which the economist lives. It consists of two interrelated views: one involving a perceived relationship between social and economic forces within a society; the other pertaining to an interpretation of human behavior. A conceptualized reality gives direction to the economist's analysis by influencing both the problems chosen for investigations as well as the conceived interrelationships between economic and non-economic factors. See Jensen (1976, pp. 262–72).
7. The distinct periods are offered for the sake of exposition. The author recognizes that these time periods are distinguished by artificial boundaries and may overlap. Particular studies written and published within a certain period (for example, the population issue) may have had their inception in Myrdal's mind during an earlier period.

CHAPTER 1

8. See Angresano (1996b, pp. 3–19) for a full description of an economy from the evolutionary-institutional perspective.

9. Such as What to produce?, How much to produce?, How to produce?, and How to distribute what is produced?

10. Attitudes in this context are the views of society's members regarding what economic, social, political, and cultural conditions should prevail along with a conception of the same types of conditions as they actually exist in that society.

11. Economic historians agree that the major technological inventions and innovations in the late 18th and early 19th centuries were instrumental in the evolution of 'capitalism'. The dramatic reversal of key performance indicators in the 1980s contributed significantly to the political revolutions of 1989 throughout Central and Eastern Europe, and to the subsequent commitment to establish a new economy.

12. The philosophical basis for an economy is a viewpoint which specifies the place of an individual within society, an ideal state of political, social, and economic reality to serve as a set of ultimate goals for society, and a general program suggesting broad policy measures that will guide society from its actual conditions towards the ideal reality. This economic philosophy will be multidimensional in the sense that social, political, and cultural as well as economic elements are contained therein. An example is Adam Smith's philosophical basis for a laissez-faire market economy.

13. A recent comparison was made of China's and Russia's economic performances (Nolan 1995). Russia has introduced transformation policies based upon the 'transition orthodoxy' that characterized Poland's 'shock therapy' (Nolan 1995, p. 8). Evidence indicates that while adopting a transformation strategy which 'runs counter to the transition orthodoxy', China's economy has outperformed that of Russia in every major area while not experiencing a deep recession (Nolan 1995, pp. 7–8). Nolan evaluates the contrast between the two performances (China vs. Russia) as being 'breathtaking', with China experiencing more favorable outcomes in almost every economic and social indicator. Overall, this comparison suggests that the contrasting outcomes in these economies' performances could be attributed to their different transformation strategies, and that the transformation policies introduced in China could be deemed more productive than those adopted in Russia.

14. This was certainly the case in Poland, where shock therapy has received criticism for being a social experiment 'untested beyond the economic laboratories of Cambridge, Massachusetts' (Komarek 1992). As with the Laffer Curve, there was no 'analytical proof' that shock therapy would work. Rather, its neo-liberal basis and its array of policy prescriptions and proscriptions offered a 'mode of proof [that] was generally "argument by assertion" – the better known the advocates of shock therapy, the less rational argument was provided, as a rule' (Amsden *et al.* 1995, p. 12).

15. For a detailed description of the particular problems and obstacles faced by Hungary see Angresano, 1992 (a, b). It is noteworthy that China faced similar, if not more difficult obstacles when it embarked on its transformation path in the late 1970s.

16. *The Economist*, 'Survey Perestroika: And Now for the Hard Part', April 28, 1990, p. 19.

17. *The Economist*, 'Survey Perestroika: And Now for the Hard Part', p. 19.

18. Rather than evaluate the examples of profitable state-owned enterprises in CEE, France, Italy and Latin America which were widely recognized as being viable, there was a 'deeply rooted skepticism about the possibility of state-owned enterprises ever achieving a level of efficiency comparable to that of private ones, even if they were to undergo some radical reforms' (Mujzel 1993, pp. 3–4).

19. Hoen (1995) offers the Austrian alternative conception of economies, arguing that the transition should be 'viewed as a historical process and that institutions are important'. Even before the initial package of Poland's transformation policies was approved and implemented critics attacked the assumptions upon which these policies rested as being seriously flawed when it comes to the analysis of transformation. Leading Polish ana-

lysts argued that '[t]his entire reasoning rested on false premises that were completely divorced from reality. Experience has shown that the scale and above all the durability of social support initially enjoyed by the new elites was overestimated. A more important mistake was to assume that the recession process set off by the supply shock would automatically be reversed, that the realization of the stabilization programme would lay the foundations for "creative destruction"' (Hausner and Owsiak 1992, pp. 70–71). Other analysts chide advocates of shock therapy for their assumptions which 'ignore or supersede economic logic and economic history – especially their failure to study lessons of the past … [arguing that] macroeconomists, who seem to possess a trained incapacity to recognize economic reality, don't seem to have open minds' (Amsden *et al.* 1995, p. 1).

20. Lipton and Sachs (1992, p. 246). These authors offered no further justification for this assertion.

21. Simple solutions such as shock therapy for CEE or cutting taxes to reduce the United States federal budget deficit offered by 'experts' and purported to be scientific often gain broad appeal, for as Thorstein Veblen once noted 'the bearer of the universal solvent is irresistible'.

22. Rosenberger (1992, p. 273). What was not taken into consideration was the ability of interest groups to take advantage of quick schemes by obtaining assets cheaply and reselling them for substantial profit.

23. Metzger (1996) provides a scholarly, convincing presentation of the philosophical basis for the Chinese economy, particularly the role of Mao Tse Tung thought. He emphasizes that one justification for China's socialist market economy which retains the ability of the state to influence the ideology and direction of the economy is that 'it is in the interest of the Chinese to rely on state guidance not just to "regulate capitalism" … but also to cultivate an ethos throughout society somehow distinguishing between the desirable effort of free individuals to compete for profits [which is desirable] … and an undesirable tendency to "put the pursuit of selfish interests above all other considerations"' (p. 30). Therefore, the state remains the guardian of the ethos which is consistent with China's historical legacy under which the people 'have believed that the social good depends more on making the individual and the government good than on leaving the individual free to choose how to define and pursue what is good for him or her'. Therefore, a strong state presence is consistent with Chinese attitudes who look to the state 'to serve as the indispensable agent of political and economic improvement' (p. 30).

24. This section draws heavily from Angresano (1994a, c, d and 1996a).

25. This viewpoint consists of the analyst's vision regarding the ideal economic, political, and social conditions the analyst prefers for the economy(ies) in question, and the analyst's conception of the actual realities.

26. Some accounts provided by the architects of shock therapy as well as by IMF and World Bank analysts contrast (but do not compare) the experience of China with that of Poland. Some have done so in a strongly biased manner, such as the evaluation by Wing Thye Woo (1994) in which the author ignores selected unfavorable indicators and praises transformation policies in Poland for their effectiveness. However, he criticizes China for adopting similar policies. Woo focuses only on performance indicators for which the trend became positive after shock therapy was introduced, and gives shock therapy credit for this performance. On the other hand, unfavorable performance indicators in Poland either are ignored or attributed to exogenous factors.

27. These are the criteria Myrdal has used in all his transformation studies.

28. In Hungary it is estimated that purchases on the black market account for up to one quarter of the average family's total spending.

29. For an in-depth, comprehensive analysis of changes in social and economic conditions throughout Central and East Europe see UNICEF (1993). Overall, the study concluded that coinciding with transformation policies have been a 'considerable and lasting decline in output, employment and incomes and by the worsening of many social indicators … [as well as] the spread of poverty, birth contraction, escalation of death rates, decline in school enrollments and an unstoppable crime wave [which] have reached truly alarming proportions' (UNICEF 1993, p. iii). This is particularly true in Russia where the

impact of the economic crisis includes a reduction in average life expectancy for men from 62 to 59 years since 1989.

30. Throughout CEE, without exception, 'real wages have fallen massively... Wage survey data show that, in general, the sharpest falls coincided with the introduction of "big bang" reforms on price and trade liberalization' (UNICEF 1993, p. 37).

31. See Brady, 1993, and *The Economist*, 1994 and 1993. There has been 'open physical violence' against commercial bank officials perpetrated by organized crime networks seeking to control these institutions. In 1993 alone 10 senior Russian bankers have been shot in Moscow. An American hotel executive who won a court case against alleged Russsian mafia leaders over control of one of Moscow's most popular hotels was murdered gangland style during the fall of 1996.

32. The three countries in which this has not been the case are the Czech Republic, Latvia, and Estonia.

33. Note that the conclusion drawn by UNICEF is that the gravity and relative extent of the decline in CEE nations' social and economic indicators is both 'unprecedented and more pronounced, in relative terms, than those observed in Latin America and Africa' during the 1980s (UNICEF 1993, p. 2). The study also concludes that the 'largely unexpected deterioration in human welfare' (especially rising poverty, mortality and crime rates) has been 'certainly aggravated' by 'policy design problems' (UNICEF 1993, p. 45).

34. As shown in the next section, comparable performance indicators for China indicate high rates of GDP and real income growth, low incidence of poverty and unemployment, and lower rates of inflation than in CEE. New firms are developing rapidly in importance, the transformation policy adopted has been pragmatic, less ideological than in CEE, and there has been political stability. On the negative side the distribution of wealth and income is becoming more unequal, and there is no democracy.

35. The free market exchange rate was about 23,300 by the end of 1995 versus about 22,200 in early 1994. Note that about 60% of the zloty basket depreciated while 40% (based upon the Deutschmark and Swiss Franc) appreciated.

36. One analyst believes that 'analyzing the level of real wages in the years 1990–91 does not demonstrate the real changes in consumer purchasing power and personal consumption brought about by the implementation of the "Balcerowicz Plan". In 1990, total consumption was 11.7% lower than in 1989. This combined the effects of a 15.3% fall in consumption financed by personal incomes with a 0.7% increase in consumption financed by transfer payments and a 0.2% increase in social consumption figures released by the Central Office of Planning show a 6–8% growth in consumption financed by personal incomes in 1991.' Overall, however, the data indicates a painful fall in living standards in 1990–91 as evident by the large increase in 'households registered in 1990 of households on low incomes' (Czarny and Czarny 1992, pp. 66–67).

37. In reference to the history of debt negotiations one analyst points out that '[w]hen political interests of the creditors correspond with political interests of the debtor, then the creditor governments prefer to seek a balance between their own short-and long-term economic concerns and short- and long-term interests of the debtors', arguing that the Polish case 'supports that conclusion' (Mesjasz 1995, p. 15).

38. The Paris Club agreements pertain to 'all of Poland's liabilities to 17 creditor countries for medium- and long-term credits' granted prior to 1984, and consolidated in 1991 (Ministry of Economic Affairs 1995a, p. 22). Favorable re-negotiation of the debt and the economy's performance rating (Poland is ranked fourth in CEE behind Slovenia, the Czech Republic and Estonia according to an evaluation using IMF-type indicators of macroeconomic performance, political stability, foreign investment and business climate rating) helped the nation improve its ranking in the world credit rating from 58 to 57 in 1995 (*The Economist* Intelligence Unit 1995a, June 26, p. 1). Improvements in its external financial position also will reduce the waiting period before Poland hopes to become a full member of the European Union – although such status is not likely within the next seven to ten years during which time Poland will have had to reduce its foreign debt problem dramatically.

39. Unemployment was believed to be overstated in the early 1990s as some people may

have willingly taken unemployment compensation as they left state-owned enterprises for a private or informal sector job. Those likeliest to do so may already have had substantial accumulated savings, had acquired business skills, and had more savvy than others who may have tried to leave state-owned enterprise positions at a later date. Evidence of prolonged unemployment since 1993 indicates that the official unemployment rate may no longer be overstated.

40. The radical shock therapy has created some 'special problems' including a growing 'anxiety and uncertainty among the Polish population ... [especially] widespread fears of involuntary unemployment due to job layoffs (Berg 1994, p. 412). Throughout Poland attitudes are shifting away from the overly optimistic view that elimination of communist party authorities and most vestiges of central planning would enable Poland to transform its economy rapidly so that it resembled those in the European Union. This shift reflects the fact that much unemployment is prolonged, and recent studies have indicated that in 1994 'over 45 percent of the unemployed were without jobs for over a one-year period, and 55 percent have lost the right to unemployment benefits' (Orlowski 1995, pp. 13, 14). These conditions, combined with heavy demands on the state for social services from those suffering the effects of the transformation, have meant that over half the total number of unemployed are not entitled to unemployment benefits. In addition many people do not register as unemployed once their benefits expire, so there may be a growing number of discouraged workers – and thus those out of work but desirous of a job at market wages may be higher. Another analyst points out that 'official data on the state and dynamics of unemployment does not, however, reveal the true complexity of the problem. Above all, official statistics show the numbers of registered unemployed ... approximately 30–35% of unemployed people are not registered at unemployment benefit offices. ... Apart from the registered unemployed, there is also a large section of jobless peasants usually working both on farms and in industry, who are not entitled to benefits and whose chances of finding work are minimal' (Pestoff 1995, pp. 226–7).

41. Adam (1994, p. 615) argues that 'neo-liberals [architects of shock therapy] are not very concerned with the hardship affecting the population; they view it as a surgeon views post-operative pain – a necessary accompaniment of the treatment. In addition, they see the unequal distribution of the transformation burden as a way to create a prosperous, property-owning middle class'.

42. The incidence of poverty increased from about 17 to 34% of the population from 1989 to the end of 1991 (Milanovic 1992, p. 31).

43. There are differing conclusions concerning the contribution of shock therapy, to the 1990–93 performance of Poland's economy. Institutional adjustment has taken place within Poland during the past two years, and this adjustment was initiated by the shock therapy's macroeconomic reforms (Berg 1994, p. 377). Many other analysts agree, crediting shock therapy's liberalization of the economy as the prime factor responsible for the favorable macroeconomic trends – especially growth and structural change – and praise shock therapy for promoting rapid development of the private sector they believe has become the 'driving force in the recovery' (OECD 1994, p. 53). They argue this performance confirms the efficacy of shock therapy. However, other analysts offer a mixed evaluation of the 'historical achievement of Leszek Balcerowicz and his team', arguing that 'the effects of his programme range from highly positive to highly negative' (Hausner 1995, p. 4). On the positive side, shock therapy is praised for averting prolonged hyperinflation. However, critics argue that the negative effects of shock therapy, especially high inflation, excessive social costs due to the rapid destruction of the state-owned sector in treating privatization as an end in itself, and for prompting an economic crisis which led to a state financial crisis (Hausner and Owsiak 1992, pp. 44–6), outweigh its positive effects. Criticisms also are leveled at the narrow range of economic performance indicators selected to the neglect of social indicators such as unemployment, poverty, and income distribution (Gomulka 1995, p. 344), and failure to support those state-owned enterprises or cooperatives which were economically viable (Boczar et al. 1993, pp. 16, 20).

44. Kwasniewski's reputation for being pragmatic rather than ideological, which gave him

credibility with voters, was enhanced when shortly after the election he resigned from the Social Democracy of the Republic of Poland party (which had been newly created by 'reformed' ex-communists). He claimed this decision was based upon his desire to reach out to supporters of Walensa as well as to give himself more freedom to govern.

45. Continued strength of the state and its ability to quickly impose stringent monetary and fiscal measures has contributed positively to the economy's performance, albeit at the expense of human rights. For example, the state has been able to control inflation by applying a credit squeeze when strong inflationary pressures appeared. Further, credit to burgeoning private enterprises has been easier to obtain in China (than in Poland) as the growing power of local governments over revenue has enabled authorities at this level to 'pressure local banks to extend credit to private sector' (Liew 1995, p. 889).

46. As compared to the 1979–82 period, direct foreign investment grew from $7 billion to over $110 billion (Nolan 1995, p. 186).

47. An example concerns what Western observers would consider corrupt activities by state officials. It is widely assumed that managers of state-owned enterprises divert resources from their firms as they begin to engage in market activity. According to one analyst this is a form of 'de facto privatization' which permits public officials to use state assets for private benefit. The analyst concedes that this type of privatization 'is inferior to official privatization, if the latter is legally and properly [and substantively] carried out... But [that] in an imperfect world, the choice is less clear cut' (Liew 1995, p. 887). Instead of treating privatization as an end in itself, assuming Schumpeterian entrepreneurs will quickly emerge and assume control of all privatized enterprises, Chinese policy makers have permitted a different process to evolve – with semi private-sector activity developing as a result. China has permitted cadres to make the transition to private sector entrepreneurs, even if corruption was an interim stage in the process. As Liew argues '[t]he market provides a window to these employees – it reveals what is potentially possible. It provides employees of state enterprises examples, as well as opportunities, for potentially higher living standards'. In some southern Chinese provinces thousands of officials have left state-sector jobs for private-sector jobs (Liew 1995, p. 888).

48. Boris Yeltsin told Chinese President Jiang Zemin, 'We pay much attention to studying the experience of economic reforms in China'. The Chinese response was that 'the international community should acknowledge that there is no single pattern for the development of all countries'. See *Austin American-Statesman* (1994, pp. A1, A12).

49. Evidence from all over CEE indicates that some state-owned enterprises that were destroyed could have been viable if shock therapy transformation processes had not been implemented, and that managers of these firms may have learned and adjusted to the new environment – much as some state-owned enterprise managers are doing in China.

50. State intervention can be productive in a number of areas. The Asian experience illustrates the potential for effective state-guided industrial and trade policies. The state is also necessary, particularly now in CEE, to prevent competition of the quality of goods and services offered from becoming 'savage'. The extensive network of organized crime prevalent today in CEE illustrates the pressing need for greater state regulation of economic activity. The state is also necessary for providing a social safety net to its citizens who have come to expect social insurance and welfare schemes – much as they are provided by Western nations. State activity in this regard will become more necessary as privatization of previously state-owned enterprises continues and new owners have neither the desire nor willingness to provide similar schemes for their workers.

51. In a spring 1993 meeting in Prague a member of the European Community Commission, while admitting that CEE exporters faced high barriers when seeking to trade with the European Union (EU), told CEE officials that they should not retaliate or the EU would raise barriers even higher.

52. Some social scientists see a continuum (that is, what is a means in one situation becomes an end in another, and vice versa) between ultimate and instrumental goals, the method chosen to satisfy a chosen goal is not neutral since it reflects the policy makers' (and perhaps the analyst's) viewpoint. Consequently, they argue that ends and means cannot be separated.

53. See Amsden *et al.* (1995) and Nolan (1995) for a detailed analysis of the impact of shock therapy policies in Russia.
54. Some criticize Russia's Western advisors for giving confidence and support to this radical leap by leading the 'cavalry charge' towards privatization and the 'free market' in endorsing the 500-day Shatalin Plan. Western advisors very quickly provided their shock therapy recommendations which were introduced subsequently without an effective framework of government administration or law and order – with disastrous results.
55. As a result Myrdal chides most economists (including those holding a Marxist ideology or laissez-faire advocates) for failing to account adequately for non-economic factors while placing emphasis upon some basic factor to which all other economic and non-economic variables are expected to adjust once the 'basic economic factor' has been altered.
56. For example, Santarelli and Pesciarelli (1990, p. 694) argue that Schumpeter was influenced by the 'particular cultural climate of the early 20th century, especially the importance then of the great entrepreneurs'.
57. He cited the 'Green Revolution' (introduction of hybrid wheat and rice seeds which, under ideal conditions, would boost the productivity of land by about two to four times) as an example where his conception was ignored. Technological change preceded attitudinal and institutional change, with unfavorable results for decades in terms of a majority of poor farmers realizing few benefits from introduction of the new seeds without complementary changes (such as better access to water, fertilizer or credit) being provided as well.
58. See Myrdal (1957e), (1958a, b), (1968), (1969a), (1975a), (1975b), and (1978a) for detailed criticisms of neoclassical economics.
59. Myrdal viewed the neoclassical perspective as too simplistic in its formulation of policies and representative of a monolithic, deterministic vision of the behavior of an economy. This vision viewed development as occurring in a linear, mechanical, simplified manner by which neoclassical economists assumed that once certain economic conditions had been established (such as privatization of previously state-owned enterprises or liberalizing rules pertaining to free trade) the market mechanism would emerge and prosperity inevitably would ensue.

CHAPTER 2

60. During the 1982 interview Myrdal said that he had this mentor in mind when he ended *An American Dilemma* by referring to 'the Enlightenment', by using a capital 'E'.
61. GM III retrospectively believed that studying law in order to see how society functions 'was a very silly idea, crazy, absolutely mad and against all my interests, because you couldn't possibly learn about society the way law was taught in Sweden then and even now' (Harrison 1976, p. 4).
62. Alva Myrdal deserves credit for significantly influencing all of Gunnar's contributions to the social sciences, particularly those made after 1930. For a provocative, in-depth analysis of her career see Bok (1992).
63. The 'Stockholm School' of Economics, originally known as the Political Economy Club of Stockholm, was 'founded' by Eric Lindahl in the late 1920s and 'developed by him with the collaboration of Myrdal, [Bertil] Ohlin, Eric Lundberg, and other ... [young Swedish economists]' (Uhr 1951, p. 255).
64. The other two cited by the Academy at the time Myrdal was awarded the 1974 Nobel Prize in Economics were *An American Dilemma* and *Asian Drama*. Karl Mannheim also praised it for being a 'very important book ... as it is not only an approach to the history of ideas ... but because it sharpens the eye of the theoretician to the social implications of his thought' (Swedberg 1990, p. xx).
65. Paul Samuelson wrote that *Monetary Equilibrium* 'was an important anticipation by the

Stockholm School of John Maynard Keynes's *General Theory*' (Paul Samuelson, *The Collected Scientific Papers of Paul A. Samuelson* Cambridge: The MIT Press, 1975, volume 4, p. 291, in Swedberg 1990, p. xvi).

66. Dopfer (1988, p. 228). In a document written in 1934 Myrdal appears to have described the multiplier process, including the 'primary and secondary effects of exogenous impulses, without having knowledge of published material on the subject by Cambridge economists' (Dostaler 1990, p. 212).

67. The others were Friedrich Hayek's *Prices and Production* and Keynes's *Treatise on Money*. (See Velupillai, 1992.)

68. Myrdal's contribution was 'Der Gleichgewichtsbegriff als Instrument der geldtheoretischen Analyse' in F.A. Hayek, *Beitrage zur Geldtheorie*, Vienna, 1933, pp. 361–487.

69. Egon Glesinger's unpublished biography of Myrdal, written circa 1949, was obtained from the Alva and Gunnar Myrdal Collection in the Archives of the Swedish Labor Movement in Stockholm.

70. Lundberg (1974, pp. 473–4) describes the 'essence of Myrdal's theoretical structure of dynamics' as follows: '1) the *time element* contains uncertainty as well as the inertia of capital and production structure. 2) For each entrepreneur there is some kind of *objective risk* as to his expectations of future outcomes, depending on his experience and ability. 3) There are *personal risks* with regard to the enterprise (or the entrepreneur) from the credit suppliers' side. 4) Myrdal regards the *non-neutral evaluation of risks* as a central problem. Undervaluation and overvaluation (optimism and pessimism) and the dispersion of risks and evaluations among investing enterprises will have important effects on the price of risk-bearing.'

71. In this letter Myrdal is clarifying what he believes are misinterpretations by Marschak of key aspects in *Monetary Equilibrium*.

72. For an interesting analysis of graduate school economics programs in the United States, particularly the stress upon mainstream views and narrow economic models in lieu of policy issues, see Klamer and Colander (1990).

73. At an early age GM I did not believe that matters of national policy should be influenced by the average voter. In a speech he gave in 1919 called 'The Masses and the Intelligence' he advocated the establishment of 'The Swedish Intelligence Party', arguing 'that when everybody participates in politics, the intellectual level drops catastrophically. The reason for this is that "the mass" is "stupid" and "irresponsible"' (Swedberg 1990, p. x). In 1931 he was named Professor of Political Economy at Stockholm University. There he was influenced considerably by Cassel. In becoming an 'intellectual aristocrat' by being one of a few select students admitted to Cassel's 'elite circle,' Myrdal believed he was destined for leadership (Jackson 1990, p. 53).

74. For an interesting analysis of Myrdal's 'scientific personality' see Reynolds (1974).

75. During our first interview he informed me that he earned more than $1 million in royalties from the sale of *Asian Drama* (Myrdal 1968) in Japan alone, and that he and Alva had given most of their wealth to educational and other charitable foundations.

76. In December of 1930, GM I met with Ragnar Frisch at the home of Irving Fischer in Connecticut to develop the means by which to counteract the 'advancing institutionalists'. Their response was to form the Econometric Society. Although Myrdal was not a charter member of the Society, Bertil Ohlin and Friedrich A. Hayek proposed him for membership in 1932.

77. A letter to Myrdal from a friend, Robert Schweiger (Schweiger 1933) offers a criticism of John R. Commons – one which GM I shared. 'He [Commons] changes his theories from day to day and never believes in them at all. He believes only in facts and in the infinite potentialities of new variables. ... The problem for him is not the theory but the assumptions.'

78. This article has been translated into English by Paul Streeten and published in Myrdal (1958b, pp. 206–30). It was originally published in Swedish as 'Ekonomisk vetenskap och politisk ekonomi' (Economic Science and Political Economy) Stockholm: J. Akerman. Later it was published in German in *Zeitschrift fur Nationalokonomie*, Volume IV Number 3, 1933.

CHAPTER 3

79. Among his many other written works were two articles pertaining to the issue of welfare and socialism in the USA and Sweden – both written while he was in Geneva. Unfortunately, these articles are not preserved (Appendix, Myrdal Interview 1980).

80. This book consists of a series of lectures sponsored by the Godwin Foundation at Harvard in May, 1938. The title was 'The Population Problem and Social Policy'. Harvard published his Godwin lectures under the title 'Population: A Problem of Democracy'.

81. His interest in the population question grew out of 'Sweden's low and declining net reproduction rate that reached 0.78 in 1936–9 ... (1.0 is the rate required to maintain the population in the long run)' (Kindleberger 1987, p. 395).

82. This was not unusual for Myrdal, and he described himself as 'eclectic, always changing' (Appendix, Myrdal Interview 1980).

83. According to Alvin Hansen (Hansen 1981, p. 259) Myrdal wrote this without being aware of Keynes's work.

84. Myrdal believed that Keynes was not comfortable with the young members of the Stockholm School anticipating him (Appendix, Myrdal Interview 1980). He refers to a visit by Keynes to Stockholm after *The General Theory* had been published in which Keynes addressed Stockholm's prominent economists. Myrdal recalls that '[a]fter his talk one after another of the younger members of our Club [of Economists which had been "founded around Knut Wicksell"] took the floor and accused Keynes of being too classical on this and that point ... Keynes met his younger critics with open delight ... [but] only gradually did he show some easily understandable irritation, as the discussion put him more systematically in defence against a group of youngsters who stole his pose' (Myrdal 1957a, p. 130n).

85. The title of the series of books was *Wages, Cost of Living and National Income in Sweden 1860-1930*. Myrdal wrote one of the volumes that comprised part of a large-scale project directed by Gosta Bagge on 'Wages, Cost of Living, and National Income in Sweden 1860–1930'. His contribution was to 'carefully outline the existing material ... [and also to provide] a new cost of living index' (Swedberg 1990, p. xv). He was neither impressed with the study (describing it as 'just a bit of common sense applied to some not too reliable figures', stating that 'I am not very proud of the book – I am worried about it' (Swedberg 1990, pp. xv, xvi).

86. In addition to the budgetary conclusions Myrdal also concluded that changes in domestic prices relative to the rest of the world reflected Sweden's isolation, changes in general economic variables (particularly monetary aggregates) in Sweden, and relatively undeveloped world trade for Sweden (although Myrdal argued world trade did mitigate price fluctuations for Swedish agricultural products).

87. Wigforss was a prominent Social Democrat who served as Sweden's Minister of Finance in 1925–6 and 1932–49.

88. Myrdal (1933b). According to Carl Uhr (1977, p. 119) 'Myrdal's tract represented the end product of the intensive preceding research undertaken for the Committee on Unemployment.'

89. It was in fact a shorter version of the 279 page-long *Finanspolitikens ekonomiska verkningar*, published a year later in January 1934 (Myrdal 1934d).

90. For a detailed presentation of Social Democratic ideals see Koblik (1975) and Milner (1989).

91. Myrdal (1972). Here he argues that 'curiosity about society and the urge to improve it first led me to the study of social facts and relationships. It has remained so for almost a lifetime of work in the field, interrupted only by brief excursions into the political arena, where the translation of ideas and knowledge into action for the welfare of society is supposed to take place'.

92. See Childs (1936).

93. In a 1933 letter to Professor William Rappard (Myrdal, 1933d) he discusses his concep-

tion of planning. 'Since coming back to this country I have all the time been working on problems of national "planwirtschaft" [planning]: first monetary policy, then unemployment policy, fiscal means of influencing the national "conjuncture" (public works, different modes of balancing the budget ...) and finally the planning of a housing policy on a national scale ... . The only reasons I see for stating those problems as problems of national planning is the distressing fact that only the individual states offer the homogeneity of political psychology and the legal and institutional apparatus necessary to make any line of coherent policy effective.' Myrdal believed little integration and rational planning were possible in the international arena (something GM III would advocate). GM II argued that national planning was preferable for Sweden rather than international planning because of 'the distressing fact that only the individual states offer the homogeneity of political psychology and the legal and institutional apparatus necessary to make any line of coherent policy effective' (Myrdal 1933c).

94. According to one observer, '[t]he Myrdals became active in Swedish politics in the thirties. Alva's father, though an entrepreneur, was a socialist active in municipal politics. Because of the couple's interest in reforms, the Social Democratic party was the natural one for them to join' (Harrison 1976).

95. Alva Myrdal noted that the Population Study convinced her and Gunnar that '[w]hat is needed in social policy is less interest in philosophizing about power over production, which is a complicated problem, and more interest in increasing control from the consumption side, which is a comparatively easy task for competent social engineering' (A. Myrdal 1941, p. 151).

96. As a public official he was instrumental in training many young public servants. He explained the process to one colleague. 'Academicians are used by the government as experts in the departments or commissions. They very often take with them their more mature students as secretaries and assistants, and so the young folk are accustomed to practical work from a very early time of their career' (Myrdal 1937a).

97. One student of Myrdal observes that following the Myrdals' recommendations '[w]ith stunning speed, the 'family' became a Social Democratic issue'. The Social Democrats seized it, and won a majority of the parliament in 1936 and held power for the 40 years thereafter, 'enacting policies that shifted responsibility for children from the family to the state' (Carlson 1991, p. A18).

98. Myrdal adopted a standard cost of living method of analysis in his *The Cost of Living in Sweden 1860–1930* study. This study focused on investigating changes in Sweden's real wages using indices of 'semi-wholesale prices, i.e., the price where the wholesale transaction was for a comparatively small quantity and where the transaction was the ultimate or penultimate wholesale transaction' (Myrdal 1933a, pp. 22–3). Using prices published in newspapers for data, Myrdal recognized the limitations to drawing strong conclusions because the data did not guarantee that prices of intermediate goods or raw materials were representative, there were index problems characteristic of any cost-of-living study, and there was a lack of homogeneity within social groups being analyzed. He computed average prices for each county, weighted the counties, and arrived at a national price. Due to the data limitations he was not able to account for shifting populations over the 1860–1930 period.

99. One scholar argues that Myrdal 'found the theoretical core of the conventional laissez-faire economics of the first three decades of this century to be very inadequate as the basis for an interpretation of "the era of sustained abnormality" which came after 1914 and which has continued to the present' (Gruchy 1972, p. 177).

100. In a letter to William Thomas (Myrdal 1931a) Myrdal points out that the study should rely on the following Swedish material: 'official budget investigations', 'statistics of the distribution of wealth between different ages and social groups, declarations for income taxes, [and] an intensive study of different groups of individual families ... to get occupation mobility and migration, etc. Their saving habits could be studied at the same time.'

101. At the time many Swedes lived in tenements generally owned by absentee landlords, and the relatively high income stream of this latter group was perpetuated by a high inci-

dence of poverty. Popular attitudes toward the poor, namely that they were responsible for their own plight, combined with 'do-nothing' laissez-faire government attitudes were identified as principal causes of the prevalence of declining birth rates and a high incidence of poverty.

102. GM III describes his interpretation of the Enlightenment philosophy. 'It holds that truth is willsome and that a catharsis of the public mind is possible. As man is good and has the power of reason, he can attempt to dispel the clouds of his emotions, overcome the opportunism of his ignorance, reach a fuller and more dispassionate knowledge about himself and the world, and indeed, change his attitudes so that they become more rationally related to the existing facts and to his deepest valuations, his ideals. The social scientist in this great tradition is also an uncompromising adherent to freedom of thought and expression because they create a social situation where maximum possibility is given to the individual citizen to make this great attempt towards rationality. In the end this represents our only hope' (Myrdal 1956, p. 301).

103. This appendix was called 'Some Methodological Notes on the Population Problem and its Scientific Treatment' and the principal report was published in 1936 (Myrdal 1936a).

104. GM III recalls that one night he and Alva were both unable to sleep, and began discussing the possibilities such a study offered. She encouraged him to reconsider the proposal, believing they had done all they could for Sweden at that time.

CHAPTER 4

105. In the tradition of Thorstein Veblen, Clarence Ayres, John R. Commons, and some prominent contemporary Americans who hold and put into practice an institutional perspective.

106. For example, the treaty required that Sweden export electrical equipment and machinery worth about SK 200 million.

107. Sweden needed about 100,000 additional workers just to meet its agreed quota of electrical equipment and machinery.

108. In 1955 Myrdal wrote to Tarlok Sing, Joint Secretary of the Indian Planning Commission, telling Sing that he and Alva believed Myrdal should become the Director for building up the Asian Social Science Research Centre of Industrialization (for UNESCO). This Myrdal desired so he and Alva could spend the next stage of their lives together as she was already serving as Swedish Ambassador to India (Myrdal 1955d).

109. Kindleberger (1987, p. 399).

110. Myrdal pointed out that the regional income disparities in Western Europe in 1954 were much wider in the poorer than in the richer countries; and that although in the richer countries regional disparities have been diminishing, they have been widening in the poorer European countries.

111. This criticism stimulated Myrdal to write his *The Challenge of World Poverty* (Myrdal 1970a) – discussed later in the chapter.

112. Myrdal went on to argue that 'Smith, of course, never dealt with economic problems as purely "economic", and the same can be said in general of the whole classical school, including toward the end Karl Marx' (Myrdal 1968, pp. ix–x).

113. Some scholars have criticized GM III's research for only containing citations from sources he had written.

114. Much of the material from this section has been drawn from Angresano (1997).

115. In *Rich Lands and Poor* Myrdal argues in favor of a 'vision of a theory', stating it is the 'crux of all science'. This theory contains 'an interdisciplinary approach to comprehensive research, explicit statement of value premises, an organizing principle regarding how essential facts and relations exist, an empirical basis for the a priori theory, and an analysis of social change from a perspective as free as possible from "predilections"' (Myrdal 1957d, pp. 167–8).

116. GM III argues that a Western bias among development economists represents a 'natural wish' that underdeveloped countries will follow a non-communist path and 'develop into national communities that are politically, socially, and economically like our own' (Myrdal 1968, p. 22). Some adverse effects of this bias have included: the conducting of 'diplomatic', 'opportunistic' research which has ignored certain 'facts that raise awkward problems' (Myrdal 1970a, p. 8) including institutional barriers; raising expectations within the poor nations without fulfilling them, thereby leading to disillusionment and frustration; and the encouragement of a complacent attitude within the underdeveloped countries as well as 'lack of solicitude' in the richer nations, both of which have served 'shortsighted interests' while inhibiting economic development (Myrdal 1975b, p. 88).

117. Myrdal believed that social laws do not exist as do physical laws. He argued that 'what distinguishes valuations from beliefs and theories about reality is that they cannot be proved or disproved, but merely exist as social facts. [He lamented that] this has never been honestly recognized, at least not by economists ...' (Myrdal 1975b, p. 35).

118. For the study of race relations and poverty in the United States he selected the 'American Creed', see Myrdal (1975a), pp. 3–25. For poverty in underdeveloped nations he identified his 'modernization ideals', see Myrdal (1968), pp. 49–69.

119. For a presentation of a model of these interrelated factors as they comprise an economy see Angresano (1996b).

120. GM III believes that it would be very difficult to carry out reforms that threatened those in power of established institutions and attitudes, since those in power had a stake in preserving the existing institutions. In addition there were other 'social obstacles' which resisted societal transformation, especially prejudices as well as irrational behavior shaped by customs, especially religion, and the economic and social power held by a minority of elite within a community, all of which are imbedded in prevailing attitudes and institutions (Myrdal 1969b, pp. 97–101).

121. Current advisors to Central and East Europe, who do not share Myrdal's conceptualized reality, purport that their sweeping macroeconomic stabilization and privatization policies are a panacea for all nations throughout the region. Such policies, based upon narrow, closed economic models which emphasize easily quantifiable variables to the neglect of non-economic factors such as attitudes, health, and education would be soundly criticized by Myrdal as inappropriate and misguided – for they ignore the primary impediments to societal transformation and development. In the case of Central and East Europe these include absence of achievement-oriented individualistic competitiveness, lack of a civic culture by which people willingly adhere to laws concerning commerce, absence of a business culture wherein people would be consumer oriented, and corrupt political authorities.

122. See Myrdal (1957a, e), (1958a, b), (1968), (1969a), (1975a), (1975b), and (1978a) for detailed criticisms of neoclassical economics.

123. A study of economic history would lend support to Myrdal's criticism, for it indicates that in almost every OECD nation the state's active involvement in development efforts included creating the conditions for markets to perform an efficient allocative function, as well as promoting investment in leading sectors.

CHAPTER 5

124. Myrdal was highly critical of neoclassical economists' economic models for being based upon an unrealistic conception of reality, ignoring variables for which quantifiable data was not easily available, and for presenting oversimplified mathematical depictions of an economy.

125. For a detailed discussion see Angresano (1996a).

126. Much of the material in this section on goals and the following section on policies is taken from Angresano (1994a).

127. During a meeting in Prague during the spring of 1993, a member of the European Union Commission, while admitting that CEE exporters faced high barriers when seeking to trade with European Union members, told CEE trade officials that they should not retaliate or the European Union would raise trade barriers even higher.
128. The following section is taken from Angresano (1993).
129. Much of the material on privatization is taken from Angresano and Mladenova (1996c).
130. A Bulgarian saying is appropriate in this regard – 'If you try to carry two watermelons under the same arm you will be left with none.'
131. Renata Ingova, former Bulgarian Prime Minister who is now in the Academy of Sciences, has estimated that about half of state enterprises had been spontaneously privatized by the end of 1994, and therefore argued the state needed to speed up the privatization process to prevent further such privatization and to avoid larger losses of state assets. See Institute of Economics (1995).
132. Much of the material in this section is drawn from Angresano (1992a).
133. For an in-depth analysis of Russia's institutional conditions and other factors faced at the beginning of its transformation period see Nolan (1995), pp. 110–59.
134. See Nolan (1995) pp. 110–59, especially pp. 150–59.
135. Obviously no study of CEE by Myrdal was ever done. The alternative policies included in this section are drawn from actual proposals he made in his transformation studies. These policies, combined with his goals, are offered as a part of an alternative, more useful perspective for transformation policy making.
136. Nove pointed out that rather than entrepreneurs profiting from production of goods and services it was those making deals buying and reselling goods who were getting rich from such deals. Rather than being converted to capital accumulation, such profits were used to purchase foreign luxury goods or were deposited in foreign bank accounts.
137. Some researchers argue that 'hybrid forms of enterprise' (such as the township and village enterprises in China) are making positive contributions to development, and that transformation policies therefore should recognize the potential benefits of such enterprise forms (Bim , Jones, and Weisskopf 1993, p. 33, and McIntyre 1992, p. 91).
138. For example, the gradual changes in attitudes and institutions stimulated productivity increases, which spurred income growth. As a result there was increased demand for capital and consumer goods, thereby stimulating profits, savings and investment. As investment increased production facilities were improved so that it became possible to produce goods that became competitive on international markets. Greater sales meant higher incomes, and the process repeated itself in a circular, cumulative manner.
139. This section contains material from Angresano (1994c).
140. This section contains material from Angresano (1994b).
141. Marshall Goldman points out that although many of these firms specialized in domestic American concerns or arms control, 'the vast majority have virtually no experience with Eastern Europe, the Soviet Union, or communism. But they are good at preparing and submitting proposals and rounding up relevant consultants' (Goldman 1994, p. 220).
142. The material in the remainder of the chapter is drawn from Angresano 1994b.
143. This is based upon the author's observing and evaluating teaching activities by (primarily) American economists and graduate students in economics at universities throughout CEE during the 1991–3 period.

References

Adam, Jan (1994), 'Commentary – The Transition to a Market Economy in Poland', *Cambridge Journal of Economics*, **18**, 607–18.

Amsden, Alice, Michael Intriligator, Robert McIntyre, and Lance Taylor (1995), 'Strategies for a Viable Transition: Lessons from the Political Economy of Renewal', *American Expert Report – Moscow*, 13 June.

Andreff, Wladimir (1995), 'Corporate Governance of Privatized Enterprises in Transforming Economies: A Theoretical Approach', paper presented at the European Association For Evolutionary Economy Conference, Krakow, 18–20 October.

Angresano, James (1997), 'Towards Developing a 21st Century Economic Perspective: Lessons from Myrdal, Schumpeter and Hayek', Kenneth Taylor and William Halal (eds.), *21st Century Economics*, New York: St. Martin's Press.

—— (1996a), 'Poland After the Shock', *Comparative Economic Studies*, **38**, 87–112.

—— (1996b), *Comparative Economics*, 2nd edn, Upper Saddle River, NJ: Prentice Hall.

—— and Zoya Mladenova (1996c), 'Privatization in Bulgaria', *East European Quarterly*, **30**, 495–516.

—— (1994a), 'Evolving Socio-Economic Conditions in Central and East Europe: A Myrdalian View', *Development Policy Review*, **12**, 251–75.

—— (1994b), 'The Pedagogy of the Transformation: Economics Education in Central and Eastern Europe', *Higher Education in Europe*, **19**, 112–18.

—— (1994c), 'An Alternative Scenario for Central and East European Transformation', *Journal of Economic Studies*, **21**, 22–38.

—— (1994d), 'Institutional Change in Bulgaria: A Socioeconomic Approach', *The Journal of Socio-Economics*, **23**, 79–100.

—— (1993), 'Bulgarian Transformation: The Need for an Evolutionary-Institutional Approach', *Transformation Processes in Eastern Europe – Challenges for Socio-Economic Theory, Seminar Paper Number 20*, Krakow: Cracow Academy of Economics.

—— (1992a), 'Political and Economic Obstacles Inhibiting Comprehensive Reform in Hungary', *East European Quarterly*, **26**, 55–76.

—— (1992b), 'A Mixed Economy in Hungary? Lessons from the Swedish Experience', *Comparative Economic Studies*, **34**, 41–57.

—— (1990), 'Sweden: An Example of a Viable Social Economy?' *International Journal of Social Economics*, **17**, 12–31.

—— (1986), 'Gunnar Myrdal as a Social Economist', *Review of Social Economy*, **44**, 146–58.

—— (1981), 'Gunnar Myrdal's Intellectual Development as an Institutional Economist', Ph.D. dissertation, University of Tennessee.

Austin American-Statesman (1994), 'Russia Signs Peace Agreement with China', September **4**, pp. A1, A12.

Balapkins, Nicholas W. (1988), 'Gunnar Myrdal (1899–1987): A Memorial Tribute', *Eastern Economic Journal*, **14**, 99–106.

—— (1979), 'The Influence of the Philosophy of Enlightenment on the Work of Gunnar Myrdal', paper presented at the Annual Conference of the History of Economics Society, University of Illinois – Urbana-Champaign, 23–6 May.

Barry, Norman (1993), 'The Social Market Economy', *Social Philosophy and Policy*, **10**, 1–25.

Berg, Andrew (1994), 'Does Macroeconomic Reform Cause Structural Adjustment? Lessons from Poland', *Journal of Comparative Economics*, **18**, 376–409.

Bim, Alexander S., Derek C. Jones, and Thomas E. Weisskopf (1993), 'Hybrid Forms of Enterprise Organization in the Former USSR and the Russian Federation', *Comparative Economic Studies*, **35**, 1–38.

Boczar, Kazimierz, Tadeusz Szelazek, Franciszek Wala (1993), *Poland's Agricultural Cooperatives as they Move to a Market Economy*, Economic and Social Policy Series, Number 27 Warsaw: Friedrich Ebert Foundation.

Bok, Sissela (1995), 'Introduction' to 'An American Dilemma Revisited', in *Daedalus*, **124**, 1–13.

—— (1992), 'Introduction', in Gilles Dostaler, Diane Ethier, Laurent Lepage (eds), *Gunnar Myrdal and His Works*, Montreal: Harvest House, pp. 3–10.

—— (1991), *Alva Myrdal*, Reading, MA: Addison-Wesley.

Brady, Rose (1993), 'Four Years That Shook My World', *Business Week*, 26 July, pp. 48–9.

Campbell, John (1992a), 'Institutional Theory and the Influence of Foreign Actors on Reform in Capitalist and Post-Socialist Societies', paper presented at the Third Conference on The Negotiated Economy and Neo-Liberalism as Institutional Frameworks for a Market Economy – Implications for Post-Socialism, Ambleside, England, 3–6 July.

—— (1992b), 'Reflections on the Fiscal Crisis of the Post-Communist States', *Seminar Paper Number 11: Transformation Processes in Eastern Europe –*

Challenges for Socio-Economic Theory, Krakow: Cracow Academy of Economics.

Carlson, Allan (1978), 'The Roles of Alva and Gunnar Myrdal in the Development of a Social Democratic Response to Europe's Population Crisis: 1929–1938', Ph.D. dissertation, Ohio University.

Central Office of Planning – Department of Information and Forecasts (1995a), *Poland 1995: Information on the Economic Situation*, Warsaw: Central Office of Planning, June.

—— (1995b), *Poland 1990–1994: Evaluation of the Economic Processes*, Warsaw: Central Office of Planning, May.

Central Statistical Office (1995), *Poland: Quarterly Statistics*, **3**, September.

Childs, Marquis (1936), *Sweden: The Middle Way*, New Haven: Yale University Press.

Chopra, Ajai (1994), 'Monetary Policy and Financial Sector Reform', International Monetary Fund, Occasional Paper Number 116 Washington, DC: IMF, October.

Chossudovsky, Michel (1992), 'Myrdal and Economic Development: A Critical Analysis', in Gilles Dostaler, Diane Ethier, Laurent Lepage (eds), *Gunnar Myrdal and His Works*, Montreal, Harvest House, pp. 89–110.

Clayton, Elizabeth (1992), 'Agricultural Privatization in Transition Economies', *Comparative Economic Studies*, **34**, 86–92.

Czarny, Elzbieta and Boguslaw Czarny (1992), *From the Plan to the Market: The Polish Experience 1990–1991*, Economic and Social Policy Series, Number 22 Warsaw: Friedrich Ebert Foundation.

Dadush, Uri and Milan Brahmbratt (1995), 'Anticipating Capital Flow Reversals', *Finance and Development*, **32**, 3–5.

Dallago, Bruno (1992), 'Debate on the Transition of Post-Communist Economies to a Market Economy', *Acta Oeconomica*, **44**, 267–76.

Delegation of the European Commission in Poland (1995), *The Polish Economy in August, 1995, Monthly Economic Report*, 6 October.

Dhanji, Farid (1990), 'Post Communist Economic Transformation: Hungary vs. Poland', paper presented at the American Economic Association Meetings, Washington, DC, 27–30 December.

Dopfer, Kurt (1988), 'In Memoriam: Gunnar Myrdal's Contribution to Institutional Economics', *Journal of Economic Issues*, **22**, 227–31.

Dostaler, Gilles (1990), 'An Assessment of Gunnar Myrdal's Early Work in Economics', *Journal of the History of Economic Thought*, **12**, 196–221.

Dugger, William (1979), 'The Reform Method of John R. Commons', *Journal of Economic Issues*, **13**, 369–82.

Dykema, Eugene R. (1980), 'No View without a Viewpoint: Gunnar Myrdal', *World Development*, **14**, 147–63.

Economist Intelligence Unit (1996a), *Business China* London: *The Economist* 15, 29 April.

—— (1996b), *Business Eastern Europe*, London: *The Economist* 22, 29 January, 19 February, 15, 29 April, 6, 13, 20, 27 May, 10, 17 June.

—— (1996c), *Hungary 2nd quarter 1996*, London: *The Economist*.

—— (1996d), *Poland 2nd quarter 1996*, London: *The Economist*.

—— (1996e), *Russia 2nd quarter 1996*, London: *The Economist*.

—— (1995a), *Business Eastern Europe*, London: *The Economist* 23 January, 13 February, 6, 13, 20 March, 3, 10, 17, 24 April, 8, 22 May, 5, 12, 26 June, 3, 10, 17 July.

—— (1995b), *Poland 2nd quarter 1995*, London: *The Economist*.

—— (1994a), *Poland 4th quarter 1994*, London: *The Economist*.

—— (1994b), *A Survey of Poland*, London: *The Economist*, 16 April.

—— (1994c), 'Poland: Not there yet', London: *The Economist*, 3 September.

The Economist (1994), 'The road to ruin', 29 January, pp. 23–5.

—— (1993), 'Rotten to the Core', and 'No Foreigners Need Apply', 7 August.

—— (1990), 'Survey Perestroika: And Now for the Hard Part', 28 April, p. 19.

Elliott, John E. (1983), 'Joseph A. Schumpeter at 100 and The Theory of Economic Development at 72', paper presented at the Southwestern Economic Association Meetings, 14–16 April.

Ethier, Diane (1992), 'Myrdal and Southeast Asia Development', in Gilles Dostaler, Diane Ethier, Laurent Lepage (eds), *Gunnar Myrdal and His Works*, Montreal: Harvest House, pp. 68–88.

Fischer, Irving (1926), Unpublished letter to Gunnar Myrdal, 15 December.

Fischer, Stanley (1992), 'Stabilization and Economic Reform in Russia', in William C. Brainard and George L. Perry (eds), *Brookings Papers on Economic Activity* 1. Washington, DC: Brookings Institution, pp. 77–126.

Fleisher, Wilfred (1973), *Sweden: The Welfare State* Westport, CT: Greenwood Press.

Fox, Louise (1995), 'Can Eastern Europe's Old-Age Crisis Be Fixed?' *Finance and Development*, **32**, 34–7.

Gibbs, Frank (1977), 'Nobel winner fears university stifles thoughts', *New University* (School Newspaper of the University of California at Irvine), **9**, 1 March.

Gill, Louis (1992), 'Myrdal and "The Third Way"', in Gilles Dostaler, Diane Ethier, Laurent Lepage (eds), *Gunnar Myrdal and His Works*, Montreal: Harvest House, pp. 52–67.

Glesinger, Egon (1949), 'Gunnar Myrdal', unpublished biographical sketch, enclosed in a letter to Gunnar Myrdal, 3 January.

Goldman, Marshall I. (1994), *Lost Opportunity: Why Economic Reforms in Russia Have Not Worked*, New York: W.W. Norton.

Gomulka, Stanislav (1995), 'The IMF Supported Programs of Poland and Russia, 1990–94: Principles, Errors, and Results', *Journal of Comparative Economics*, **20**, 316–46.

Gordon, Wendell (1980), *Institutional Economics: The Changing System*, Austin: University of Texas Press.

Grossman, Gregory (1990), 'Sub-Rosa Privatization and Marketization in the USSR', in Jan S. Prybla (ed.), *The Annals of the American Academy of Political and Social Science* **507**, January, 44–52.

Gruchy, Alan (1972), *Contemporary Economic Thought: The Contribution of Neo-Institutional Economics*, Clifton, NJ: Augustus M. Kelley.

Hanke, Steve H. and Sir Alan Walters (1993), 'The high cost of Jeffrey Sachs', *Forbes*, 21 June, p. 52.

Hansen, Bent. (1981), 'Unemployment, Keynes, and the Stockholm School', History of Political Economy, **13**, 256–77.

Harris, Seymour E. (ed.) (1951), *Schumpeter: Social Scientist*, Cambridge, MA: Harvard University Press.

Harrison, Paul (1976), unpublished biographical sketch of Gunnar Myrdal.

Hausner, Jerzy (1995), 'Dilemmas of the Economic Strategy', unpublished manuscript prepared for the Polish Deputy Prime Minister for Economic Affairs.

—— (1992), 'Doctrinal Aspects of the Transformation Process and Factors Affecting the Financial Crisis of the State', paper presented at the Third Conference on The Negotiated Economy and Neo-Liberalism as Institutional Frameworks for a Market Economy – Implications for Post-Socialism, Ambleside, England, 3–6 July.

—— and Stanislaw Owsiak (1992), *Financial crisis of a State in Transformation: The Polish Case*, Economic and Social Policy Series, Number 26 Warsaw: Friedrich Ebert Foundation.

—— and Andrej Wojtyna (1992), 'Privatization as a Restructuring Device: Can it Substitute for Industrial Policy in the Transforming Economies: Some Lessons from Poland', paper presented at the Association for Evolutionary Political Economy conference, Paris, 4–6 November.

Hayek, Friedrich A. (1944), *The Road to Serfdom*, Chicago: University of Chicago Press.

Hodgson, Geoffrey M. (1988), *Economics and Institutions*, Cambridge: Polity Press.

Hoen, Herman W. (1995), 'Theoretically Underpinning the Transition in Eastern Europe: An Austrian View', *Economic Systems*, **19**, 59–77.

Hollander, Samuel (1987), *Classical Economics*, Oxford: Basil Blackwell.

Institute of Economics (1995), *Economic Outlook of Bulgaria: 1995–1997* Sofia: Bulgarian Academy of Sciences.

International Monetary Fund (1995), 'Progress Report on Commercial Bank Debt Restructuring', *Finance and Development*, **32**, 14–15.

Islam, Shafiqul (1993), 'Russia's Rough Road to Capitalism', *Foreign Affairs*, Spring.

Jackson, Walter A. (1990), *Gunnar Myrdal and America's Conscience: Social Engineering and Racial Liberalism, 1938–1987*, Chapel Hill: University of North Carolina Press.

Jensen, Hans (1976), 'Sources and Contours of Adam Smith's Conceptualized Reality in The Wealth of Nations', *Review of Social Economy*, **34**, 259–76.

Johnson, B. and B. Lundvall (1992), 'Catching up and Institutional Learning under Post-Socialism', unpublished paper presented at Aalborg University.

Keppel, Frederick (1937), unpublished letter to Gunnar Myrdal, 12 August.

—— (1942), unpublished letter to Gunnar Myrdal, 4 September.

Keynes, John Maynard (1964), *The General Theory of Employment, Interest, and Money*, New York: Harcourt, Brace & World.

Kindleberger, Charles P. (1987), 'Gunnar Myrdal, 1898–1987', *Scandinavian Journal of Economics*, **89**, 393–403.

Klamer, Arjo and David Collander (1990), *The Making of an Economist*, Boulder, CO: Westview.

Klusak, M. and P. Mertlik (1992), 'Transformation and Macroeconomic Stabilization of the Czechoslovak Economy', paper presented at the Third Conference on The Negotiated Economy and Neo-Liberalism as Institutional Frameworks for a Market Economy – Implications for Post-Socialism, Ambleside, England, 3–6 July.

Koblik, Steven (ed.) (1975), *Sweden's Development from Poverty to Affluence: 1750–1970*, Minneapolis: University of Minnesota Press.

Komarek, Walter (1992), 'Shock Therapy and its Victims', *The New York Times*, 5 January, p. 14.

Kornai, Janos (1990), *Vision and Reality, Market and State*, Budapest: Corvina Books.

Koves, A. (1992), 'Shock Therapy Versus Gradual Change', *Acta Oeconomica*, **44**, 13–44.

Kowalik, Tadeusz (1992a), 'Can Poland Afford the Swedish Model?' paper presented at the Third Conference on The Negotiated Economy and Neo-Liberalism as Institutional Frameworks for a Market Economy – Implications for Post-Socialism, Ambleside, England, 3–6 July.

—— (1992b), 'The Great Transformation and Privatization: Two years of Poland's Experience', working paper prepared for a seminar at the Stockholm Institute of Soviet and East European Economies.

Kregel, Jan and Egon Matzner (1992), 'Agenda for the Reconstruction of Central and Eastern Europe', *Challenge*, September–October, pp. 33–40.

—— and Gerhard Grabher (eds) (1992), *Market Shock: An Agenda for the Socio-Economic Reconstruction of Central and Eastern Europe*, Vienna: Austrian Academy of Sciences.

Lalonde, Francine (1992), 'Gunnar Myrdal and Social Democracy', in Gilles Dostaler, Diane Ethier, Laurent Lepage (eds), *Gunnar Myrdal and His Works*, Montreal: Harvest House, pp. 37–51.

Lange, Oskar (1957), *ECE: The First Ten Years 1947–1957*, Geneva: United Nations Economic Commission for Europe.

Laski, Kazimierz (1993), *Transition from the Command to the Market System: what went wrong and what to do now?*, Vienna: The Vienna Institute for Comparative Economic Studies.

Li, Elizabeth (1995), 'Market Reform and the Chinese Urban Labor Market: Evidence from a 1992 Labor Market Survey', paper presented at the Southern Economic Association Meetings, New Orleans, November.

Liew, Leong H. (1995), 'Gradualism in China's Economic Reform and the Role for a Strong State, *Journal of Economic Issues*, **29**, 883–94.

Lipton, David and Jeffrey D. Sachs (1992), 'Prospects for Russia's Economic Reforms', William C. Brainard and George L. Perry (eds), *Brookings Papers on Economic Activity 2*.

Lundberg, Erik (1985), 'The Rise and Fall of the Swedish Model', *Journal of Economic Literature*, **23**, 1–36.

—— (1974), 'Gunnar Myrdal's Contribution to Economic Theory: A Short Survey', *Swedish Journal of Economics*, **74**, 472–8.

Marquid, Judith (1995), 'Cultures in Transition: The Educational System in Poland', paper presented at the European Association for Evolutionary Political Economy Conference, Krakow, 19–21 October.

McIntyre, Robert (1992), 'The Phantom of Transition: Privatization of Agriculture in the Former Soviet Union and Eastern Europe', *Comparative Economic Studies*, **34**, 54–67.

Mesjasz, Czeslaw (1995), 'Institutional Determinants of Commercial Debt Negotiations Between Poland and the London Club', paper presented at the European Association for Evolutionary Political Economy Conference, Krakow, 19–21 October.

Metzger, Thomas A. (1996), *Transcending the West – Mao's Vision of Socialism and the Legitimization of Teng Hsiao-p'ing's Modernization Program*, Stanford, CA: Hoover Institution.

Milanovic, Branko (1992), 'Social Costs of Transition to Capitalism: Poland 1990–91', paper presented at Cracow Academy of Economics, Krakow.

Milner, Henry (1989), *Sweden: Social Democracy in Practice*, Oxford: Oxford University Press.

Ministry of Economic Affairs (1995a), *The Republic of Poland – Data Tables*, Confidential Report, April.

—— (1995b), *The Republic of Poland – Credit Rating Presentation to Moody's Investor Services*, Confidential Report, April.

Ministry of Industry and Trade (1995), 'International Competitiveness of Polish Industry – Industrial Policy Program for 1995–1997', Warsaw: Ministry of Industry and Trade, April.

Mokrzycki, Edmund (1993), 'The Social Limits of East European Economic Reform', *The Journal of Socio-Economics*, **22**, 29–30.

Moskoff, William and Nader Nazmi (1992), 'Economic Stabilization in the Former Soviet Union: Lessons from Argentina and Brazil', *Comparative Economic Studies*, **34**, 67–81.

Mujzel, Jan (1993), 'State-owned Enterprises in Transition: Prospects amidst Crisis', paper presented at Cracow Academy of Economics, Krakow.

Murrell, Peter (1992), 'Evolution in Economies and in the Economic Reform of the Centrally Planned Economies', in C. Clague and G. Raussen (eds), *The Emergence of Market Economies in Eastern Europe*, Cambridge, MA: Blackwell.

Myant, Hla (1968) 'Review of *Asian Drama: An Inquiry into the Poverty of Nations*', *Swedish Journal of Economics*, pp. 242–5.

Myrdal, Alva (1941), *Nation and Family*, New York: Harper & Brothers.

Myrdal, Gunnar (1982), *Hyr styrs landet?*, Stockholm: Raben & Sjogren.

—— (1978a), 'Institutional Economics', *Journal of Economic Issues*, **12**, 771–82.

—— (1978b), *Increasing Interdependence between States but Failure of International Cooperation*, Gothenburg: Gothenburg University Press.

—— (1978c), *Political and Institutional Economics*, Eleventh Geary Lecture. Dublin: The Economic and Social Research Institute.

—— (1977a), unpublished draft of the 'Preface to the New Swedish Edition 1972' of *The Political Element in the Development of Economic Theory*, May.

—— (1977b), 'The Meaning and Validity of Institutional Economics', in Rolf Steppacher, Brigitte Zoggwalz, and Hermann Hutzfeldt (eds), *Economics in Institutional Perspective: Memorial Essays in Honor of K. William Kapp*, Lexington: D.C. Heath & Co., pp. 82–9.

—— (1976), 'Remarks Upon Receipt of the Veblen–Commons Award', *Journal of Economic Issues*, **10**, 215–16.

—— (1975a), *An American Dilemma: The Negro Problem and Modern Democracy*, Two Volumes, New York: Pantheon.

—— (1975b), *Against the Stream: Critical Essays on Economics*, New York: Vintage.

—— (1975c), 'The Unity of the Social Sciences', Plenary Address to the Society for Applied Anthropology, Amsterdam, 21 March.

—— (1975d), *The Equality Issue in World Development*, Stockholm: The Nobel Foundation.

—— (1974a), 'What is Development?' *Journal of Economic Issues*, **8**, 729–36.

—— (1974b), 'What is Political Economy'? *Papers in Economic Criticism: Commemoration of the First Frank E. Seidman Distinguished Award in Political Economy*, Memphis: Memphis State University.

—— (1974c), Interview with Barbara Taylor in Stockholm.

—— (1972), 'The Social Sciences and Their Impact on Society', in Teodor Shanin (ed.), *The Rules of the Game: Cross-disciplinary Essays on Models in Scholarly Thought*, London: Tavistock Publication, pp. 347–59.

—— (1970a), *The Challenge of World Poverty: A World Anti-Poverty Program in Outline*, New York: Pantheon.

—— (1970b), 'An Economist's Vision of a Sane World', in Oka Keibunsha, (ed.), *Gunnar Myrdal: Essays and Lectures*, Chapter 7, Tokyo: Keibunsha.

—— (1970c), unpublished letter to Andre Schiffrin (Pantheon Books), 1 July.

—— (1969a), *The Political Element in the Development of Economic Theory*, Cambridge, MA: Harvard University Press.

—— (1969b), *Objectivity in Social Research*, New York: Pantheon.

—— (1969c), unpublished letter to Elizabeth Blackert, 11 January.

—— (1969d), unpublished letter to John E. Booth (Associate Director of the 20th Century Fund), 18 August.

—— (1968), *Asian Drama: An Inquiry into the Poverty of Nations*, three volumes, New York: Pantheon.

—— (1966a), unpublished letter to August Heckscher (Twentieth Century Fund), 16 May.

—— (1966b), unpublished letter to August Heckscher, 1 October.

—— (1963), *Challenge to Affluence*, New York: Pantheon.

—— (1961), unpublished letter to August Heckscher, 18 September.

—— (1960), *Beyond the Welfare State*, New Haven: Yale University Press.

—— (1958a), *Value in Social Theory: A Selection of Essays on Methodology*, Paul Streeten (ed.), London: Routledge & Kegan Paul.

—— (1958b), 'Ends and Means in Political Economy', in *Value and Social Theory*, Paul Streeten (ed.), London: Routledge & Kegan Paul, pp. 206–30. This article was translated into English by Paul Streeten. It was originally published in Swedish as 'Ekonomisk vetenskap och politisk ekonomi' (Economic Science and Political Economy) Stockholm: J. Akerman. Later it was published in German in a *Zeitschrift fur Nationalokonomie*, **4**, 1933.

—— (1957a), *Economic Theory and Under-Developed Regions*, London: Gerald Duckworth.

—— (1957b), in ECE Press Release 17 April, 1957, published by the Information Service of the European Office of the United Nations, Geneva.

—— (1957c), 'Opening Statement by Executive Secretary to the 12th Session of the ECE', 29 April.

—— (1957d), unpublished letter written to Alva Myrdal (written from Moscow).

—— (1957e), *Rich Lands and Poor*, New York: Harper & Brothers.

—— (1956a), *An International Economy: Problems & Prospects*, New York: Harper & Brothers.

—— (1956b), unpublished letter to Dag Hammarskjold, 16 October.

—— (1956c), unpublished letter to Charles Dollard (Carnegie Corporation), 16 January.

—— (1956d), unpublished 'Scope and Purpose of the [Asian] Study', attachment to letter to Norman S. Buchanan, The Rockefeller Foundation, 19 June.

—— (1955a), unpublished letter to Paul Samuelson, 14 March.

—— (1955b), unpublished letter to Frau Dr. Gerhard Machenroth, 5 October.

—— (1955c), unpublished letter to N. Koestner (Chief of Research Department, National Bank of Egypt), 11 October.

—— (1955d), unpublished letter to Tarlok Sing (Joint Secretary of the Indian Planning Commission).

—— (1954a), unpublished letter to W. Arthur Lewis, 21 April.

—— (1954b) unpublished letter to Arnold Rose, 13 April.

—— (1953), 'International Economic Cooperation and European Integration', Address to the United Europe Movement Lunch-time Forum in Westminster, England, 26 March.

—— (1952), unpublished letter to Raoul Prebisch, 29 January.

—— (1951a), unpublished letter to Richard Kahn (King's College, Cambridge), 20 April.

—— (1951b), unpublished notes for the Marshall Lecture in Manchester, England.

—— (1951c), 'The Trend Towards Economic Planning', *The Manchester School of Economic and Social Studies*, **19**, 1–42.

—— (1947a), 'Statement about the Origin of the ECE', Geneva: United Nations Economic Commission for Europe.

—— (1947b), unpublished letter to Arnold Rose, 11 February.

—— (1940), *Population: A Problem for Democracy*, Cambridge, MA: Harvard University Press.

—— (1939a), *Monetary Equilibrium*, Glasgow: William Hodge.

—— (1939b), 'Fiscal Policy in the Business Cycle', *American Economic Review Part 2 Supplement*, **29**, 183–93.

—— (1938a), unpublished letter to Dorothy Thomas, 1 March.

—— (1938b), *Betankande i naringsfragan* [Report Concerning the Food Problem], Stockholm.

—— (1938c), unpublished letter to Eva and Arthur Burns, 14 February.

—— (1937a), unpublished letter to Roy V. Peel, 3 February.

—— (1937b), unpublished letter to Dr. O.E. Baker, Bureau of Agricultural Economics, Washington, DC, 30 August.

—— (1937c), unpublished letter to Frederick Keppel, 7 October.

—— (1936a), '*Nagra metodiska anmarkningar rorande befolkningsfragans innebord och vetenskapliga behandling*', [Some Methodological Notes on the Population Problem and Its Scientific Treatment], *Bilaga 1* – SOU, **59**, 149–58.

—— (1936b), '*Aktuella beskattningsproblem*', [Present Problems of Taxation], *Nationalekonomiska Foreningens Forhandlingar*, 91–115.

—— and Alva Myrdal (1934a), *Kris i befolkningsfragan* [Crisis in the population question], Stockholm: Almquist and Wicksell.

—— (1934b), unpublished letter to Dr J. Marschak, All Souls College, Oxford, 2 October.

—— (1934c), unpublished letter to Dr Brinley Thomas, 9 May.

—— (1934d), *Finanspolitikens Ekonomiska Verkningar* [The Economic Effects of Fiscal Policy], Stockholm: Arbetsloshetsutredningens betankande 2 *Bilagor* – SOU, **2**.

—— (1933a), *The Cost of Living in Sweden 1830–1930*, (Translated by E. Classen), London: P.S. King & Son.

—— (1933b), *Konjunktur och offentlig hushallning. En utredning* [Business Cycles and Public Finance. Memorandum Concerning the Effects of Various Measures within the Public Sector on the Business Cycles in Sweden], *Kooperativa Forbundet*, Stockholm.

—— (1933c), 'Industrialization and Population', *Economic Essays in Honor of Gustav Cassel*, London: G. Allen & Unwin, 435–57.

—— (1933d), unpublished letter to William Rappard, Institut Universitaire de Hautes Etudes Internationales, Geneva, 16 February.

—— (1933e), *Bostadsfragan sasom socialt planlaggningsproblem* [The Housing Question as a Problem of Social Planning], SOU, **14**.

—— (1932a), unpublished 'Appendix – Short Note on an Investigation of the Swedish Population at present being carried on at the University of Stockholm'.

—— (1932b), unpublished letter to Jacob Viner, 20 December.

—— (1932c), 'Socialpolitikens dilemma' [The Dilemma of Social Policy], *Spektrum*, **2** (3), 1–13, and (4), 13–31.

—— (1931a), unpublished letter to William Thomas, 2 February.

—— (1931b), 'Socialism eller kapitalism i framtidens Amerika?' [Socialism or capitalism in the United States of the Future?], *Tiden*, **23**, 205–30.

—— (1930), 'International Double Taxation', unpublished lecture delivered at the Post Graduate Institute of International Studies, Geneva.

—— (1929), 'Sparandets plats i realinkomstberakning' [The Place of Savings in Calculation of Real Income], *Ekonomisk Tidskrift*, **31**, 157–69.

National Statistical Institute (1995), *The Socio-Economic Development of Bulgaria in 1990–94*, Sofia: National Statistical Institute.

Nielsen, Klaus (1992), 'The Mixed Economy, the Neo-liberal Challenge, and the Negotiated Economy', *The Journal of Socio-Economics*, **21**, 283–309.

Nielsen, Klaus and Ove Pedersen (1990), 'From the Mixed Economy to the Negotiated Economy: the Scandinavian Countries', paper presented at the Second International Conference on Socio-Economics, Washington, DC, 16–18 March.

Nolan, Peter (1995), *China's Rise, Russia's Fall*, New York: St. Martin's Press.

Nove, Alec (1992), 'Economics of the Transition Period', *Forum*, **5**, 6–7.

O'Brien, John C. (1977), 'Ethics in Economics in Gunnar Myrdal', paper presented at the Annual Conference of the History of Economics Society, University of California, Riverside, 24–6.

OECD (1994), *Economic Survey: Poland*, Paris: OECD.

Ohlin, Bertil (1981), 'Stockholm and Cambridge: Four Papers on the Monetary and Employment Theory of the 1930s', in Otto Steiger (ed.), *History of Political Economy*, **13**, 189–255.

—— (1978), 'On the Formulation of Monetary Theory' (Translated by Hanse E. Brems and William P. Yohe), *History of Political Economy*, **10**, 353–88.

Orlowski, Lucjan T. (1995), 'The Social Impact of Preparations for Admission to the European Union on Transformation Strategies in Central Europe', *Comparative Economic Studies*, **37**, 29–48.

Pejovich, Svetozar (1993), 'Institutions, Nationalism, and the Transition Process in Eastern Europe', *Social Philosophy and Policy*, **10**, 65–78.

Peltier, Jacques (1992), 'Myrdal and Value Loaded Concepts', in Gilles Dostaler, Diane Ethier, Laurent Lepage (eds), *Gunnar Myrdal and His Works*, Montreal: Harvest House, pp. 188–206.

Pestoff, Victor A. (ed.) (1995), *Reforming Social Services in Central and Eastern Europe – An Eleven Nation Overview*, Krakow: Cracow Academy of Economics.

—— (1992), 'Third Sector and Co-operative Services – An Alternative to Privatization', *Journal of Consumer Policy*, **15**, 21–45.

Population Index (1942), Review of Alva Myrdal, *Nation and Family*, **8**, January.

Porter, Michael (1990), *The Competitive Advantage of Nations*, London: Macmillan.

Prybla, Jan (1995), Review of Nicholas R. Lardy, *China in the World Economy*, *Journal of Comparative Economics*, **21**, 124–30.

Reynolds, Lloyd G. (1974), 'Gunnar Myrdal's Contribution to Economics, 1940–1970', *Swedish Journal of Economics*, **76**, 479–97.

Ringen, Stein and Claire Wallace (1993), *Societies in Transition: East-Central Europe Today: Prague Papers on Social Responses to Transformation* Volume 1, Prague: Central European University.

Rosati, Dariusz K. (1993), *The Politics of Economic Reform in Central and Eastern Europe*, London: Centre for Economic Policy Research.

Rosenberger, Leif (1992), 'Economic Transition in Eastern Europe: Paying the Price for Freedom', *East European Quarterly*, **26**, 261–78.

Rosier, Michel (1992), 'On the Hypothetical Character of Moral Premises', in Gilles Dostaler, Diane Ethier, Laurent Lepage (eds), *Gunnar Myrdal and His Works*, Montreal: Harvest House, pp. 174–87.

Rostow, Walt (1990), *The Theorists of Economic Growth*, Oxford: Oxford University Press.

—— (1949), unpublished letter to Barbara Ward (*The Economist*), 9 February.

Sachs, Jeffrey D. and Wing Thye Woo (1994), 'Introduction – Experiences in the Transition to a Market Economy', *Journal of Comparative Economics*, **18**, 271–5.

Santarelli, Enrico and Enzo Pesciarelli (1990), 'The Emergence of a Vision: the Development of Schumpeter's Theory of Entrepreneurship', *History of Political Economy*, **22**, 677–96.

Schweiger, Robert (1933), unpublished letter to Gunnar Myrdal, 7 February.

Seccareccia, Mario (1992), 'Wicksellian, Myrdal and the Monetary Explanation of Cyclical Crises', in Gilles Dostaler, Diane Ethier, Laurent Lepage (eds), *Gunnar Myrdal and His Works*, Montreal: Harvest House, pp. 144–62.

Steiger, Otto (1978), 'Substantive Changes in the Final Version of Ohlin's 1933 Paper', *History of Political Economy*, **10**, 420–52.

Streeten, Paul (1992), 'Myrdal, the Man and the Theorist', in Gilles Dostaler, Diane Ethier, Laurent Lepage (eds), *Gunnar Myrdal and His Works*, Montreal: Harvest House, pp. 111–27.

Surdej, Aleksander (1992), 'Politics of the Stabilization in Poland', *Transformation Processes in Eastern Europe – Challenges for Socio-Economic Theory, Seminar Paper Number 9*, Krakow: Cracow Academy of Economics.

Swaan, Wim and Maria Lissowska (1992), 'Enterprise Behavior in Hungary and Poland in the Transition to a Market Economy: Individual and Organizational Routines as a Barrier to Change', in Wolfgang Blaas and John Foster (eds), *Mixed Economies in Europe*, Aldershot: Edward Elgar, pp. 89–121.

Swedberg, Richard (1990), *Introduction to: The Political Element in the Development of Economic Theory by Gunnar Myrdal*, Stockholm: Sociologiska Institutionen.

Sztompka, Piotr (1992), 'Civilizational Competence: The Prerequisite of Post-Communist Transition', unpublished paper presented at Jagiellonian University, Krakow, November.

Taylor, Lance (1988), *Variations of Stabilisation Experience*, Oxford: Oxford University Press.

Thomas, Dorothy Swain (1941), *Social and Economic Aspects of Swedish Population Movements: 1750–1933*, New York: Macmillan.

Tilton, Timothy (1992), 'Gunnar Myrdal and the Swedish Model', in Gilles Dostaler, Diane Ethier, Laurent Lepage (eds), *Gunnar Myrdal and His Works*, Montreal: Harvest House, pp. 13–36.

—— (1979), 'A Swedish Road to Socialism: Ernst Wigforss and the Ideological Foundations of Swedish Social Democracy', *The American Political Science Review*, **73**, June.

Todaro, Michael P. (1989), *Economic Development in the Third World*, 4th edn, New York: Longman.

Uhr, Carl (1977), 'Economists and Policymaking 1930–1936: Sweden's Experience', *History of Political Economy*, **9**, 89–121.

—— (1951), 'Knut Wicksell – A Centennial Evaluation', *American Economic Review*, **41**, 829–60.

UNICEF (1993), *Central and Eastern Europe in Transition: Public Policy and Social Conditions*, Florence: UNICEF International Child Development Centre.

Velupillai, Kumaraswamy (1992), 'Reflections on Gunnar Myrdal's Contributions to Economic Theory', in Gilles Dostaler, Diane Ethier, Laurent Lepage (eds), *Gunnar Myrdal and His Works*, Montreal: Harvest House, pp. 128–43.

Woo, Wing Thye (1994), 'The Art of Reforming Centrally Planned Economies: Comparing China, Poland and Russia', *Journal of Comparative Economics*, **18**, pp. 276–308.

World Bank (1993), *The East Asian Miracle*, Washington, DC: World Bank.

—— (1991), *World Development Report 1991*, New York: Oxford University Press.

Young, Susan (1995), *Private Business and Economic Reform in China*, Armonk: East Gate Book.

Two Interviews conducted by the author with Gunnar Myrdal, Stockholm 8, 9 July 1980, and July 1982.

Interview conducted by the author with Walt Rostow, Austin, 23 February 1996.

Index